"MR. BUCK"

The Autobiography
of

Nash Buckingham

"MR. BUCK"

The Autobiography

of

Nash Buckingham (signature)

by

NASH BUCKINGHAM

Edited by
Dr. Dyrk Halstead and Steve Smith

COUNTRYSPORT PRESS
Traverse City, Michigan

To
Jim Brinkley, Sr.

CONTENTS

FOREWORD

Irma Buckingham O'Fallon

Nash Buckingham was an author, an athlete, a conservationist, a scholar, and the most gentle man I've ever known. He was honored for his contributions to each and every field. He corresponded with "captains and kings," as they say, with statesmen, heads of state, chairmen of notable corporations, and presidents. He has been memorialized and eulogized. Nash Buckingham was my grandfather.

When I think of this man – his wisdom, his idealism, his courage – it is no wonder that I've been able to weather the many storms that life so generously bestows upon us all, and which now must be considered those proverbial "blessings in disguise." for without them, I might never have come to know (or even perceive) the depth of Nash Buckingham, "his Irma," my precious, adorable grandmother, "their Irma," my glorious, incredible mother, all of whom have been the angels on the shoulder of their "Fat Rat" and "Jimbo" and "Kelly-Poo." To have known him was a privilege (to many); for him to have been my grandfather is now overwhelming.

Nash Buckingham's life was not limited to a duck blind. His life was an expression of unselfish love that (in my lifetime) spanned four generations. He was a loving husband, a devoted father, grandfather, and great-grandfather whose wise, quiet ways ultimately touched his family, his love of the land, and his fellow man.

I remember that he used to take me on endless trips to the park across from the house on Stonewall in Memphis where he would swing me in what seemed to me as a child an enormous rope swing. He would tell me stories of "The Three Billy Goats Gruff." Each billy goat had his own distinctive voice, individual dialect, and personality. He took me to see my first dog show, my first horse show. We would go to the zoo. There was a great brown bear that would hold one of his back feet with one of his front paws and wave to us with the other.

I remember the life-size rag doll my Aunt Annie (his youngest sister) made for me. I do not recall that doll's name, but I do remember that one day she disappeared. I suspect that after she had been dragged to the the zoo and the park and to bed and through the house and yard, my grandfather, grandmother, and Aunt Annie all agreed it was time to replace her with a new rag doll exactly like the old one. I would have none of that! So while I was mourning her loss, "Nonny," as I called the great man, went to the "doll hospital" and retrieved the worn-out but wonderful doll. My mother confided to me much later that if the Health Department knew of her whereabouts, they would come after us all!

I remember him taking me to the Pink Palace, which housed all the treasures of his dear friend Berry Brooks and his wife Virginia, to whom *Hallowed Years* is dedicated. We arrived at the house, a virtual museum in itself, and upon walking through the front door, we were standing between two huge bull elephant tusks next to which stood a medieval suit of armor. He could sit for hours and tell stories of the Brooks safaris and their adventures together. They were exciting and funny and wonderful. I remember them so vividly.

Later, he would take me to see every movie Esther Williams ever made. He admired her grace and beauty and discipline – "She was a fine athlete." He would write to my mother and say, "…take her to see *Young Bess*," to see *Scaramouche*. I saw every movie Stewart Granger ever made and to this day could see them all over and over again!

So much has been written and said of my grandfather. So few could ever imagine his rendition of "The Three Billy Goats Gruff" or his trip to the "doll hospital" for a tiny toddler. But then again, perhaps, just maybe they would. For if the pen is mightier than the sword, then a mighty man was he. His quiet, gentle manner is magnified, yet sometimes contradicted, by the eloquent appeals that blazed away for the present laws to protect the environment.

And blaze the way he did. He took out his pen to burn through the beauracracy, to fire away at hypocrisy. He never backed away from a fight to right a wrong. Whether it was man's inhumanity to man, man's indifference to the land, or the creatures great and small that inhabited the earth, Nash Buckingham's ire could be aroused.

And what a special gift he had for confronting the issues. He did not discuss or debate appealing to emotion, but met it head-on with a common sense approach. To him, if something was as clear as the nose on your face, he would simply approach the matter as: "Sir – or madam – there is a nose on your face. Powder it or blow it or do whatever needs to be done with it, but, by all means recognize it as a nose!" Most of life is really that simple – we only make it complicated. Our eyes often take our noses for granted and fail to see.

And the years pass.

I know this man never failed to thank God for a lavender and pink and gold sunset or a "diamond morning" with the dew fresh on the grass and trees …the tear he kissed from my grandmother's eye after nearly sixty years of marriage and said, "You are still as beautiful to me as the first day I ever saw you."

The depth of Nash Buckingham was as deep as the Mississippi itself. Humanity shines so brilliantly in his works that found warmth in a puppy's cold nose on a frosty morning and coffee with chickory, sweetened with black strap molasses.

Yes, there was wisdom and knowledge tempered so evenly with grace and reverence and humor. He was prophetic. His heart was kind and dear. He did not lead a charmed life; life charmed him.

Here is a man who kept his springer spaniel Chubby's collar for over forty years so that it could be buried with him – and it was. There are two photographs of Chubby in *Tattered Coat*. One with Nonny and one with Barbee (my pet name for my grandmother) – "his Irma," as he called her – "Bunksey," as they affectionately referred to each other. She was raised amidst the plantations and magnolias – light copper-colored hair and twinkling blue eyes. Their love knew no bounds. In this day and age it is difficult, if not impossible, to find such an incredibly beautiful relationship. I can tell you that their devotion to each other was real. It existed.

I share this intimacy because of all his many, many attributes, this particular facet of his life has never properly been addressed. They loved each other and were in love with each other for an entire lifetime. I can say this without any hesitation because I witnessed it. Had I not, I would have never believed it could be possible. This is not a childhood memory, a fantasy passed down from one generation to the next. A grown woman with two children of my own, I was with them both, along with my father and my mother, when Barbee was taken to the nursing home. Both of them – so frail and aged, but such a deep, abiding love I have never seen before – and strength, my God, what strength! With her blue eyes still shining and his shoulders broad, but stooped with the passing of time, he held both her little hands in his.

I will never forget that day. It would have been one of the saddest days of my life, but the sadness was so totally overshadowed by the tenderness and inspiration of the moment. Tears of joy and elation come to my eyes when I think of that time, but never, never will I think of it with sadness. Their cup was indeed full and runneth over with an abundance of sharing that time cannot erase.

Nash Buckingham died on March 10, 1971.

His Irma died on January 17, 1974.

Their Irma, my mother, passed away on October 1, 1979. I found this poem the night she died while going through her papers. Words cannot describe my feelings when I opened this piece of paper, but in today's vernacular, it will suffice to say, "I lost it." In retrospect, on what was undoubtedly the saddest day of my life, Nash Buckingham's magic was there reaching out once again. Out of an insignificant drawer packed with mundane bits and pieces of things I read:

– A LETTER TO SANTA CLAUS –

Dear, wee grand-daughter, precious Heart Of Ours,
This is Nonny's and Barbee's letter to Santa Claus and GOD –
"Dear Saint Nick, before you drive your reindeer'd sleigh across
HIS moonlit voids and earthly chimney tops,
Kneel down beside your own warm, feather bed as this child kneels
And say our prayer for her to HIM.
'Oh! GREATEST GIVER of all LIGHT and GIFTS
Oh! STAR of BETHLEHEM serene
Make same to shine upon our grandchild's soul.
'Of such,' said HE, 'suffer their coming unto ME.'
Bring first to her, DEAR LORD, the radiant gift of faith in THEE
To thus enrich through life and after-life her faith in prayer
That renders doubly deep our duty in her being brought THY way.
However humble be her passage through this life
Bring her next, DEAR LORD, that priceless gift of character
That only YOU instill – and courage, too,
To help her fight THY battles for the RIGHT.
And though, among wee souls, her way be rose or thorn,
Leave first CHRIST'S blessing, Santa Claus, on this our grandchild's
earliest Christmas morn.' "

Nonny.

And I wonder why we are blessed. *A La Belle Etoile.* He said it of my grandmother, now I say it to them both. What a legacy to have had you. What a miracle to understand.

Love,

Fat Rat

INTRODUCTION

Dr. Dyrk Halstead

That I am writing this is something of a story in itself. In September of 1989, my shooting partner and friend, Robert Urich, and I were lamenting the fact that we didn't get afield nearly as often as we "needed." Unfortunately for doctors and actors (and I'm sure for many of you), we don't get paid unless we're present and accounted for. To make matters worse, my wife has adopted the "matching funds" policy – despite my conviction that I haven't lost a dime on a high-grade shotgun and have yet to recover one on a used dress.

Anyway, Robert suggested that we look into the possibility of hosting some type of outdoor, conservation-oriented television show, "not like anything that's ever been done. I mean Hallmark Hall of Fame quality. Great locations, great camera work, ethical, sportsmanlike conduct...," he said before I interrupted. "What a great idea," I said, "it sounds like a television show that would make you feel the way you do when you read one of Nash Buckingham's stories."

"That's it! Let's try to buy the rights to Nash Buckingham's books and develop the material," Robert said.

I suppose greater ideas have been born of lesser conversations, but I took Robert literally and started making calls. Copyright searches of 50-year-old books aren't exactly my area of expertise. One look at last September's phone bill and you'll know I'm telling the truth. But persistence paid its dividend. On a Thursday afternoon, I confirmed a Sunday brunch engagement with Nash Buckingham's granddaughter in Knoxville, Tennessee.

My wife Tina and I met with Irma Buckingham O'Fallon over a nice buffet. I indicated to her that my partner was in the entertainment industry and that we were interested in purchasing the underlying film and literary rights to her grandfather's works. If this was something that she felt inclined to pursue, Robert would come to Knoxville the following week for a meeting. Before leaving, she wanted to show me a few things that might be of interest. She laid on the table several original photos that appeared in the Derrydale editions, letters to and from Nash, and an unpublished story. I conceded that I might be interested.

A week and a half later, Robert and I were introduced to Glen Claiborne and his charming wife, Jean, at Irma's Knoxville home. Glen is the epitome of a Southern gentleman lawyer, agreeable, affable, and quite attentive to his client's interest. We had a most enlightening discussion that afternoon and conceptually agreed on matters. I couldn't help but notice the old boxes on the dining room table. To a Buckingham aficionado, what I was about to see was…well, I had arrived.

Hundreds of photos – many of which had appeared in his books, correspondence from Havaliah Babcock, Robert Churchill, John Olin, scrapbooks, and the original manuscript of *Tattered Coat* passed from my hands to Robert's with quiet reverence. In the bottom of a water-stained box were old orange and manila folders, ten of them. I gasped audibly as I read the first label:

> Nash Buckingham
> Letters, Documents, Text, Photos
> Material for AUTOBIOGRAPHY

I had just found Nash Buckingham's autobiography more than 25 years after it was written. I gulped the words from that old Smith-Corona typewriter, words that were crammed to the edges of yellowed paper and punctuated like no other author ever did. For those few glorious minutes, etched into memory, I was the only man alive that *knew* Nash left us his life's story. I had collected all of Buckingham's first editions, twice actually, since I helped Bob acquire his. I had read and reread them and honestly believe them to be the finest outdoor literature ever written. I couldn't have been more thrilled if I had discovered Noah's Ark or an unfired Parker *Invincible*.

No autobiography can be considered anything except a work-in-progress, because the subject of it is the author himself. Nash was no different than anyone else would be in a similar situation. Correspondence he had saved indicated this book had been in progress for a number of years before his death in 1971, but it had never been fully pulled together into final, publishable form.

But, Nash had left files and folders and notes and material he wanted included into his story, things he had written and things others had written and said about him. In some cases, these materials were letters with his handwritten comments on them; in other cases, they were personal photos or the transcripts of speeches delivered by others or by himself. In all cases, they were necessary, and have been included in this book with fidelity to what Nash wanted.

But moreover, there was a message that he wanted to leave behind, not – as he said – a mere recitation of his shooting prowess and experiences, but rather a systematic recounting of his life so the reader will *know* him, and also so that the reader will share the fervor he felt for conservation and saving those gifts of Nature he treasured and that were so much the fabric of his being. The photo captions and other notes made throughout are to help you, the reader, enjoy and understand his story a bit more.

Nash felt that his well-lived life had a value, and that value was in his being a spokeman for the ethical, caring hunter-shooter: the true conservationist. It is this that he had intended to publish while he was writing and gathering it together; it is this that is published here.

The only thing left to do was to find a publisher for the material, a company that felt – to a man – the way Bob and I and Irma and her children felt about Nash. Countrysport Press, who I consider the pre-eminent outdoor book publisher in America, more than meets that requirement. What you hold in your hands is the finished product.

This, then, is Nash's story. His life and his life's work written by himself, the summation of his career and the things, people, and events he considered important to him. It has been a labor of love for all of us involved in it. Throughout it all, we have all – everyone involved with the project – felt that Nash was there with us. We are proud to be able to bring such an important work to light and to life.

PART I

THE
EARLY YEARS

Miles Sherman Buckingham, Nash's father, who Nash regarded as a fine shot, good sportsman, and the man who gave him his early love for the sporting life.

A
BUCKINGHAM
FAMILY HISTORY

Our immediate family traces directly from the original settler, Thomas Buckingham, who, after touching at Plymouth 1637 with the Pruden & Hall expedition, went on to Milford and Saybook, Connecticut. Some of his original holdings are now in New Haven (1639). A grandson was one of the ten founders of Yale. He died in 1659 at Boston while there seeking a minister for their Milford flock.

Thomas' son Samuel, born 1641, had a son, Samuel, born 1668. And his son, Thomas, was born 1699. His sons Thomas and Benjamin were born, respectively, 1727 and 1737. We descend from Benjamin, whose son Nathan was born 1767 and his son, Sherman, was born 1793. And his son, Henry Gunn, our Grandfather, was born in 1821. His picture appears in my book, *Blood Lines*.

His oldest son, Miles Sherman Buckingham, was born May 16, 1846. His first son, Miles Gifford Buckingham, was born October 17, 1877. I was born May 31, 1880, in Memphis, and my younger brother, Henry Gunn, in 1887. Our two sisters, Cornelia Beckwith and Annie Gifford, were born in 1882 and 1889 respectively. Our grandfather, Henry Gunn Buckingham, drygood merchant out of New Orleans, settled in Memphis in 1828. He married Miss Mary McIntosh. My maternal grandfather, Theophilus Nash (born 1790), for whom I was named, son of a British ship owner, studied architecture in Philadelphia and was on the Chickasaw Bluffs (site of present Memphis) in 1810, en route via keelboat to New Orleans. He hunted with the Chickasaw Indians, and their chief, Johnny, at parting gave him a lock of hair, which I still have.

Grandfather Nash prospered in New Orleans and married Virginia Haynes of Baltimore, daughter of an editor of the old *Baltimore Sun*. There were three children: my mother Annie Gifford, Aunt Jessie, and an infant son who is buried with his parents in Brighton, England. My grandfather was a world traveler for many years; my mother had crossed the Atlantic thirty-two times from childhood to her marriage. My older brother, Miles Gifford, was a brilliant young banker under my parent, Miles Sherman Buckingham, president of the old State National Bank of Memphis, Tennessee. He died at 45 of a heart attack.

My younger brother, Henry Gunn (Princeton '10, where he played football), was a prep-graduate of Culver Military Academy. He coached the Colorado School of Mines, Denver University, and at Santa Clara University on the Pacific Coast. He was of the 305th Engineers, 80th Division in World War I, promoted on the field of battle and cited. He was badly wounded and spent his life at Biloxi, Mississippi, coaching prep football and writing. He died in 1951. Cornelia Beckwith Buckingham died in 1958. My younger sister, Mrs. A. J. V. Ware of Memphis, has two living children. I was married in 1910 to Irma Lee Jones, of Memphis, daughter of a pioneering and distinguished family of the state's settlings. We now enter our fifty-third year of married happiness. Our daughter, Mrs. R. E. Witt of Knoxville, has a daughter, Irma Buckingham O'Fallon, and there are two great-grandchildren, James Nash O'Fallon and little sister, Kelly Louise O'Fallon.

1637-1963. With the Lord's will to go.

Theophilus Nash Buckingham

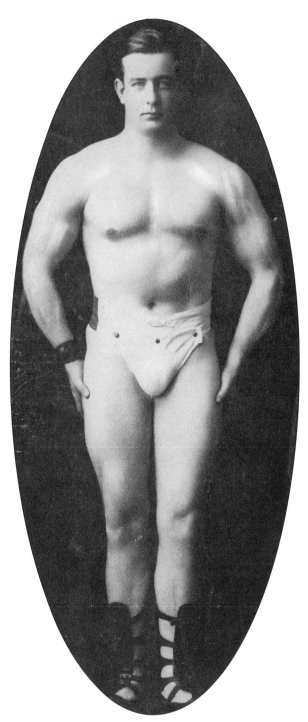

Nash was an exemplary physical specimen, owing to a lifelong interest in athletics. This photograph was made in 1902 while he was at the University of Tennessee. The back of the photo records his physical measurements as follows:

Height	5 10½
Weight	190
Chest	45
Chest Expanded	49
Waist	34 ½
Neck	16 ½
Arm	16 ½
Calf	16
Thigh	25 ½.

The photo also records that Buckingham was a member of the Milo Trio with August Dewell and B. W. Dudley. Nash notes: "This (photograph) was made in 1902; I had been in vaudeville with the Harvard physical culturist Dewell, and we had a weightlifting, boxing, and wrestling act at University of Tennessee's June Jubilee to raise money for the football coach's salary. I was coming twenty-two. I boxed pro out West in '07 and '08 and then turned 'amateur' to win the Southern AAU of America (heavyweight) in New Orleans."

AN
OVERVIEW

W hat follows is a brief overview of my life, a listing of the things I consider important to me. It will help as this book unfolds to follow the facets of a perhaps too-many-faceted career.

I was born Theophilus Nash Buckingham, May 31, 1880, in Memphis, Tennessee, son of Miles Sherman and Annie Gifford Nash Buckingham. I was educated in kindergarten and public schools until 1895, when I entered and completed the Memphis University School. I played football, baseball, and track, and had begun shooting, hunting, and fishing with my father and older brother when I was eight years of age. I shot my first wildfowl – swan, geese and ducks – when I was ten at the famous old duck clubs – Wapanoca in Arkansas and Beaver Dam in north Mississippi.

I entered Harvard in 1898 with the Class of 1902. In the spring of 1901, because of a malarial siege, I left Harvard and entered the University of Tennessee Law School. My first story, in dialect, was published in the *Harvard Monthly*, 1902.

At Harvard I fell under the influence of a famous physical culturist, August Dewell, partner of Eugene Sandow, to such an extent that I appeared with him in Vaudeville. I played football at Tennessee in 1901 and was elected Captain for '02. The 1902 team had a 6-2-season, defeating Sewanee, University of Nashville, Georgia Tech, and the University of Mississippi.

I also played baseball and was with the track and boxing teams. As a schoolboy I boxed with the "Real Kid" McCoy, and at Harvard I had come under the tutelage of Heavyweight Champions James J. Corbett and Australian Steve O'Donnell. I left Law School within a month of graduation in 1903 to enter a lucrative insurance business in Memphis and a position as

A page from Nash's scrapbook from his days at Harvard University. The top telegram is from "Papa," and tells his son that money is on the way, no doubt stimulated by a request from Nash – like all college men. The lower telegram tells Nash that he has to take time from classes to see to his sister's welfare. Nash's obvious delight at being freed for a short time is at the bottom.

The Harvard Monthly.

My Dear Sir:

Your MS. has been accepted, and by presenting this card at *13 Houghton 20 Grays* Hall you will receive three copies of the number in which it appears.

....
WMorrow

----- *Editor-in-Chief.*

The acceptance for publication of Nash's first piece, a story written "in dialect," and published in 1902, after Nash had left Harvard for the University of Tennessee.

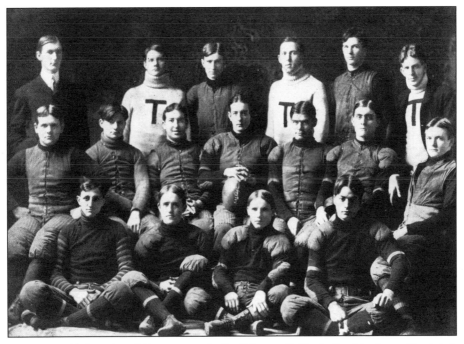

"The 1902 University of Tennessee football team, T. Nash Buckingham, Captain" (holding ball, center). Although Nash was a fine football player, it was not his favorite sport. He enjoyed baseball more, and boxing the most.

sportswriter for the *Memphis Commercial Appeal*.

While at Tennessee I was named All-Southern tackle by the late Heisman – then coaching Clemson. I had become an avid hunter and fisherman and soon placed in trap shooting circles with the famous "Gin Squad" of the original Memphis Gun Club. I sold my first outdoor story about ranching and big game hunting in Colorado in 1909, and I ranched on the North Fork of the White River for the years 1904 through 1913.

In 1899, I played baseball with the famous Chickasaw "Chicks" baseball team, and later, in 1905 with the Collegians. In 1908-9-10, I coached the earliest football elevens of the University of Tennessee "Doctors," and also played some early pro football.

In 1910, I married Miss Irma Lee Jones of Memphis (Her great-grandfather owned and built the home on the Ames Plantation, Grand Junction Tennessee, in 1847) a splendid shot, equestrienne, and golfer of those early days. We've been married at this writing 57 years. In 1910, I won the AAU of America heavyweight boxing title at New Orleans in their Southern Open Tournament.

About 1912, I began writing for the country's outdoor magazines, especially *Field & Stream*, of which I eventually became an Associate Field Editor. In 1916, I spent the summer at Camp Rye, Tennessee with the Chickasaw Guards that became part of the 1st Tennessee Infantry mobilizing for the Mexican Border.

In 1917, I entered the sporting goods business in Memphis with the late Major Enoch Ensley and stayed at it eight years, meanwhile writing in a broader field of the out-of-doors. While at the mobilization camp in 1916, I had written and sold to *Recreation* magazine a story entitled "De Shootinest Gent'man," destined to be an outdoor bestseller, and eventually a collector's item in book form.

In 1925 I was invited by the Western Cartridge Company, of East Alton, Illinois, to become director of their newly established Game Restoration Department and remained with them three years before accepting another bid to become Executive Secretary of The American Wildfowlers, a Foundation for Remedial Legislation and Waterfowl Betterment in their Breeding Grounds. Work of the American Wildfowlers from 1928 through 1932 has been characterized as "highly effective." The organization evolved into the Ducks Unlimited of today.

I was one of the original founders of the Outdoor Writers Association of America in 1927 at Chicago, and in 1941 I became chairman of its Waterfowl Committee. In recognition of this committee's work, in 1947 I was awarded *Field & Stream's* national trophy for Outstanding Service to Conservation for

Newspaper advertisements for Nash's sporting-goods business he and partners Enoch Ensley and Jim Carrigan started in 1917. Nash continued his writing career, and many articles appeared in the trade magazine, The Sporting Goods Dealer. *It was here and in the outdoor magazines of the day that his writing came to the attention of John Olin, who hired Nash to be Winchester-Western's first Director of Game Restoration. Nash left the sporting-goods business in 1925. The poem in the smaller ad is Nash's.*

our fight to cease the slaughter of Canada geese in the Horseshoe Lake, Illinois area during 1944-'45, and '46 which brought the "padlocking" of two counties for two years and eventually saw a lasting reform in many phases of the sinister operation. Had this battle with the Fish & Wildlife Service not occurred, the chances are the Mississippi Valley's flock of Canada geese would have been exterminated. I also led the fight that saw the mergansers saved from an equally evil fate.

The Waterfowl Committee of OWAA was solely responsible for the founding of what became the Mississippi Valley Flyway Council. In 1935-36, I was called to Missouri to lead a statewide survey which led to the formation of the great Missouri Conservation Commission, a model for other states to follow to relieve conservation from political grasp.

In 1934, at the invitation of Mr. Hobart Ames, I became an associate judge of the National Field Trial Championships held since 1896, and since 1902 at the vast Ames Plantation, Grand Junction, Tennessee. I served in this capacity for seventeen years, reporting the National annually for *Field & Stream* magazine. I was fortunate to judge practically every other top field trial feature in the country, and was later elected to the Field Trial Hall of Fame. I also became a Jade of the Chieftains of the Outdoor Writers Association.

Through the years I had compiled a history of the National Field Trial Championship – *National Field Trial Champions*. My other books consist of: *De Shootinest Gent'man, Mark Right, Ole Miss, Blood Lines, Hallowed Years, Game Bag, Tattered Coat*, and a reissue of *De Shootinest Gent'man*, in 1961. On its release, the *Memphis Commercial Appeal's* Paul Flowers "Greenhouse" column, to which I had been a contributor for many years, honored me with a public dinner at the Peabody Hotel, Memphis. I was presented with plaques from the University of Tennessee, the West Tennessee Sportsmens Association, and other gifts revealing the friendships I treasured over the years.

On January 18th, 1963, at the Lochhaven Club, Alton, Illinois, I was named 1962 "Outdoorsman of the Year" for Western-Winchester's national election by the 4000 Outdoor Writers Association members. In the run-off among six finalists, among them such luminaries as Dwight Eisenhower, Stewart Udall, Joe Foss, and John Alden Knight, I was elected and presented the Great Scroll and a magnificent custom-made Model 21 Winchester shotgun.

During my four years as Executive Secretary of the American Wildfowlers at Washington, D.C., I helped lay the groundwork for readjustment of the besieged Game Refuge Bill. My close friend J. N. "Ding" Darling was responsible for President Roosevelt's Executive Order that resulted in the curtailment of magazine guns to not more than three shots. In those years I probably saw more of and was concerned with some of the greatest national wildlife measures now on the books – including the Federal duck stamp that has raised millions for waterfowl.

Two years before his passing, Ding Darling and I were considering a plan for a bill that would remove administration of the Migratory Bird Law from jurisdiction of the Department of Interior and place it, and its enforcement, under an authority consisting of international lawyers, hydraulic engineers, and highly placed biologists from our four flyways, its enforcement to be placed under those agencies specializing in the seizures and convictions of criminals. In short, a last and determined effort to remove probably the finest piece of wildlife legislation ever devised for the benefit of this nation's out-of-doors from its political shadows of today. From where I sit, and with the knowledge that highly placed biologists agree, I feel we are today shooting "remnant wildfowl populations."

I feel that just about one more severe drought on the breeding grounds of Canada and the U.S., plus enforcement that has become a pallid pretense, and national duck shooting, now in last place on the totem pole for sporting interests, will pass into its final resting place with the buffalo.

At one time in my perhaps too-many-sided career, I worked in harmony and close friendship with two of this nation's greatest gun editors and outdoor authors in their own right – Colonel Harold P. Sheldon, former Chief Conservation Officer of the U. S. Fish & Wildlife Service (author of the Famed *Tranquility* stories), and Capt. Paul Curtis, Gun Editor of *Field & Stream* magazine. Both those gentlemen, now long gone, were kind enough to write testimonials to my shooting. Wrote Capt. Curtis, in 1927, "When a shooter like Nash Buckingham says that sort of thing about a shell (Western's 3-inch, copper-coated No. 4 Magnums) it is time to listen. For Nash makes a practice of shooting at ducks and bringing them down dead with surprising frequency at ranges where I leave off shooting at them. I have shot with him on the Mississippi, and I can say, irrespective of whatever other value he may have to his company, he is the best exponent they could get. I have helped a lot of men kill ducks, and at his special forte of knocking them cold at a distance, he has forgotten more than most of us get a chance to learn. The Nash Buckinghams are scarce."

And Colonel Sheldon, in an inspired foreword, wrote, "With an inherited love of sport and great opportunity at his door, it is not strange that Nash Buckingham became one of our best game shots as well as a most skillful and seasoned observer of the habits and habitats of wild birds and creatures. An experienced live pigeon shot and for years possessor of a worthy trap shooting average, Buckingham profited through access to gun and shell manufacture that rounded out his natural bent for gunning and its tools. Much has been written of his skill at upland game, and particularly of his ability at 'high ducks' with his now famous 12 bore Burt Becker Magnum. It has been my pleasure, educationally, to spend a good many days with him in duck blinds or behind his dogs after bob whites in Tennessee and Mississippi. I have myself written of seeing him bring down a limit of fifteen ducks with seventeen shells. I sincerely doubt if any duck was closer than fifty yards and the two extra loads were used to second-shot badly winged mallards."

For the kind words of these two greats, I am eternally in their debt.

THE
OLD HOME
PLACE

As a child I used to watch our old Negro cook, Lucretia Moody, and in after years, attempt rather unsuccessfully to imitate the nonchalant ease and elephantine grace with which she so confidently pinched up, sifted, and whipped together unmeasured ingredients (save by eye and touch) resulting in tasty beaten or butter-milk biscuits, satin-like mush muffins, cracklin' pone, Dally Lunn, batty-cakes, and other comestible blandishments in the bread and pastry lines too numerous to mention. Cooks have gone to Heaven for less than Lucretia's molasses and chess pies, the former heavily studded with pecan halves.

Suet, hasty, Indian, and bread-and-butter puddings, sluggish sluicings of golden or alabaster, plum-studded batter were pushed from thick, yellow crocks into which, with Lucretia's broad back turned for even a jiffy, went my swiftly explorative and quickly licked finger. Maybe dodging blows from her long-handled wooden spoon aimed at my head in feigned anger helped my ring dodging and football swerving abilities in more mature but locust-eaten years.

But for the life of me, I've never completely recaptured the words to made-up tunes Lucretia hummed or sang while waddling about her kitchen. Thanks to a fair ear for music, however, I can still carry the quavery but on-key strains of some of her melodies. They were all praises to Him. Or gladness at her own surety of being nestled within Salvation's wings. Others were of different mood. Lamentation, supplication, but, invariably, implicit trust in "De Lamb."

Like many of her day (these ninety years a-gone), Lucretia made up her own words and music. Forerunners, perhaps, of today's exquisite spirituals.

31

And praise God if that be so. For, as hymns, such rhythmic and sonorous bursts of creative belief and holiest imagery express spontaneously an individuality swelling with an acceptance of Salvation and divine implacability that has no more worthy counterpart in religion since time began.

I carry Lucretia's old refrains in my heart just as I still bear in mind the picture of her moving about in her beloved domain. Lucretia means as much to me today as, when a shaver, I fled to her huge, protective arms in many a close place when it paid a fellow to have a friend. To rest, with a sense of supreme safety, upon her capacious bosom and defy the elements or ailments of a child's world. Lucretia and her husband (who never deserted Confederate states), and her folks before her had been with our family for many, many years. Many and many a night we children said our prayers at Lucretia's knees before being tucked into bed while Dad and Mother went visiting or to the theatre. Lucretia is undoubtedly in Heaven. And I'll gamble a noggin of nectar that because she loved all of us as truly and loyally as we cared for her, that she'll be right there with our parents if and when we children manage to gather at the river of her songs. There was never but one River.

Lucretia's kitchen was a full thirty feet square with a twelve-foot ceiling. Its heavily plastered lath walls were kept flawlessly painted in either a peculiar shade of robin's-egg blue or a tender, virginal pink, according to Lucretia's flair for decor. And with such selections, Mother never disagreed. It was Lucretia's kitchen: She lived in it, reigned over it – and what she wanted or said, went. Over her giant range ran a square framework of piping ringed with hooks. From these hung the heavier copper spiders, pots, and roasters. All she had to do was reach up and lift off the desired utensil.

To one side of the range was a deeply inset open hearth burning four-foot wood. In front of that sat the servants' dining table, a marble-topped affair seating ten in case of parties or extra help. Many a school lesson we youngsters studied at that table, for the great house had no central heating unit and the kitchen was always toast-warm. We still possess that table, too. There were two matched walnut cupboards with fretted tin fronts and a huge pantry around the corner from the fireplace.

The cupboards were inviolately Lucretia's and not even Moody, her husband, was permitted to "mess with them." The kitchen floor was of twenty-inch, hand-hewn poplar planks invariably scrubbed to a bluish white.

A comfortable bedroom opened off the kitchen's northwest corner. Nights when torrential rains or snows and bitter cold prevented their going home, Lucretia and Moody bunked there rather than trudge several blocks to their cottage on Suzette.

Between the kitchen range and tub-like sink for dishwashing stood the pride of Lucretia's very being: the oak and cedar block with its movable marble top upon which she flogged the dough for beaten biscuits and rolled pie crusts. Her tremendous arms floured to the elbows, Lucretia piled a mound of dough upon the marble expanse, flourished a groove-headed hand-maul, grinned at us children gathered to watch and beg a lick, and, poised for the initial wallop, struck an Amazonian pose. But she was only waiting for a bid of perhaps two pennies as a church offering. Lucky the youngsters who climbed upon a chair, seized the beater in both hands (after surreptitiously spitting on them), rose on his or her toes, and let go with intent to splatter.

In after years it occurred to me that perhaps Lucretia got her dough bashed on the same basis Tom Sawyer used to get his aunt's fence whitewashed. For there were also penny consolation prizes in exchange for permission to use the fancy animal dough-cutters and fashion the last remnant for a personal biscuit or cookie. But somehow, preparation of supper was my choicest time for being in Lucretia's kingdom.

In winter's early dusks, the vast kitchen was shadowy and fragrant with sweet, meaty blends. The range had a sort of low, engine-like pant that air-waved coffee and spice aromas. Jerry Lee, the yard-man and waiter-at-table, sat in a cane-bottomed chair while I climbed into his lap and ground the coffee in a squat, yellow hand-mill. I was not allowed to drink coffee but sniffed the drawer-full and liked it better after Lucretia had cooked even that a shade blacker in the pan.

Above all else I recall the flawless neatness of her kitchen and her almost tigerish resentment of anything or anyone's disturbing it. She worked with a dishcloth notched in one elbow, and any untoward spilling of flour or grease was instantly eradicated with a swipe of her eraser. And woe unto Moody or anyone else's bringing boot-mud into her kitchen. I can hear Moody now, patiently raking and scraping his footgear on the porch doormat. And, invariably, Lucretia's first glance flew to Moody's brogans.

On the north end of our long, latticed back-gallery sat an enormous, vault-like ice-box or refrigerator. It housed several hundred pounds of ice and kept fresh the butter, eggs, meat, poultry, and game it took to feed an overall ten. That cold storage outfit was Moody's special duty to end all such, and he practically stood at attention when Mother inspected it daily.

Strange to say, Mother did all the table-carving at our home, except on hams and cold joints. That was father's assigned specialty. I have seen quite a few accomplished carvers in my time, but never one, much less a woman, remotely in Mother's class at hitting joints cleanly and shaving off slices of hot gobbler, eight-rib roast, or leg o' lamb. She was small and stood up to carve, but invariably her first glance and feel was at the knife's edge with a flash of approbation or questioning at Jerry Lee.

As I recall the story, she had been taught to carve while a member of the graduating class at Bolton Priory at Pelham, New York. The Priory very wisely brought in a famous meat-chef from a New York City hotel and the girls were given instruction in the fine arts of carving. Keeping knives sharp was a remembered "must," and Mother could flash her knife along the steel and hone the stone with the best of such cult. Father, equally keen on knives and carving, prided himself at slicing hams and cold roasts. He would give one glance at some highly prized country ham or spiced round of beef and run an accusing eye along the line of his three sons. At such moments, Jerry Lee usually chose to look the other way. It took ten mallard ducks a meal to feed our household. Mother carved for herself and the girls, but Father and each of us three boys were simply handed a whole duck and left to our own devices, which had better be correct.

My mother was an Englishwoman by birth, and, prior to her marriage in 1875 had, with her widower father and younger sister, crossed the Atlantic many times, living abroad in England and on the Continent a great deal. Beautifully educated and a gifted linguist and pianist, she reared her brood of five with a devotion to educational and religious tenets utterly unassailable in its completeness. Each evening, after lessons, we three eldest were read aloud the world's best literature: from Uncle Remus and Diddy, Dumps and Tot, to Dickens, Thackeray, Lorna Doone, and *Westward Ho!* By the time I had entered pre-school, much less through college, their combined parallel-readings were behind me. My grandfather, a world-traveler, left behind a library whose incalculable value was spared me until 1922, when a fire at my then-residence destroyed the rare volumes. Autographed books and letters from Edgar Allen Poe who played in a troupe of Baltimore amateur thespians with my grandparent, Hogarths, and original surveys of Mexico were among the treasures lost. Somehow I managed to salvage early editions of Fox's *Book of Martyrs*, the *Spectator*, and *Chronicles of the Bastile*.

Our home sat in a tree-shaded grounds that sloped from front to rear, our front and rear portions being two and one story respectively, the latter high off the ground on brick piers. Thereunder was another cold-room where Moody cut up the heavier meats, picked ducks, and saw to it that all neighborhood give-aways of waterfowl were cared for on a personally delivered basis. There was usually a boat or two stored there for painting and a specially wired dog-kennel for special occasions, quarantines, and breedings, and doubling as a maternity ward.

Between the main house and the rear was a cross-hall sixty by twenty feet with a downstairs rear-bedroom opening off it and a bath for company. It was nothing unusual on Friday nights to find from six to ten lads housed there and upstairs in my brother's and my room. You came up into the front great hall by three steps, and just inside sat the huge base-burner. The library, walled by bookcases, was fifty by twenty with bay windows at each end. The hall was fifteen feet wide and the dining room and parlor, beyond, were close by twenty-five feet square and with twelve-foot ceilings and large fireplaces. It took a lot of wood and untiring activity by the yard-man to keep that establishment comfortably warm in winter. But, we grew up reasonably healthy kids and only a few serious sicknesses, providentially, knocked at our door.

Roy, the greyhound who came to us in 1885, lived to be seventeen years old. The giant animal was complete master of a magnificent destiny. He was known the city over and when my younger brother and sister went walking with their nurse Aunt Lucy Lee, Roy stalked with them as a feared protector. He could clear the high iron-guarded picket fence of St. Agnes' Academy and snatch squirrels off the oaks before they knew what was happening. And if country dogs, coming to town under farm wagons, wanted to start something, they rarely tried it a second time.

Roy slept on a special mattress with a horse-blanket in winter, when he didn't choose to use my or my brother's bed. That vast, cold back-hall often saw huge rats scamper across it after night, so my brother and I devised a method of gunning them while lying on Roy's mattress with a dim gas jet in the hall and ourselves in darkness, though supposedly studying lessons. Through a crack in the door would be stuck our sixteen-gauge double barrel Parker with Roy watching – his ears cocked. But he was never allowed to touch the slain rats – for fear of a bite or contamination. But afield, Roy was a treasure. Broken to sit, heel, and fetch, he was a rabbit agent supreme, one whose like I never expect to see again.

In sunshine or shadow he was a great comfort and confidant. Many a night I've lain on the library hearth rug, with the household abed, reading by the firelight such tales of Poe's as *The Pit and the Pendulum* or the *Fall of the House of Usher*. I'd become so frightened that I'd read with one arm around the sleeping Roy's neck and ears keened for the arrival of the Lady Madeline's spook. And when I retired up the long, spiral staircase, Roy's was a consoling presence.

My
Early Years

M y life's first memory impressed me so vividly that it stood me in good stead later on. It is crystal clear even today. I was probably between three and four years old (1883-'84). Standing on a wide sloping lawn all brilliantly green-gold in warm summer sunshine, I watched a squirrel run along the picket fence rail between our home and our neighbor's to the east. To me the whole world seemed bathed in that wondrously tinted light.

I laughed and shouted and clapped my hands and shouted at the scampering, tail-waving, strange little creature. It fascinated me and naught I reckoned then of how many many squirrels I would sight in my lifetime. Then I heard my older brother shout – and his words still ring – "There's little Nash away down yonder on the lawn in the hot sun by himself. I'll go get him." He led me back to our shady magnolia mall on our upper lawn past the carriage driveway.

Thereafter, tiny glimpses flit past like cinema rushes. Peeping over a big bed's footboard to spy for Santa Claus and actually seeing him on hands and knees arranging toys around the big fireplace. It was Santa all right, there in a faint glow from log embers. Next morning there'd be drums and horns and building blocks and hobby-horses and the servants all in for gifts, egg-nog, and pretending to get caught for "Cris'mus gif'."

Memories of Pullman berths, enormous mountains, drinking mineral waters from springs of the Blue Ridge, and of digging in the sand by the seashore with a sort of deep rumble in my ears from pounding surfs. I retain a faint impression of colored lights from the Capitol's dome at Washington, with Mother holding my hand tightly and pointing away down yonder into a vast dim pit. It's all very swift and blurry.

Then, three little stair-stepped, long flannel-nightgowned figures snuggled about our Mother's knees to be read fairy tales and then repeat after her, "Our Father Which Art In Heaven." She was very, very lovely with her smiling gray eyes and deep-brown hair that hung past us almost to the floor. Then, one by one, we were tucked into our high-sided cribs and given a last good-night kiss to sleep on.

But how did that squirrel I first saw running along the fence come in handy later? Well, one late September or early October forenoon fifteen years later when "English A" for Harvard's class of 1902 was broken up into sections, mine was presided over by a slender, very dark-haired prof with an extremely resonant and beautifully pitched voice. His name was Copeland, and whispers went around that this was "The Great Copey." Without parley or preliminary he said, "Young gentlemen, as our first theme, to cover not more than two note-pages, you will set down the first impression you remember of life." Mine had never left me, so that was a natural.

Next day he asked for some short scene of levity or drama we recalled. I wrote of hearing an old Negro preacher deliver a funeral oration while standing in the deceased's nearly filled grave. "Brethren an' sistern'," he shouted, "dere's comin' a time when dere'll be a weepin' an' a wailin' an' a gnashin' o' tooths, an' dem as ain' got no toofs, dey gums'll hav' t' take it." Professor Copeland (God rest his great stature) read my little theme to the class next morning and said – reflectively – "A voice from the South – at least I sense freshness and diversion." The compliment toward my writing stayed with me throughout the years, and perhaps influenced me where dialect pieces were concerned, for my "De Shootinest Gent'man" has remained one of my best-known stories.

T he earliest recollection I retain of where summers were spent is the sound and scent of the sea. A sort of murmur and boom of big waves tumbling snow-ridged onto the sand and a tangy saltiness. The waves would rush up the beach all spread out and chase my brother and me like something alive as we scampered ahead with Mother in her bathing suit out in the ocean calling to us (she swam beautifully) and Aunt Lucy Lee keeping us from getting bowled over by the pelting breakers. The place? The recent great storm that so severely damaged the Atlantic Coast recalled it, Atlantic City.

My first real memory of travel and summering is of Blue Ridge Springs, Virginia – about seven miles east of Roanoke. The big frame hotel stood alongside the railroad overlooking a valley behind it, with towering mountains in the distance. A long covered bridge led across the valley full of lovely trees and weeping willows and springs from which the guests drank medicinal waters.

On the hill opposite the valley stood cottages, and that's where Mother and nurse with three chicks bedded down – most comfortably, too. I can remember the soft beds, lamplight and candles, long walks through the mountain trails, and Mother's playing tennis and dancing in the big ballroom at the hotel. We children played games in the valley, made rounds of the springs, and guzzled various dosey waters and visited the neighboring country store about half a mile up the road. I can still smell the interior of that store, a blend of tobacco, coffee, molasses, and drygoods.

And, most vividly, I recall men in black suits who wore beards and big floppy black hats and their women in dresses that looked like a nun's habiliments. The men, instead of shaking hands, pulled each others' beards. I heard Aunt Lucy Lee calling them the Dunkards (a religious sect), but I got it phonetically as "The Drunkards" and was terribly frightened of them.

I remember that when we left Blue Ridge at night we had to change cars somewhere (probably Lynchburg) in order to get to Richmond, Virginia where Mother had relatives from her young girlhood during the Civil War. As we left the Pullman before daylight, I was the last in line, and, passing Mother's still-lighted berth, I saw her pocketbook lying there on the blanket – she had forgotten it. I put it into my pocket and when at the hotel Mother suddenly missed her wallet and was about to have a spasm, I became a hero by producing same.

I remember Richmond but vaguely as of then but was shown the house where Mother lived, next door to the headquarters of General Robert E. Lee. Mother showed us where his couriers used to tie their horses to a fence and one day a shell killed one of their favorite riders, a red-bearded Irishman. Mother told us, too, of how they used to go to market with a wheelbarrow full of Confederate money but bring back only a few parcels. She had two trunks full of Confederate money years later in our lumber room.

One day Mother took my brother and me over to Petersburg, Virginia to visit friends and we visited the battlefield of the Crater. Miles and I found quite a few spent rifle balls while rooting around in the scene of the awful conflict; I kept them for years. I also have a recollection of Mother's showing us in Richmond where some famous church or theatre burned with great loss. Her father was in the fire but escaped, along with old Chief Johnny of the Chicasaw Indians whom he had known in 1810 at the site of Memphis. The Chief was back there for some sort of a convention or treaty.

We were shown, too, the Episcopal church where Mother used to lay out Bishop Stringfellow's robes for communion services and told of how one day a young Greek minister, who changed his name to Patterson, came for a tryout sermon. He was very short, so Mother put a soapbox in the pulpit. He mounted it and gave his text, "Now ye shall see me and now ye shall not." The box slipped and he disappeared. But he later came to our city of Memphis and was a beloved pastor for many, many years – Dr. George Patterson.

From that Atlantic City summer we brought home two big "concher shells" – at least that's what the name sounded like to me – white on the outside and pale pink inside. When you held them up to the light they had the color of a mouse's ear inside and when you held them to your ear you could hear the booming roar of the surf and restless sea.

After Atlantic City I vividly remember Niagara Falls; we summered out in the country from there at a pleasant farmhouse where we went for long walks and played with a lot of nice children. I remember crossing the great bridge across a foam-clouded canyon that scared me and watching the thunderous waterfall that made me grip Aunt Lucy Lee's hand tighter. I remember the good food at the farm and the names of the two young waitresses, Edith and Bay. Of the gettings-there and comings-home, I recall best being tucked into a Pullman berth, of kissing Daddy goodbye, and then the long trip where the porter put cinder-boards into our section to keep the cinders out of our eyes and we played up and down the aisles while the news-butchers and candy-men came through with tempting wares.

There was always the excitement of getting into and out of cities. That must have been my first visit to a city called Chicago. I was taken to a zoo, probably Lincoln Park, and we stayed at the old original Palmer House, where the floor of the lobby or barbershop had silver dollars imbedded in it. Mother sent my brother Miles to get his hair trimmed (25 cents) and when she got there the barber had thrown the book at him for shampoo, various oils, etc., to the tune of nearly $2.00. I remember Mother's giving the Boss Trimmer a lecture, putting a silver dollar on the counter, and walking out, with a threat to tell the hotel proprietor and, if necessary, the police.

In 1887 we were somewhere in Virginia and I distinctly recall on the way home visiting cousins in Winchester, Kentucky and being in Louisville at the old Galt House where we could look out of the window and see the Ohio. Then an evening at the Fair with giant fireworks and pyrotechnical clown. My mother's folks lived in a big house of white plaster with large gardens full of hollyhocks and a high brick wall we couldn't climb.

But 1888 was a summer I've never forgotten. We traveled three nights on the sleeper before we got to Kennybunkport, Maine, stopping off first at Washington where about all I recollect is being taken away up high in the Capitol dome with bewildering colored lights away down yonder and hearing what must have been a guide explain details while I held tighter to Mother's hand. It was scary. Then I recall arriving in Boston and being at a Hotel Vendome on what was probably Commonwealth Avenue and then being taken out to see Harvard and the Yard. Little did I dream then that one day I'd live nearly three years on the Yard and cross it many and many a time, old dorms, pump, and all. Then Kennybunk where some of Mother's schoolgirl friends had a summer home. We were put into a hack, Mother, Aunt Lucy, Miles, "me," Cornelia, and little year-old new baby brother Henry, and driven along a river out to where a great hotel stood along a curving beach and a giant seawall of great blocks where the river emptied into the ocean. There were little bathing houses on the beach's upper shelf.

Maine coast waters were cold, but nearly every sunshiny day we went bathing, hunting amid the rocks for star-crabs, prize pebbles and such, and taking swimming lessons from Mother with dog-fashion paddlings. Then there'd be long walks up the coast to Spouting Rock and Blowing Cave where tremendous rollers billowed in to strike the reefs and boom high into the air. And always there were ships going in and out of the river: tall-masted schooners, sometimes so close to the seawall we could shout to sailors on deck.

The first boat ride I ever had was from Kennybunkport down the river with Mother's friend Nan Bolton and her sister – two lovely young women with a racy cedar skiff. They had blonde hair and their strong young arms were tanned brown and they could really send their skiff dancing down the tide. Miles sat in the prow, Mother and I in the stern, and they finally landed us at the Seaward House. Mother didn't care for the big hotel so the Boltons got us into the Seaward House, a lovely inn run by a Mrs. Hughes, an Englishwoman from Boston. It sat along an embankment of the river that ran for several miles back into the lovely countryside where we went to pick blueberries to be turned in to the cooks for the finest muffins I've ever eaten.

There was a small dock down front on the river and the Seaward House lawns and gardens were lovely. Off the dock I caught my first fish, hand-lining with Aunt Lucy Lee holding onto the back waist of my pants. I felt something tugging at the bait and yanked. Then up – in response to frantic jerks – up came a flapping flounder that I finally managed to get off the hook and rush for the cook with my special prize for supper. Sometimes the Bolton girls would come in their skiff and we'd pull far up the embankment – I recall one afternoon seeing an Indian youth diving from a towering rock along shore. I can see his lithe, bronzed, beautifully muscled body now, shooting through space.

It was on the steps on the Seaward House a few days after our arrival that a Second Civil War broke out but was quickly settled. There were two boys and their parents there from Boston, the kids just about Miles' and my age and size, but they were not nice to us and began calling us "dirty rebels." Finally we met on the veranda steps above the flowerbeds. The older boy sneered at Miles and shoved him with a cry of "dirty rebel." The younger brother was backing him up. Thereupon Miles swung from his shoetops on the Boston boy's nose and over he went backwards and down into the (fortunately) soft flowerbed. And I, lowering my head, butted the other in his tummy and sent him after his brother. They arose squalling and out rushed their parents, Mother, Mrs. Hughes, and Aunt Lucy. A tremendous pow-wow.

There was an old gentleman sitting in a rocking chair, reading. He wore a bright plaid cap and pince-nez. He arose and shutting his book, demanded silence. "Those two boys," he said, pointing to Miles and me, "are perfectly in the right. Those two boys," pointing to the Bostonese, "began calling them dirty rebels and shoving them around whereupon the older rebel knocked hell out of that one – I would have done the same thing myself – and I fought in the Union Army, too." That settled it. The Boston kids were chivvied away and with their parents left Seaward House next day.

For a long time in our library at home we had large photographs of Blowing Rock and Spouting Cave, Indian bows and arrows, and baskets that smelled of the sweet salt marshes. And the big shells that we put to our ears to hear the sea roar again. I wasn't to see the state of Maine again until 1907 when I went moose hunting into New Brunswick. We left Kennybunkport and went to New York for a visit with Mother's relative, Bishop Spaulding of New York, who lived up the Hudson at Riverdale. I recall across the river something called the Spuyten Divvil, a great wooden estate with an old Irish gardener in a smock, pottering about a hot-house full of flowers. An old ivy-covered stone house, and ice-cream at meals. I distinctly remember demanding seconds on the ice cream and getting a call-down.

In New York we stayed at the old Fifth Avenue Hotel and I can still hear the jangle of mule car gongs and see the hurrying through and being taken to a museum. Then the long trip home and first school days.

I have little adequate recollection of the earlier Christmases when I was five or six years old, other than that of hanging up stockings amid suppressed excitement to awaken next morning to find drums, horns, rocking horses, wooly sheep on wheels, and apples and oranges galore. In those days, too, people made a lot of early noise at Christmas, the point being to catch other folks for a "Cris'mas gif." It was along in there, too, that I recall father's bringing home a set of boxing gloves, and, on his knees, he would don a pair and give Miles, my older brother, and me boxing lessons. Afterward we would have a brotherly set-to.

It came in handy, too. One day, while I was still in kilt-skirts, an up-the-street boy named Garnet Parker (a close friend in later life) came by with a colored man fetching home a cow. He had graduated into knee-pants and roughly shoved me out of his way on the sidewalk. Then he pushed me. The colored man stopped to watch and several older boys roller-skating across the street came running. Their leader was Mike Gavin, son of our good neighbor and he at once took over as my second. Mike lived to be a great and wealthy New York lawyer, passing on at eighty-five. Recalling the boxing lessons and how to throw a right-hand punch, I let fly and landed squarely on "Kitty's" beak and set him back on his heels, whereupon I charged in with flailing lefts and rights that sent him howling and the onlookers stopped it. I was two years away from my second battle.

And in that old home where I was born, and it is still standing though much changed, I developed a fright complex. Out in the wide high-ceilinged downstairs hall the gas jets' three reflections made long arms flick across the ceiling and, apparently, reach for me. I was secretly terribly frightened of them. Mother must have discerned reluctance on my part when asked to get something for her upstairs, and I know now that she deliberately tested me watchfully. I would, on orders, go to the parlor-library door, crack it open, and watch the ceiling for those wigging, clutchy arms. Then, shutting my eyes and holding my breath, I'd dart across the hall and rush upstairs, repeating the dash when I came downstairs. Finally Mother took me on her lap and gave me a long, quiet talking to; the gist of which was that it was all fancy on my part, that the wiggly, clutching arms meant nothing; if they did she and father would be right there – now then – let's try it two or three times, just to show you. That did it, for above all else I loved Mother.

The other fright complex was dead chicken heads. It used to take six or eight chickens a meal for our family and down in the long backyard, our cook, Lucretia Moody, used to wring chicken necks and the poor fowl would hop all around, spouting blood from headless feather masses. The boys found I was

"September 1887, Miles Buckingham aged 10 years, Nash Buckingham aged 7 years, Cornie Buckingham aged 5 years, Henry Buckingham aged 6 months, and Lucy, our old mammy nurse. Photo taken in New York while Mama was visiting Aunt Cornelia Beckwith."

afraid of dead chicken heads and used to throw them at me to see me run or shrink. And, strangely enough, when Mother found it out, she told me that while I was en route to the universe, she had been hit by a carelessly thrown chicken head – so I was prenatally marked. Strangely, too, it persisted, although the heads of any other type fowl have no such antipathy for me.

But I have very vivid recollection of 1887 and 1888 at Christmas time. I recall having typhoid fever in '87 and of having to be taught to walk again by the colored nurse "Aunt" Mammy Frances Daniels, at that time about the only "trained nurse" in Memphis. I remember being held up to the window to see my grandfather's funeral pass our house on Vance Street on its way east to Elmwood Cemetery.

But Christmas 1888 is very vivid. My younger brother, Henry, was about a year old – we had spent the past summer in Kennybunkport. That Christmas we three children, Miles, Cornelia, and I, were expectantly around the lighted Christmas tree. All the servants were on hand, too. Father walked over to the big black square piano on which Mother used to play songs and hymns for us, and picked up a double-barreled shotgun. We knew it wasn't his because it was smaller. It was a sixteen-gauge hammer Parker, for Miles, two and a half years my senior. Gunningly, we were off to the races – and a long, long race it's been.

After church and a wonderful Christmas dinner of turkey, roast suckling pig, and plum pudding (the same fare every Christmas until death did us part), Father called his two setters, Nip and Tuck, and he and Miles with their shotguns and ammunition and I along to learn walked out east into the country into what was known as "Snowden's Field." It was ideal quail country as we knew from having watched Dad and his friends run their field trial dogs many times. Starting in at what is today's St. John's church on Peabody at Bellevue, we hunted east to within a quarter-mile of where I type these lines. The dogs pointed a good many times, and Miles, with some previous experience with Dad's gun, sacked a half dozen bobwhites strictly on his own. I was very proud of him, and justly so, because as the years advanced and he began to hunt ducks and geese, too, he developed into one of the finest wingshots I've ever seen.

I recall that we ended at what is now the northwest corner of McLean and Central where the fine old Carter home was to later stand, but it was a canebrake then and paths led to it from a clearing where some sort of contractor's camp was pitched. It was getting dusk and we were nearly three miles from home. The contractor, however, recognized father and sent us home in a big surrey with a driver. A wonderful, wonderful Christmas.

I t was not until mid-January of 1889 that I fired my first shotgun – Dad's 12 bore. I accompanied him and Mister Edward Moon on a quail hunt on the Lemaster farm east of the city and beyond Nonconnah Creek, an eight-mile drive from our house. We used the surrey and left home before daylight, with Dad and Mister Ed on the driver's seat and the three dogs, Nip, Tuck, and Dan, and I on the back seat under a buffalo robe. We went southeast on the Pigeon Roost road, crossed the rickety wooden bridge over Nonconnah, past the hamlet of Shakerag, and, farther on, where the Germantown road turned north, we entered Winchester Pike's dirt road and the Lemaster antebellum cottage home lay just beyond. Today, that is all suburban Memphis and heavily populated with expressways running everywhichaway around Nonconnah.

There was a breakfast of country ham, red gravy, eggs, and batty-cakes at the Lemaster home and then we mounted good walking horses with a mule-mounted Negro along with lunch and saddle bags. Our dogs were ramblers and finders. We lunched down in the bottoms by a fire Clabe, the guide, built, and you could drink clear creek water in those days without fear of disease. Father let me shoot twice at single birds that afternoon and I missed both times, but I found the gun didn't kick a bit and was eager for next time's try. That eagerness was to last a lifetime. Too, father had joined a duck club in Arkansas and came home with sacks full of mallards and other species including geese and swan and promised us that in another season we boys would be taken along to Wapanoca. Right along there I followed up the typhoid fever with scarlet fever, but with the aid of Mother, Dr. Maury, and Mammy Frances, I made it through.

Looking back on our family life of the eighties and early nineties, I recall that the big household was early astir, with turns in the bathroom and assembly at breakfast for grace and grub, Mother behind the coffee service, but only she and father partook; we children got no coffee until we were sixteen. Ham, bacon steak, fish, biscuits, batty cakes, pitchers of milk, and eggs galore. Appetites were carefully scrutinized by Mother and Aunt Lucy Lee the nurse.

Little sister Annie was to be born in '89 and, of all us children, Aunt Lucy loved her best. I can see her now rolling the baby-buggy containing Annie, with little brother Henry walking along behind, and the great black greyhound, Roy, stalking solemnly beside Aunt Lucy. They were known all over our end of town, which was the 7th or "Kid Glove" ward. The New Frontier, in sepia, now hangs over the 7th. After breakfast, lunches were packed for Miles and me, and, with children of the neighborhood, we took off for first schooling at Miss Clara Conway's coeducational preparatory two miles north of Vance street – on Poplar. Four miles a day and no sport cars or family limousines with chauffeurs for the little darlings. If it rained hard enough, we got to ride all the way around on the mule cars or later (1892), on the first electric trains.

I was in the kindergarten (kids got to school later in life in those days) "Sunbeam Class" of lovely Miss Florence Acree. One of my first jobs after learning to write my name by ear and sight was to copy a picture in watercolor of a Chinaman with two buckets of water hanging from a shoulder carrier. Miss Florence complimented it highly but that is as far as I ever got in art – the brushy kind, that is.

But I had a fight the first day in school. We were let out on the playground for what was known in those days as "little recess," but I took a biscuit sandwich along, ate half of it, and sailed the remaining biscuit half as far as I could – watching it curl – and hit a boy named Allen Ullathorne, a Poplar Street denizen, in the back. He whirled around angrily – several lads pointed me out – and over charged Allen. I started to say, "I didn't mean to hit you," but the look on his face decided me to drop apology and mend defense fences,

A crowd gathered. He barged in so I met the assailant with an overhand right, remembered from early parental tiffs and the skirmish with Kitty Parker, that landed flush on Allen's beak and rolled him to one side. Then, for the first time, I realized how the world cries for the kill in the prize ring. He was off balance and when one of the spectators shoved him, he went down, got up and – ran – with the crowd after him. Miles, two years ahead of me in school, got there about that time and we waited until they brought him back to see if he wanted any more. We both drew a good talking to from Miss Conway and were made to shake hands. I think she had a hard time to refrain from laughing. But anyway, Allen and I got to be fine friends that lasted his lifetime – a fine man and citizen.

I never had another unfriendly personal fight until seventy years later and got restrained from that encounter. I am thankful I didn't get to K.O. that guy, because a month later he had a heart attack and I might have put him away for good, and myself along with him. At that, he didn't want any part of it and, poor fellow, he also had a lot of other trouble. With amateurs and professionals I donned boxing gloves for many years, and I can honestly say that I never emerged from a battle with any sense of unfriendliness for an

47

opponent. You got and gave lumps and there were rough, tough customers – yes. But some of the best friends I've ever known have been prizefighters.

We spent the summer of 1889 at Waukesha, Wisconsin with a final week or so at Madison amid its nest of beautiful lakes. At Waukesha we were cared for at Mrs. Wardrobe's comfortable home almost next door to the lovely high school and splendid grounds. It was directly opposite one of the top hotels. Of the several noted springs, I recall Bethesda and Silurian. One of the big hotels had a swimming pool, too. And near town was a ginger ale bottling plant where you could really fill up. Beautiful parks abounded, there were lots of archery contests going, and for us, some particularly grand playmates.

Across the street from Mrs. Wardrobe's, a family from Louisville, Kentucky had rented a summer home and brought their servants, carriages, and horses. The Powhatan Wooldridges, Mr. Wooldridge also did landscapes and portraits in oil. Their son, "Pow" was our age and his two sisters were lovely little girls and beautifully reared. We had great times. One I particularly recall was a fishing trip to nearby Peewaukee Lake. Mr. Wooldridge, "Pow," and their Negro coachman, the big surrey, and Miles and I – about daylight. By the time we reached the lake it was cloudy, spitting rain, and windy, but we bought bait, got a good seaworthy boat, and flew at it. Down the lake a piece we turned into some probably wild rice inlets and began fishing. By two o'clock that afternoon we had two strings of big perch and pickerel and bass that took Mr. Wooldridge and two of us boys to lift. Fifty years later I was returning from judging the Saskatchewan field trials and crossed the trestle over a long narrowish lake between Milwaukee and Chicago – I knew it instantly: Peewaukee – and sure enough, in a moment the Hiawatha passed that station.

The youngest of the five children was born in 1889, and that necessitated father's buying the bigger Murray house next door on Vance and the families merely swapped houses. Shortly thereafter Mr. Murray built another home adjoining him on the east (our old, big sideyard grove). Both our houses had been built during or immediately after the Civil War by a gentleman who went away to fight but never came back except as a ghost and that's how Mr. Murray came to buy the homes.

There was a scare-legend that the ghost sometimes came around to see how matters were going – a feeble, emaciated man in uniform who merely walked wistfully around but never bothered anyone. The servants were all frightened when he was reported seen, but personally, while constantly on the lookout, I never saw him. My grandfather's valet, a Negro man named Jones, who, unfortunately was somewhat addicted to liquor, reported having been chased by the ghost – who after carrying Jones at a terrific pace for several blocks, suddenly went up in smoke. We lived in the old house for twelve years until father practically tore it down and rebuilt a huge modern home, with six bedrooms and three baths

Nearly all homes of those earlier days had front-porches, "piazzas," or verandas where the occupants, under awnings, took the early morning or evening shade and cool. Air conditioning was of Jules Verne vintage. Screening was not known, and after overflows in the Mississippi, mosquitoes could get mighty bad. But, it was wonderful to sit at dusk with the birds in the big trees and the katydid chorus striking up all at once and dying away just as swiftly. That was a wonderful old home with a big sideyard where Annie later had her big dollhouse and we played baseball in the big vacant lot next door.

By the time I was eight years old I had shot quail on the wing behind top bird dogs. Mr. Bryson, owner and handler of the great setter, Gladstone, was our next-door neighbor. In 1889, my father joined the Wapanoca Outing Club at Turrell, Arkansas and one Thanksgiving Day, 1890, I had my first duck hunt. All this is more thoroughly covered in a story, "Comin' Twenty-One," which appears in my book, *The Hallowed Years.*

That same year I also began wildfowling at the old Beaver Dam Ducking Club, Tunica County, Mississippi, forty-two miles south of Memphis, and hunting on the Mississippi River. Railroads hadn't been in vogue long to either point – Wapanoca or Beaver Dam. The counties were just beginning to have the timber cut, and the masses of wildfowl were incredible. I was also taken to the Grand Prairie of Arkansas, west of Memphis, where with my elders we camped and shot prairie chickens. By 1989, these birds, due to the grossest exploitation, were gone. I was taken goose shooting from pits on Mississippi River sandbars. We'd go downriver on steamboats and be put ashore at some friendly planter's land. But very few people goose hunted this area in those days.

Between 1890 and 1900, I saw swans practically disappear. Market hunting held full sway legally and publicly approved. By the time 1901 rolled around, I had shot a lot of wildfowl and upland game. We boys were taken to Minnesota for early shooting. I wish I had a picture showing my last shoot on Wapanoca Lake, Washington's Birthday, 1901. The late Judge George Gilham and I bagged a

49

hundred pintails, almost all drakes. The club limit was fifty ducks per person per day – there was no Federal or state limit. In those days, and earlier, as a well-grown lad, I shot twelve, ten, and even eight-gauge shotguns. There were, of course, many wild turkeys shot in those formative years. Many of those hunts are recorded in my nine books, including *National Field Trial Champions*, a history of the National Field Trial Champion Association, where I served for seventeen years as an associate judge and reported for *Field & Stream*.

I left the University of Tennessee Law School a month before graduation in 1903 to take over an insurance company my dad had gotten hold of. He was president of the State National Bank in Memphis. I was also of the Class of 1902 at Harvard, but a bad dose of malaria laid me out in my junior year, so I came South to the law school. I recall gunning the prairies of the Dakotas for prairie chickens and sharptails, as well as wildfowl, in 1904, and then on to Saskatchewan. It was all market gunning in that country. Our private car was sidetracked, and we'd shoot for a week from buckboards with rambling dogs. But at every stop there'd be barrels of birds being shipped by farmers to Eastern markets.

In 1904 I began hunting big game and fishing on the North Fork of the White River in Colorado, and "took up" there summers for the love of the country, staying until 1913. In those years, too, I had penetrated the Texas and Louisiana coastals at the old Delta Duck Club, and spent many days shooting canvasbacks off Rockport, Arkansas, San Jacinto Bay, with some other time after prairie chickens in the Texas Panhandle. While at Harvard, I recall gunning shelldrakes from a fisherman's island off the coast. We lived with the fishermen and shot from sand holes above the tides walled with wet seaweed – but it made good blinds.

By those years, too, with wildfowl conditions unchanged as to state or Federal attention, I was thoroughly familiar with what is today the ricelands of Arkansas. Rice was just being "discovered" then. The continental supply of wildfowl was incredible, but there were certain signs showing even then that the future should have very serious care. There were many duck clubs in the nation. I have shot the famous old Winous Point Duck Club on Sandusky Bay, as well as the private clubs of Currituck Sound. Incidentally, I think that Winous Point is the oldest duck club in the nation, with Beaver Dam – privately owned for these many years – the next oldest.

"The ranch sprawls in the lethargic inertia of siesta. My ranch on Beaver Creek just off the White River – 240 acres, great deer, elk and fishing. Irma and I honeymooned here in 1910."

Nash "with a 2-pounder." The only photograph in existence in which he sports a mustache. This was made at the E-X Ranch in Colorado, 1908.

Although not well-known as a big-game hunter, Nash's Western period acquainted him with the sport, and an early fall trip to New Brunswick produced this trophy.

The back of the photograph records: "Backward – turn backward! The big salmon of the Upper Little Mirimichi, Ghost Trout," indicating Nash's use of this photograph in the story of that name.

Some Reflections
On Athletics

"The Old Chicks"

Recounting the Deeds of Memphis' Greatest Team by T. Nash Buckingham
(From the Memphis Commercial Appeal, *circa 1919, recalling some of*
Nash's baseball exploits)

The Flight From Friar Point

While the Chickasaw-Selma series of 1899 was undoubtedly the most interesting, there was one contest the memory of which will linger longer with the boys. The Chicks had played some 20 games, were well shaken together and their fame had spread throughout the land. The personnel of the team had about settled down to brass tacks when a challenge was received from the ball team at Friar Point, Mississippi.

Louis Mosby, who had played some mighty good ball for the Chicks at first base, had been called away and the bag, with an odd change or so for circumstance, was looked after by Greer or Newt Ford. The Chicks had never played a game away from home, but after due deliberation it was decided to travel to the delta and engage the enemy.

Now, in those good old days, baseball in the half carved out delta was a matter to be entered into, like matrimony, "not lightly nor unadvisedly"; win, lose or draw, it was usually a case of "fight and fly." Friar Point had imported a battery – "Sheeny" McGill and Veasy – for the occasion, and their ranks bristled with talent from the university and baseball stardom of the grand old sovereign commonwealth.

The Chicks left Memphis one afternoon on the good ship Jim Lee. A large delegation accompanied us, and much money, for it was rumored that the Friars had a roll to wager. We had a lovely trip downstream; it was, if we recall accurately, the last of July, and an exquisite sunset had Greer expatiating upon its highlights and shadows. Next morning we disembarked, climbed the levee and were housed in the local hostelry. About all we remember of the tavern was that some poor soul was ill and the management requested as little disturbance in the house as possible.

It was a reeking hot day, and after a brief survey of the town we were of the opinion that the crowd wouldn't be much to split the gate over. But that afternoon when we dressed and went across the road to the ball lot, it looked as though half the population of the state had sprung from somewhere. They came afoot, horse and muleback, in wagons and in those fine turnouts for which country folk were noted in those times. And they were all there to see justice done, too.

The Festive Bat Boys of '99

The Chicks began to find their old rival, McGull (who had visited Memphis with teams from Louisville), and collected several runs, holding Friar Point at every angle, meanwhile. Shields and Hurlburt were doing the honors, with Newt Ford at first that day, Mallory, Hutton, Taylor, Scarborough, with Monedonico in left, "Cap" Collier in Center and the writer staked out in right field. Somewhere along the middle of the game, with excitement intense and partisan feeling rapidly mounting to that atmosphere involving equal parts of menace and caution, some Friar Point batter tipped up a foul. Ed Hurlburt ran up the third baseline and muffed the ball ingloriously.

A local Negro lad set up a shrill cry of derision and joy and a young fellow sitting in a group of habitants along the third base sector kidded Hurlburt. Ed was really addressing the former, but at any rate, what he said was construed to mean the latter, and that settled the matter right there. Immediately thereafter some kind soul on the gate, having given warning to Manager Finley, was besieged with requests for passes. Scarborough came up, warned by the aforementioned angel, and told our manager that those gentlemen who had been after passes had gone, to be brutally frank, for their pistols. The issuing of passes ceased abruptly.

Serious Trouble in the Offing

Next inning we were standing out in right field, hoping that the next man up wouldn't hit one in our direction, when a great commotion took place around the gate and home plate. We saw a young man advancing upon the infield and we do not feel that we are doing truth much wrong when we say that the pistol he bore was of great length and girth.

We could see it plainly from afar right field and it glistened in the sunlight and was not good to look upon. But for the quick thinking and action of T.G. Scarborough there might have been serious trouble, but he rushed in from shortstop and other cool heads dashing from the grandstand averted tragedy.

Hurlburt, really having meant no offense to the lad, apologized "as though his life depended on it," and the game was resumed. To make matters worse, some other kind soul came over to our bench and let it be remembered that immediately upon the adjournment of the contest it was in contemplation by certain losers to "fog up the park" and treat the spectators to a foot race with the Chicks furnishing the leading role. But some heaven-sent friends from Helena, who had come down on a little steamer to see the game, offered us aid. We were invited to come aboard their craft and go to Helena for a game next day. We were instructed not to go to the hotel and dress, and to grab suitcases and go right on down to the boat. Our three last batters struck out without a murmur and then the foot race started.

We thought we were the first ballplayers to reach the floating haven but, mounting to the top deck and turning into the shelter of a smoke stack, we found the huge frame of Ed Hurlburt occupying the only shell hole in sight. We asked him what his trouble was and he replied by a nod of the head – meaning *he* was. About that time we heard a loud disturbance taking place to starboard and tiptoeing across, we peeped over the good ship's bulwark to investigate. There upon the gangplank stood our noble second baseman, Mr. Albert Mallory, his hands aloft, and just ashore, sitting upon a mule and leveling upon Albert's bosom the business end of a Winchester rifle, sat the young man to who Ed Hurlburt had addressed his unfortunate remark.

We forget just now the exact words spoken by Mr. Albert Mallory, his hands aloft, and the gentleman of the mistake in identity, but they came right from the heart. Our ship's captain came forward at this juncture and with great presence of mind seconded Mr. Mallory's motion and cut away the gangplank. Up the river we steamed, while the insulted party followed us up the levee seeking a chance to fire at Hurlburt. 'Tis said that he did actually turn one loose across our bow, but we cannot substantiate that – we were in no position to. Score: Chicks 4, Friars Point 0.

I had three most thrilling experiences at UT. In baseball, 1902, at old Baldwin Park we were playing Vanderbilt. I shut them out with three hits on Friday and was supposed to play first base against them on Saturday. But they talked me into trying the "iron-man" stunt and pitching again in the second. When we were ahead with two outs in the ninth I based my first free-pass. The next batter hit a weak pop-fly to the first baseman. He didn't have to move to make the catch. I took off my glove, intending to sail it from Baldwin Park over to The Hill, because I would rather have whipped Vandy those two games than been President of the United States. But the first baseman dropped the ball!

We had been using a substitute centerfielder since the sixth inning when our fine fielder, Mack Gamble, had been injured while sliding. After the pop-fly error, the next batsman hit a soft fly ball to center. Mack's substitute not only muffed the play but fell down trying to recapture it.

I'll tell you one thing. The deep sorrow of those two fine teammates, after the game, hurt worse than losing...

That fall, 1902, we had a terrific football game with Vanderbilt. I got loose for a long run, no one t'wixt we and the goal line except Vandy quarterback Kyle, an Old Fox and a good 'un, too. We didn't know about, or have, the downfield blocking for which the Vols are famous nowadays. So, in desperation, I tried hard, but unsuccessfully, to hurdle Kyle.

Sitting there disconsolate in defeat that could have been victory, I realized to the fullest how those erring teammates on the baseball team felt. Thrills can be two-edged.

Once at a track meet, after participating in the shot put, hammer throw, discus, and pole vault, I was forced to replace a guy who ran the last 440 yards on the mile relay team. Our team won. I have since heard about guys walking a mile for their favorite brand of cigarette, but I'll bet that's the first time and last that I'd run a quarter-of-a-mile for a bunch of bananas – the prize.

Memphis Hall of Sport Fame— T. Nash Buckingham, No. 4

NASH WAS A CLEVER HARD HITTING BOXER.

"BUCK" WAS AL-WAYS A GOOD CLEAN SPORT.

WAS STAR PUNTER FULL FOR U of T.

T. NASH BUCKINGHAM.

By Jimmie Frank 1920.

By Herbert Caldwell.

A LOVER of sports, an advocate of clean sports and fairness in all competition and a true sportsman in all that the word "sportsman" implies is Theophilus Nash Buckingham, one of the most versatile athletes Memphis ever produced. Although he has not actively engaged in any competitive athletic events for probably ten years, "Nash," as he is familiarly known, keeps abreast of the times and is probably as well informed in various sports as any of the present-day stars.

Buckingham is a native son. He first saw the light here in Memphis on the 31st day of May, 1880. A robust youngster, "Buck" took to out-of-door games at about the age a duck would take to water. He says he can't remember of ever having played dolls, but that as soon as he discarded the kilties, donned his first pants and became a full-fledged boy he was either playing or "butting in" the games of the larger boys in the neighborhood.

Buckingham during his days of activity as a college athlete played an important part in football, baseball and track and field events. After his college days he kept up his indulgence in athletics as an amateur boxer, and today is an enthusiastic trapshooter and a devotee of the golf links. Golf, states "Buck," is his favorite of all sports and he thinks is the greatest conditioner and health retainer for persons of 35 years of age and over.

After playing a prominent part in athletics on the Memphis High School teams, Buckingham entered Memphis University School, where he was a member of the baseball, football and track teams of 1895-96-97. He was a big factor in the

success of the school in athletics during those years.

Buckingham entered Harvard in the fall of 1898. He played on the class teams that fall and with the class teams and scrubs in baseball and football the following year. With prospects for his most brilliant career in athletics, and it practically assured that he would make his letter, in 1900 Buckingham suffered a setback with an attack of fever early in the summer. He was prevented from trying for the baseball team and did not recuperate sufficiently to resume football practice in the fall.

Discouraged by his illness at Harvard, Buckingham returned home and entered the law department of the University of Tennessee in the spring of 1901. He pitched and played first base on the baseball team and played fullback and tackle on the football team. He was also a member of the track team. His second year at Tennessee, Buckingham was elected captain of the football team. For the first time in the athletic relations of the two schools Tennessee defeated Sewanee in 1902. The season wound up with a three-cornered tie for the S. I. A. A. football championship, with Vanderbilt, Tennessee and Sewanee filing claims for the title.

Under most peculiar circumstances Buckingham in 1902 broke the S. I. A. A. record for shot-putting. He was pitching a game for Tennessee and between innings-went into the circle and put a 16-pound shot something over 40 feet—he does not remember the actual distance—setting a new record and one which may still stand, although Buckingham lays no claim to the present record.

Following his collegiate athletic career Buckingham continued to play a prominent part in athletics in the south. During the years 1907 to 1910, inclusive, he was a member of the famous "Gin Squad" of trapshooters, who represented Memphis in trapshooting meets throughout the country. Other members of the team were Bayard Snowden, Bright Goodbar, Hugh Wynne and Fontaine Martin. The "Gin Squad" gained much notoriety.

In 1910 Bucknigham, representing Memphis, won the heavyweight championship of the Amateur Athletic Union boxing tournament held in New Orleans. "Buck," who weighed about 180 pounds, made a clean sweep of the heavies.

During the latter years of the Chickasaw baseball team Buckingham pitched and played first base in several games for the Chicks, and later played the same positions for the Collegians, a team which included several members of the old Chickasaws.

After leaving Tennessee Buckingham played in several football games, making his last appearance on the field as a member of a team of local stars banded together as the Memphis Athletic Club in 1909.

Buckingham is a member of the Memphis Country Club, where he spends much time . on the links. He is also a member of several hunting and fishing clubs and is an enthusiastic hunter and fisherman. Love for the sports probably dictated "Buck's" destiny in the business world, for he is an active member of the firm in a thriving sporting goods business here in Memphis.

An article from the Memphis Commercial Appeal *proclaiming Nash's induction into the* Memphis Hall of Sport Fame *with a rundown of his formidable athletic achievements.*

THE TULANE UNIVERSITY OF LOUISIANA
NEW ORLEANS

Oct. 25, 1910

OFFICE OF THE
PRESIDENT

Mr. Nash Buckingham,

Memphis, Tenn

Dear Sir:-

Can you officiate between Mississippi A & M and Tulane at New Orleans on Nov.5 and at what price. Also Nov.19 at New Orleans when we play Auburn. Your immediate reply will be appreciated. If you will come for a definite amount and expenses please state what your expenses will probably be.

Yours truly,

Secretary

Nash was highly regarded as a football official. This letter from Tulane asking Nash to officiate is dated a mere 11 days before the first game.

Nash was an inveterate golfer with a somewhat less than skillful touch that he overcame with strength. With him is Chubby, his springer spaniel.

(From the Memphis Commercial Appeal, *date unknown, that told of Nash's fascination with golfing.)*

Nash Buckingham Could Hit 'Em.

Whenever someone starts talking of 300-yard drives, there's always someone else to be a bit sarcastic about the feat. When 400-yard drives are mentioned, disbelief is a mild word for the reaction.

But consider the case of Nash Buckingham. Not even Nash himself knows how far he hit a golf ball in the olden days, but it was very much farther than anyone else around here has hit 'em. Nash didn't always know where the ball was going, but it always went for a long, long ride.

For instance, one day at the Memphis Country Club he drove a ball from the second tee clear across the road that runs along the east side of the course. If you're familiar with that layout you'd judge that the carry is at least 350 yards.

Buckingham says, "I was a wild palooka on the golf course in those days – back around 1923 or '24. On this particular occasion I would up and let go with all I had. The ball started sailing on a straight line over the ditch and toward the road. It was very dry, the course was hard and the wind was behind me. We looked all over for the ball, and finally I discovered it a few feet outside the fence bordering the road.

That was some knock. Nash has hit others. Once when there was a bridge crossing the creek on the 13th he slammed a ball on the bridge that bounded past the green and he had to play back after his drive. He was over the ninth green with a drive before sand was placed in front of it. And there are other records.

And here's a pair of weird ones.

Once Buckingham had two balls out of bounds on the third hole and made a four – which is one under par. It was done this way: His first drive was sliced badly and disappeared. His second was a wide hook that hit the hard macadam road out of bounds and took a weird hop back into the fairway. He laid his second dead and ran down a putt for a four.

Then again. He was playing with Leo Carter in the qualifying round of a club tournament, Nash was even fours, through the 13th. He drove the ball under this same bridge that was mentioned above, and unwisely tried to play out. In the end he had to sink a long putt to get a 13.

MY
IRMA

She was born Irma Lee Jones, June 24, 1885. She was educated at St. Paul School, St. Mary's School, and Miss Brown's, New York (finishing school). We were wed on June 1, 1910 at St. Mary's Cathedral, Bishop Thomas F. Gailor officiating. We have a daughter, Mrs. R. E. Witt, Knoxville; a granddaughter, Mrs. Irma O'Fallon, Knoxville; and two great-grandchildren, James Nash O'Fallon and Kelly Louise O'Fallon, Knoxville.

N.B.

Mr. and Mrs. Thomas B. Jones

request the honour of

presence at the marriage of their daughter

Irma Lee

to

Mr. T. Nash Buckingham

on the evening of Wednesday, the first of June

at half after six o'clock

at Saint Mary's Cathedral

in the City of Memphis

The wedding invitation of Nash and Irma Lee Jones, one of Memphis' social lights, a skilled outdoorswoman, and a fine shot on waterfowl, doves, and quail. Their wedding was one of the social high points of the spring of 1910.

Playful honeymooners at Big Beaver Ranch. The photograph reads: "June 1910. Mr. and Mrs. T. Nash Buckingham."

Irma in the Colorado mountains shortly after she wed Nash. He regarded her as "an excellent equestrienne."

Duck hunting at Beaver Dam with Perry Hooker and "Pat" the Chesapeake, and...

...fishing for bream in the spring, and...

taking a drink from the Mississippi. Nash's note on the photograph: "Irma drinking from the Mississippi off O. K. Sandbar. Pure, filtered, cold water after a long hike. She would not dare do so today."

Irma, Nash's wife of over sixty years. The writing in Nash's hand on the photo reads: "Irma and Chubby – his last dove hunt at the Spicer Farm. 1940. N. B."

Irma Jones Buckingham, Nash's daughter, "with roaches and pole at Beaver Dam, 1920."

"Irma Buckingham and Little Irma, aged 8, bream fishing at Beaver Dam, 1920."

Irma landing a trout at Big Beaver Ranch in the Colorado high country during their honeymoon. Irma was an accomplished fisher, wingshot, and outdoor person when they met. In May, 1970, with Irma in a nursing home, and Nash less than a year from death, he wrote of her: "My most priceless debt of life is to have had the honor of being her husband." Before she was hospitalized, Nash cared for her at home. He wrote his good friend Lea Lawrence about her: "I've had a rough two years of it; my Irma's convalescence has been slow and there are complications requiring chores involving intern, nurse, cook, small-time 'doc,' and lessons with the walker. But to one who has made marriage a melody for me and our own, it is a pleasure and returns to that June 1, a muslin-minded day when we both, in a clear voice, agreed before the Bishop to help each other 'in sickness and in health and for richer or poorer.' There's been sunshine and shadow, but we both meant it and have kept God's trust."

PART II

THE REAL "SHOOTINEST GENT'MAN"

One of the best-known photos of Nash as a young man.

...I'm on my way to 91 and would like to get some missing history out of my system, because many of these old-time shooters and hunters are gone and there are not many left who've kept in touch and are still at it. You might say that the serious business of shooting game began in 1870 (the Parker gun was first and the greatest ever). Fred Kimble, with whom I maintained correspondence, inventor or discoverer of choke boring and clay pigeons. A real champion. The '70's and '80's passed, and, as a youngster, I saw and knew all those great old-time men and bird dogs. By 1890, I was learning to shoot clays and act as trap boy and live bird tending at the traps. My Dad and his friends were great sportsmen.

By the early 1900's, and ever since, I knew most of the all-time greats at the traps, live birds, and clays. There were no game laws to amount to anything and wildfowling was "for the birds." The duck clubs were the first to ever clap on bag limits – fifty ducks a day and all the geese and swans you could lower. The trap shooting and live birds greats, amateur and professional, were treated like bullfighters. The gun and ammo companies had pro squads that traveled. I knew 'em all. By the time I was 20 years old I had shot probably as much wild game as many of today's shooters have put together since.

They are now, those oldsters, all gone. And with them, the game. What the great Ira N. Gabrielson now refers to as "remnant populations."

There are a lot of hidden things. For instance, in Fred Kimble's writings (about 90% of my education in gunnery), his accounts of his early duck shooting contests with the big muzzlers – there isn't a word about the use of duck calls. There must have been a sight of game, when men stage contests, entailing the kills of over 100 ducks, muzzle-loading. Yet, south of Illinois, in the Big Lake and Reelfoot countries, Beckhart and Glodo were making their own calls and blowin' 'em for market. John Olin has a Glodo I gave him that the great Guy Ward gave me.

I've been and am still asked innumerable questions about game kills and skills of the "ancients," including myself. Who were the best shots at what? Is there a difference 'twixt "hunting" and "shooting"? Name the best wildfowl hunters and shots I've ever actually hunted with. What about long-range shooting?

For instance, if I had to name a group I've gunned with and considered the "greatest," there'd be Harold Money (De Shootinest Gent'man), Guy Ward, the old Reelfoot pro and marketeer (a grand chap), P. C. "Perry" Hooker

Showing the shooting form that made Nash one of the all-time great shotgunners. The note reads: "On Western trap grounds at factory, 1926."

Gibbs of Union City, Tennessee (Remington), Herb Parsons (Olin's great exhibition shooter), Henry Bartholomew of Washington, D. C., Hugh Buckingham, Sr., Charles P. Williams of Greenville, Mississippi (the late), the late Col. Harold Sheldon of Vermont, Chief Game Warden, U.S.A., Robert S. Anderson, my gun pal of 35 years, next to Hooker the top "hunting" caller, Col. Wm. Howard Stovall of Stovall, Mississippi, and Dr. William F. Andrews of Memphis, who holds a ranking spot at hitting and calling any game. And Henry P. Davis.

And the late Bayard Snowden of Memphis, my boyhood and lifetime "companero" afield, was as sound a shotgun operator as the rule book notes. We were "raised up" together.

If H. D. "Jake" Gibbs of Union City, Tennessee is still alive he'd be right at 97. I'll find out shortly. A splendid character.

Now, all over the U.S.A. there are areas or regions that have produced storied game shots. I've met and known many of them, including most of the older "gun editors," down to the newer "outdoor writers." I just happen to be the oldest surviving outdoor writer...

Nash's close friend Henry Davis on a quail shoot. Nash regarded Davis as a first-class shot.

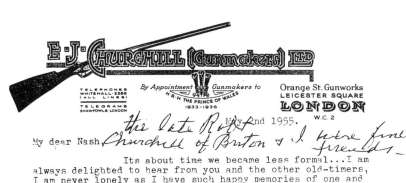

the late Robert Churchill of Briton & I were fine friends –

My dear Nash, May 2nd 1955.

Its about time we became less formal...I am
always delighted to hear from you and the other old-timers,
I am never lonely as I have such happy memories of one and
all and it warms me again to receive your kindly offer of help
with the American edition.

I told Michael Joseph I would like him to ask you to edit it
and I enclose copy of letter from Denhard & Stewart to Alfred
Knopf showing how they took matters into their own hands...
do you know them ?

I dont quite get your "controlled" pheasant shooting over dogs...
Mick Carney wrote me that he took part in a shoot involving over
a thousand released birds......I think the book stopped Naval
Operations in Formosa for a few hours as he says I did a little
more than scanning - perhaps to the detriment of my work"

One of the most charming of Ira's many lady friends Elise Watts
wrote me about pheasant shooting at so much per shot...I hate
walking up pheasants...the poor so-and-so has'nt got a chance
and if he flies straight away you cant reach a vital part...its
big odds you've got a runner.....and as the Lord Bishop would say
if he escapes he still feels sore around that part of his body
which the Lord Chancellor puts on the Woolsack.

In spite of lack of reviews owing to the newspaper strike, in
spite of it being out of season the publisher is delighted having
sold 1800 advance orders and repeats coming in hourly (they showed
the book and spoke about it on Television)
The English are not such readers as you are, also you have one or
two more shooters than we have, so the U.S. edition should sell
well......God help me..I just realise..these Americans also are
inquisitive and also write letters....and I already have quite
a fan mail over here which keeps me as busy as Mark Twain's wood-
chopper (you remember Mark said he was the busied man in the whole
world...he had only one arm...he had a lot of wood to chop...and
a bad dose of the itch)   Thumping this wripetriter I am
also reminded of Mark and his two worst complaints to have at once
Gout & St Vitus Dance....well I have the gout ...in my right hand
and although I am shooting I havent much grip or sensitive touch
so am going to Bad Gastein in Austria for their cure

*A letter from the famous gunmaker and shooting coach Robert Churchill of England
with Nash's handwritten notes. Churchill and Nash shared a common respect and
affection for one another.*

74

Thanks for your invitation...if I could only chuck work and
travel the world...I must go to Spain this winter...I enclose
photostat of one of their best days 3267 Partridges...some of
the guns use my XXV gun which is ideal for the job....my memory
isnt as good as it was but I recall something about the best
shooting gun I have ever heard of...Becker 12x32" weight 10-lbs
left barrel @ 41 yards = 92%....have you still got it and does
it still pattern as good......wish I could patter measure the
insides from breech to muzzle.

Ira will be over next month and I hope to shoot grouse with
him in August.... Very many thanks for your kindly introductions
and best of wishes,

                    Yours always sincerely,

                         Bob

*I first met Robt.
Churchill when he
visited us at alton, Ill.
in '26 & I showed him
around St Louis —
Fine man.
I still have the big
guns. N.B
69 —*

THE *American Rifleman*

1600 RHODE ISLAND AVENUE ··· WASHINGTON 6, D.C.

ELMER KEITH
Salmon, Idaho

June 14th-55.

Mr. Nash Buckingham,
Box 720,
Memphis, Tenn.

Dear Mr. Buckingham:

In over 30 years of writing I have answered
a lot of letters and they run 350 to 450 a month now, but I can
tell you damn few of them brought me the genuine pleasure of
yours of the 9th May. Been to busy finishing up a big work for
Stackpole on Sixguns to answer sooner as wanted to write a letter
, not a note. Of all the compliments on my book Shotguns I have
received, I value yours the highest. Old Charley Askins coached
me over 20 years and taught me a lot and whe he got to old to
keep up his column in S.A. I wrote and sent his wife several of
his last articles so she could read them to him and let him sign
them and keep his job going. He was a grand old man of the good
old school. I am just a kid only 56, but was raised in the Montana
cow country from 1905 on. Think we see about exactly alike on
shotguns. All my shooting has been on game no targets and I
prefer full choked guns for all except quail both barrels and
30" tubes for the 16 and 32 for the 10 and 12 bores. I have just
one shorter gun and that a 12 Westley Richards best quality single
trig ejector hand detachable lock 26" bbls imp and mod for
a quail gun. My pert pheasant guns are a pair of 30" doubles in
full choke 16 bore. One is Major Askins old No 5 Ithaca that he
had them make up to order and which he wanted me to have and the
other an Aya best qaulity on the Purdey system. For ducks and
gooses have Askins mag ten the first one built No 500,000 and
got a chance for one 90 yard double last fall with 2 Ox Western
coppered twos and got four the year before and for ducks have
a B.H.E.Parker double trap, 32" both full that goes 84 and 86.%
The 16 Ithaca throws full 90 percent with 6s both tubes with
Super X and the mag ten threw two strings of straight ten shots
with each barrel with Western Super X 3s coppered that went
93% for each barrel, no fouling shot and no patterns thrown out
each barrel exactly duplicated patterns thrown with the other
at some point in its ten sot string. That is best shooting gun
I ver owned and it does only 85" with Copp ered twos and not as
good with lead twos.
     I asked my old freind Capt Hopkins of Western to get me a case
of two ounces No 3 coppered again last year and he promised
but never got them as they put him to running a game farm I understand
and this gun especially tooled for threes as I sent it back to
Ithaca twice after getting it from Askins and some man that Ithaca
used to have evidently knew what to do in boreing a gun as damn
little trace of a cone left in it and it shoots. Whoever he was
and you probably know, must have been a pupil of old Burt Becker.
Think he must also have bored the 16 Ithaca as those two are my
best patterning shotguns.
     You stock dimensions would fit me to a t and I bet your guns

PLEASE ADDRESS ALL QUESTIONS TO "DOPE BAG" NATIONAL RIFLE ASSOCIATION, 1600 RHODE ISLAND AVENUE, N. W., WASHINGTON 6, D. C.

PUBLISHED MONTHLY BY THE NATIONAL RIFLE ASSOCIATION OF AMERICA

A letter from another great, Elmer Keith, and some of his own ruminations, reflections, and observations.

Page two

would also as I also shoot more like you, Askins and Nimble,
an' all my shooting has been game, never had achance to try
either live pigeon or clay targets to know what could do.
Did shoot two rounds trap in a hard wind at Winchester with
tiny Hellwig andgot 12 andthen 15 and missed about every damn
straight away and got every wide angle bird, Strage gunsboth
a 21 and a mod 12 and did not get chance to throw a pettern on
a barn or water to know elevations. Then a year ago N.R.A. sent
me out to represent them at inaugural of Natl Skket trap club house
and they instgted I shoot roundof skeet. Never saw it shot
before watched the all American team shoot scme and vorrowed
a em over under andtried it. Got 13 but missed those No 8 think
they call em anyway is where they come at you and you blow em
off end of barrel. Told them never shot agame bird that way in
my young life always let em go over andthen when in right range
bust em but they would not let me do it that way and the crossing
ones there you havent time so missed all those babies on end
of gun barrel from that statioh.
        Just had a letter from a lad who toldme I knew nothing
about sixguns and damn little about rifles, so be it cantplease
em alland life far too short for any of us to learn very much
of any one thing even. That lad will realize it in another
30 years maybe as he catalogued himself when he listed a lot
of names of men who watched him hit empty 12 guage shotgun shells
off hand with a rifle at 100 yards. e is a far better shot than
I will ever be and I served on and topped three national match
30 caliber teams at Camp perry and got 2nd, 3re, 4th and 8th
in some of the big individual long range matches and third in
a muzzle loading off handmatch at Perry three years ago.
        The Sheriff and I just took a coupletrught boys down to
the State Pen at Boise couple days ago, the Darrah brothers who
had four and five' jail breaks around here each and 7 armed robberies
in one week, plus two car thefts and armed break pit at Idaho
Falls where wetook em for safe keeping, They knocked the depty
on the head and escaped there and the next to last capture they
cam out of a rat hole in an attic under my old 44 Spl S & W
andrdroppedtheir gun when I had only couple ounces left on my
double action trigger puhkl . We came back via Sun Valley and
saw my friend Rudy Etchen, good kid Rudy and met his dad f or
first time and Fred told me to remember him to you when I wrote
as I toldhim about your fine letter. He is hale and hearty and
shooting chcuks at long rangewith scope sighted rifle and I think
  enjoying life there.
        Agree with all you say in this letter also for years
have enjoyed your fine articles on sotgun shooting as they all
ring true and tell a story that these new birds cannot ever do.
        I always liked the Super 10 bore 1 5/8 ounce load
and use it for ducks in my mag ten. gives a darn good pattern
many running up as high as 90 percent in this gun and last fall
I shot six straight doubles on jumped mallards with it and
that load of 1 5/8 ounce 4s. Once a duck I killed got up and
had to kill him again andonce another crossed my line of shot
and got killed and another time of the six doubles two flew in
he way and all three came dome so i would up with 15 mallards
for 13 shots, best I ever did on jumped mallards . Had two runs
of 17 each on pheasants with the Ithca 16 bore including some
doubles in each. Write when you havethe time and all best wishes.

Nash with John Bailey, his friend and shooting companion for many years. Nash's letters to John were set down in a book by the same name by George Bird Evans. Nash has a dark lens over his eye following cataract surgery.

Box 720 Memphis Tenn
March 25th 57

Mr. Havilah Babcock
c/ Field & Stream
383 Fourth Avenue
New York, NY.

Dear Mr. Babcock-: ,
Your article re bird dogs-retrievers etc., in Joe Stetson's column in 'just-out' F&S.

I learned about ' blowing in a dog's ear to make him drop a bird',back in late November of 1904,from a Negro named John Watkins with whom I hunted for many years-he lived on the Shepherd land,4 miles west of LaGrange Tenn--his picture over,a fine bitch of mine was a frontis piece picture in FS away back when Ray Holland became editor.I have an enlargement-framed.
That day I was tring out a big young pointer I'd bought from a country boy for $25.He had a snout like the Big Bad Wolf's when he drooled over the Three Little Pigs.But he was a bird dog,and a top one for years.But he brought me my first kill and there he stood,the bird lost to sight in that tremendous jaw and mouth.John Watkins watched me cajole,and threaten and then said-"Blow in his ear",Mist' Nash. I did so,and out he spit the bird.That did it.He finally got so,all I had to do was lean toward him,stoop down and threat-en with puffed cheeks and I got my bird.I used to run across it occasionally in other dogs,but some owners to whomI mentioned it,looked as tho they thought I was kidding'em.The last time I saw it work was in '46.I was shooting with th late(and great) 'Gene Howe,on his huge ranch along the Canadian river north east of Amarillo--quail,doves, ducks, turkey et al.'Gene had just gotten back a lovely pointer bitch from some handler,and she was a corker,too.But, 'Gene confided,she'd NOT give up a bird.Walking along I said-"That's easy,just blow in her ear".He looked at me as tho I was nuts.Shortly thereafter,we got sepa-rated and I hear him shoot and begin calling "Dead".Then I heard him shout--"Oh, Buck, Oh Buck--it-works".Never have I seen a gunner more delighted.I've puzzled as to how dogs,endowed-with all other fine attributes of skill,got th-at way?I can only attribute it to their having been sort of hard-headed natur-ally,maybe cuffed around,and gotten more so.I learned when a boy that some dogs bitterly resent being stared at closely and fixedly,so much so that some-times they break under it and jump at you.
The last double retrieve I saw was three years ago when a lit tle black and white pointer bitch I was trying out for a friend,ran for one falling bird,saw another dropped on beyond,off clear ground,-she went to the last marked fall,came back,nosed the two together and fetch'em to the young lady with whom I was shooting.
I've often wondered who started all that bourbon-stuff about southern gentlemen shooting off horses--I began in 1890,when I0, with some of the game's greatest field trial and shooting dog figures-I never saw it.I've seen dogs come back to some quiet horse and rear up and hand in a bird-BUT-the shooter and horse both knew their dog-and vice versa.In next Christmas Number of American Field,I'll have a story entitled Old Minstrels Harp Their Lays".It tells the origin of three shooting 'stories',and your mention of that Negro one about shooting off the mule,could have been included.Maybe,like the others I heard the original,out on the old Howard Plantation,Aberdeen ,Miss,in 1912. Hal Howard was asking a negro " which side his mule bridled and saddled on'(which side to walk up on him om)and then asked about shooting off him.Anyway, I always enjoy your stories and I'm glad to see something readable still app-earing instead of exploiting some foreign fields and waters or telling you how to catch more--for more,etc etc.Sometimes I wonder how we old timers ever mana-ged to bag or catch anything.I've been looking for those horseback shooters, the gun who always kills 24 X 25,the guy who shoots deadly from the hip and the chap who,always kills 6 out of every rise,all my life.No luck. Regards.
Nash Buckingham

Correspondence (pages 79-81) between two of the greatest who ever wrote: Nash Buckingham and Havilah Babcock. Babcock, a professor of English at the University of South Carolina, after an exchange of letters, suggested a collaborative work on quail hunting that would have been monumental, but Babcock's death shortly after his letter was written ended the project. Nash's regrets are noted in his handwriting. As can be seen from this and other letters by Nash, even much of his personal correspondence read like fine sporting stories.

UNIVERSITY OF SOUTH CAROLINA

COLUMBIA

Department of English

April 1, 1957

Mr. Nash Buckingham
Box 720
Memphis, Tennessee

Dear Nash,

Your letter gives me indescribable pleasure. Without knowing
it, you have exercised a rather profound influence on my life. When
I first began writing, I adopted you as a model, but I knew that I
could never attain your status as a writer and as an authority on
the outofdoors. Wherever I have been during the last twenty-five
years, I have heard people praising Nash Buckingham. If I hadn't
loved you so much I would have gotten as jealous as Hell! You have
hunted just about throughout the country. You have devoted and
admiring friends in every state and in every walk of life. Surely
you must be a happy man. I would guess that "The Shootingest
Gentleman" is the best known outdoor story ever written.

My collections of stories are between printings and virtually
impossible to get, but I should like very much to swap autographs
with you. I can send you either MY HEALTH IS BETTER IN NOVEMBER or
TALES OF QUAILS 'N SUCH — whichever you think you could stomach the
best.

Many, many thanks for your gracious letter. I shall never
forget you.

Affectionately,

Havilah Babcock
Head of English Department
University of South Carolina

HB:d

80

UNIVERSITY OF SOUTH CAROLINA

COLUMBIA

January 7, 1958

Dear Nash,

I have been thinking for some time about an
idea that might make some money for both of us---a collection
of famous shooting stories. I have had two collections of my
own stories published--MY HEALTH IS BETTER IN NOVEMBER and
TALES OF QUAILS AND SUCH, and both have done well. A third
collection, I DON'T WANT TO SHOOT AN ELEPHANT AND ORHER
STORIES, will be published in New York in June.

I believe a collection of famous shooting stories---
shotgun, not rifle or pistol, would do extremely well if the
right stories are picked and the right publisher undertakes the
project. THE SHOOTINGEST GENTLEMAN remains the most famous
and most beloved story in this field. Everywhere I go I run
into people talking about and wanting to get it. Maybe you and
I could pick a few of our own, and a dozen others that are well
known and in demand, and bring them out. I have the necessary
publishing connections. What do you think? Do you own
your copyrights? I do.

Most cordially,

Havilah Babcock

Havilah Babcock,
Head of the English Dept.

return

*A good man
who passed on
before we could
get together.*

81

"The late Captain Paul Curtis, Field & Stream,*" another of Nash's famous companions.*

Nash and companions Ira Richards and Bayard Snowden in North Dakota in September of 1945 with a mixed bag of pheasants and sharptails. Nash traveled to the plains often to shoot and write of his experiences.

Edgar Queeny, driver, and dog await Nash for a morning's quail shooting. The wagon was integral to the way Nash enjoyed quail hunting the most – from a horse following a good dog.

Nash with his cousin, Hugh E. Buckingham, at Hugh's "Whip o' Will Farm" south of Saulsbury, Tennessee. Although the photo says it was made in 1941, Nash was mistaken because the developing date on the back of the photo notes the film was processed December 20, 1935. This may be the only photo extant of Nash with an over-under.

Nice 12 ℔ Salmon
Little Mirimichi.
1920 –
Heaviest 26 ℔s.

ICE BOUND
DUCK HUNTING

My first encounter with ice while duck gunning came on New Year's Day 1891 when I turned into my eleventh year. Father and I went to his Wapanoca Outing Club amid then virgin timberlands in Arkansas, twenty-five miles north of our home in Memphis, Tennessee. Wapanoca was founded in 1887. Trains were still being ferried across the Mississippi river by transports.

From the 2,000 acre lake sprawled across their 5,000 acres of forest, sourced Big Lake. Spring fed, it flowed first into Tyronza River, then into the gorgeous St. Francis, merging finally with the Mississippi far southward. We were the only members hunting. A light snow was falling at darkness. "Uncle Phil" Gwynne, clubhouse keeper, predicted a frozen lake by morning. Sure enough, a shallow, tracking snow lay underfoot. Even currented Big Creek was making ice along its feather edges.

Father and I were in one boat with Osborn Neely pushing. Behind us, fortunately, came a second boat with veteran paddler Crockett in charge of decoys, guns, shell-boxes, coffee pot, and grub. I sat on a soapbox behind my parent. It wasn't daylight, nor snowing. Current kept Big Creek fairly well open. The cold bit like a dog.

A mile later the creek broadened into Little Lake and an outlook of fairly thin ice. From Big Lake on beyond the timber, came a sonorous grumble of swans and Canada geese. We headed for a famous blind about half way up Little Lake – Galloway's Point. Just then my soapbox slipped on the boat's iced bottom, tilted, and threw me across the freeboard. Reaching for me, Dad overbalanced and followed suit. We went all the way gracefully and sank standing in two feet of water.

Nash at Wapanoca, 1916.

We didn't immerse, but our hip boots dipped aplenty and the water was so cold it burnt. We dumped out most of the water, grabbed paddles, and lit out for the clubhouse, leaving overhead myriads of early ducks hunting open water. Did I get a bawling-out from Dad? Not on your life; he wasn't that kind. And I've remembered it with the deepest love for eighty-eight years. I hope you have such a treasure.

Glowing logs in the clubroom's cavernous fireplace soon dried us out, along with hot coffee and toddies for the grownups and a glass of eggnog concocted for me by Uncle Phil. We were soon good as new. Then old hunter Crockett suggested a wild turkey hunt down Big Creek's wilds. His proposal suited Father better than fighting ice all day. The train for Memphis wasn't due until mid-afternoon, so we had ample time. Osborn and I took a faint, snow-clad trail down the off side of Big Creek. Dad and Crockett disappeared down the opposite creek side.

I was using Dad's 12 bore, double hammer gun – a Bonehill. He packed his ten pound Greener, 32-inch magnum double chambered for 3¼ inch cases that he hand-loaded. Osborn and Crockett carried long-tubed double hammer guns from the Meacham Arms Company. We three shot handloads of 3¼ drams and an ounce and an eighth of #4 chilled shot. There weren't many factory-loaded shells around in those days. It was my first snow hunt for bigger game. "Effn' d' cold unlaxes," said Crockett, 'h'its sure gwi' snow." But it didn't.

Osborn eased ahead of me through a magnificent vista of giant hardwoods. Snow-clad ropes of wild grapevines looped to scrape forbidding canebrakes. Overall hung a spell of eerie, cathedral silence. Osborn and Crockett were born and raised of those wilds and practically lived off them. Osborn scanned every yard of our way for coon, squirrel, rabbit, turkey, deer, wolf, and even bear tracks. He would call me to his side, diagnose, analyze, and explain. In after years, he was to become the finest wild goose caller with his own voice I've ever heard.

We emerged upon a tiny cleared eminence where Big Creek curved abruptly westward. We could see above canebrake tops on the creek's far side. Osborn touched my shoulder and pointed. About seventy-five yards away, a well-racked buck and a doe stood poised – watching intently. "Ef' I jes' had my rifle," breathed Osborn. Their flashing white flags awave, the pair dove into the underbrush. I had had my first sight of big game in the rough.

Across Big Creek four shots crashed. A swarm of huge birds lofted cover and fanned in all directions. Four, flying close together, headed directly at us. We hunkered behind a huge tree and Osborn whispered, "Don't shoot t'wellst I gives d' word." He let them cross the creek and onto high ground before he straightened and said, "Let 'em have it." Three hit the ground – one wounded, that I chased down and finished off. Two handsome gobblers and a fat hen.

Crockett and Osborn compared notes across Big Creek. He and Dad had trailed a big bunch of turkeys into a weedy opening, flushed 'em, and dropped four on the rise. Seven birds for one hunt was enough. We circled back to the clubhouse and sighted two more bucks. Osborn promised to give them his personal attention next day. Uncle Phil, Crockett, and Osborn each got a turkey to "work on," and every Sunday for a month, Mother served a magnificent bird.

I still prefer stale cornbread and sausage dressing, with the moist bird-flesh a bit underdone. Seconds, of course. So the capsized boat and frigid ducking had a happy ending. As the old drinking song went, "T'was not the first time nor yet the last time." T'was only "the bee-ginning."

On a Saturday of that same January 1891, I accompanied Dad's close friend and renowned outdoorsman, the late Mr. Arthur Wheatley, to Wapanoca. They were neighbors, maintained bird dog and retriever kennels, and did a sight of hunting and fishing together. Like my father, Mr. Wheatley was a founder of Wapanoca. He had ridden with the late Lieutenant General Nathan Bedford Forrest, C.S.A. during the Civil War. He pioneered earliest American field trials and wrote for various outdoor publications under the name of "Guido," his famed gun-dog. He was a top shot at the traps and live pigeons. He was a United States Commissioner and engaged in real estate and insurance.

Again, bitter cold prevailed. Ice formed along even Big Creek's rim. Our boat, with Osborn Neey pushing, was tinned fore and aft against ice. From distant Big Lake again came the clamor of swans and geese. Day was breaking by the time we had crashed through to a blind at the passageway leading to Big Lake. There I learned how to clear ice from in front of a duck blind. The water was nearly knee-deep.

Mr. Wheatley and Osborn first drove the boat around four sides of a hundred-foot square. They then halved and quartered the inside squares. Depressing the sheets, they slid and pushed them under the outside rim, leaving the inside pool clear of ice. Into that they pitched but half a dozen wooden mallard decoys. How many similar pools of duck-shooting water I've cleared in seventy-eight ensuing years, I'd hate to say – for I am still at it. I began learning something of proper blind building, too.

Ours had been built crosswise of a willowed point and not end-to-end for

"My Daddy's Gun!"

My Daddy's gun! I touch it reverently!
While thru the vale that honest tear mist weaves,
Across the years of their brave comradeship
Drifts comfort in the pictures memory leaves.
I see again his stalwart form, and you, old gun,
Both in the primal joys of days afield,
When distance dropped uncounted from his manful stride
And all the wealth he sought was nature's yield!
My Daddy's gun!
Again the glint of golden sedge, the orchard's breath,
Again your voice that echo'd o'er the hill
When Bob Whites fled to thicket haven depths
But left behind limp, mottled tribute to his skill.
Mirage? No! Sunrise flooding all the marsh with gold,
Cold rain! Swift wildfowl circling to your blind,
Or storm blown snows that beat upon your camp,
"Two souls with but a single thought"—you didn't mind!
My Daddy's gun!
Ah! glorious days along a merry, foam flecked stream,
With all the thrills the Gods o' Luck could send
To pave the day's path deep in rich content
Yet dangle greater chances just around each bend.
I feel his arm about me when the days were done
His "Little Lad" who trudged along behind
To catch the jest or fun threat in his level eyes
And share in them the treasures real pals find!
He sought the secrets of the trees and clouds,
Shared e'er his cup or dined from berried bowers,
The nesting trysts of spring were sacred trusts to him,
His ideals fragrant as the balmy romance of the flowers.
No thought of his but leaves your sights held high,
No act of his but gives you right to pride,
In thirty years of perfect trust and faith fulfilled,
Along the trail to "Been There," side by side!
My Daddy's gun! I pledge it reverently,
That by the living strength and staunchness of your due,
"Tho storm blown snows may beat upon our camp,"
So will I bear his trust by you!
                                        —T. N. BUCKINGHAM.

91

the fourteen-foot duck boat, so that a gunner occupied each end and not fore and aft with the front hunter's back exposed to the rear gun. And the boat was staked and tied solid as a rock. "Never shoot from a boat that's the least bit wobbly," Mr. Arthur used to say, "Off balance a mite, and chances are you'll miss the shot."

He peered through his field glasses, and right there was where I began another study in wildfowling's benefits and those of other hunting fields as well. "There's open water in the lake's east end," he muttered. His glasses swung a semi-circle. "The swans and geese are heading for the Mississippi, but the duck movement's general; we'll have some visitors 'ere long." He examined the lake's north or cypress side.

"Goodness gracious," he exclaimed, "An enormous bunch of teal is leaving Trexler's Corner and heading this way around the shoreline of the Cross Arms and Tate's pocket." He released the leather cord of his glasses and picked up his gun, "Get ready, Boy." I was. The weaving black mass of teal flashed the curve to our left, spotted the open water and stools. In an unbelievable instant their saraband dipped, fashioned a half circle, and literally swarmed all over us. Their hundreds blotted out the ice-hole. We each fired twice into the black curtain and a disorganized mass resumed flight.

I've often wondered since how many we could have bagged had we been using today's pump guns or autoloaders. We retrieved twenty-eight green-winged teal after shooting several cripples. The daily bag limit of fifty ducks and as many swan or geese as one could lower had been established by the club – not by state or national regulation of which, as to waterfowl, there was none.

We shot until noon and a steady stream of many species decoyed to our pool. I was governed by Mr. Wheatley's coaching and began to understand, from my mentor's skill, when to and when not to shoot. Osborn built a small fire on a big tree's blown-over base, and we knocked off for hot coffee, sandwiches, pie, and a count-up. We had about ninety ducks but not a flight of geese or swans had returned from the river. Then we hit the trail for home. I had learned how to open a shooting hole in the ice, how a tight blind and steady boat meant better safety and shooting, and that binoculars have and always will be a must for any gunning.

Until I became of age in 1901, I shot Wapanoca many times with good scores on swan and Canada geese, to say nothing of as fine black bass fishing (fly and bait casting) as ever mortal enjoyed. Folks didn't fish or hunt much on Sunday in those times. Somehow, the swans just seemed to peter out all of a sudden. Until the turn of the century, I won and lost a lot of wildfowling ice. But travel and experience have their profits. I had able mentors to whom I am deeply grateful. Now as to other waters and joustings with ice.

Once upon a long-ago hunting time, there being no railroad available in that direction, four gentlemen from Memphis, Tennessee, set forth via Mississippi river steam-packet for a landing at Austin, Mississippi, then seat of Tunica County. They were guests of the late Dr. Richard Owen, owner of most of the land surrounding an eight-mile "horseshoe" lake several miles inland, and known since Indian times as Beaver Dam. Club records noted the year of their visit as 1878. They enjoyed such fabulous sport at swans, geese, ducks, deer, and wild turkey amid the forest primeval that their first tented camp gave way to a wide dog-trot log cabin overlooking a long, majestic spring-fed lake belted in sawgrass and lush with natural foods for game and fish.

Seven years passed before a railroad passed their way. It linked Louisville, Kentucky with New Orleans, Louisiana (with Memphis, Tennessee about midway) and only forty-two miles from Beaver Dam. Eighteen members leased the lake and built a commodious clubhouse, to be aged in the wood with fumes from pipes, cigars, lamp wicks, candlelight, toddies, and waftings from oak and hickory warming from Steamboat Bill, the stove.

The newer, inland town of Tunica, on the railroad, became the county seat, today an enlightened, prosperous, tolerant community of loyal and spirited citizens, a bustling little city going forward under God; blessed by Him with peace and dignity and progress for all. But even in 1885, the Beaver Dam Ducking Club members planned acquisition of the future Wapanoca Club's 5,000 acres of lake and land in Arkansas.

In a huge ledger, Beaver Dam's members were required by strict rule to record their daily bags of all game by species. A bag limit of fifty ducks a day with no limit on swans or geese was established as a conservation measure. Weather conditions, water levels, natural foods, and general statistics for the Good of the Order were sought. Nearly thirty years later, when the Migratory Bird Law loomed, had such records been made mandatory in Federal game management, our continental wildfowl populations would be in far better shape than today's.

Duck club life at Beaver Dam ended in the 1930's. But, with the lake's still centering increased land holdings, the son, grandsons, and great-grandsons of the late Dr. Richard Owen have kept the faith in land and water managements and protections of wildlife. Forests have fallen, but restorations have kept guarded faith against the press of civilization

Along the Mississippi River's levee system, and inland as well, other large landowners have maintained and increased not just wildlife resources, but a large measure of pride in visible evidences of what firm enforcement can accomplish. It is my own vast privilege to still hunt and fish on Beaver Dam.

Having gunned it since early November of 1890, I have come in contact with a good deal of ice.

I'm recalling a bitter morning in December 1906, when en route to my office I suspicioned that Beaver Dam would be frozen. I had come a long way since those 1890's and turn-of-the-century's wildfowlings. I'd fought ice at Wapanoca, Menasha, on Arkansas' prairies and just-starting ricelands. Currituck's sink-boxes, Minnesota, the Dakotas, Texas and Louisiana coastals were old stories. So, from the depot, I telephoned our office that I'd be home next morning, and caught the "Limb Dodger" local for Beaver Dam.

My Tournament Grade, 1897 Model Winchester pump-gun with its two tubes (quail and wildfowl) 12 bore was at home. But in my club locker there'd be the heavy, sturdy, and reliable old Bonehill double hammer gun with plenty of shells. Also those Warner & Swasey binoculars whose ancestors had been Mr. Wheatley's field glasses. My binoculars had searched the Rockies' and New Brunswick's burnt lands and bogs for moose, elk, and bighorns, to say nothing of prying wildfowling's secrets from Mississippi River sandbars and Canadian big country.

Horace Miller, late Negro clubhouse keeper at Beaver Dam who very shortly then would become relator of a story entitled, *De Shootinest Gent'man*, met my train and confirmed the ice threat. My glasses revealed complete ice coverage except for a narrow open passageway along the lake's west bank southward. But I spotted no ducks or even coots anywhere. In a tinned duck boat, we broke ice across the lake and into the narrow open water. The overhead darkened and cooled ominously.

For a mile, until we came to that belt of cypress pilings between the open lake and the hidden Teal Hole, we saw no sign of game. Inside the willows, we found a "blowdown" that made fine sitting. Horace dropped some decoys into the passageway out front. The water wasn't much more than a foot deep. There we sat dejectedly for half an hour. I had never seen the lake so utterly devoid of gunning prospects. Sensing uncanny tension, our depression deepened.

Suddenly came a faint *tinkle-tinkle*! Sleet! We could see showers of white pellets bouncing off the ice out front across the open passageway. Having our slickers along helped. "Great-I-Am," cried Horace, "Look comin' from high over the South End timber – dem ducks mus' be leavin' d' river." As he spoke, a huge bunch of mallards hovered over the decoys. I gave 'em both barrels and four or five of them splashed into the channel. Sleet began covering the ice. Visibility lessened. Thousands upon thousands of ducks of many species were lighting on the ice as far as we could peer across the lake. They were all over us, and Canada geese too.

94

Sometime I knocked ducks from crossing outfits. The extractor of the noble old Bonehill suddenly snapped and it became a muzzle-loader. Resourceful Horace solved that by quickly trimming a willow branch into two ramrods. Standing beside me he'd insert them when I unbreeched. Taking care to not knock the brass bases off the paper hulls. I was reloaded in a jiffy. My gun's tubes became hot and had to be dipped into the water.

The ice field whitened increasingly. I killed four Canadas with a right and left blast into one bunch. Falling ducks hit the ice and slid pathyways through the sleet. The limit was fifty ducks a day then, and while we had tried to keep toll, we at times became confused. "Horace," I said, "We'd best pick up while it's light enough to see – some of the ducks are in the channel but about a third of them are on the ice."

Horace was equal to the emergency again and I resumed learning. He cut down three tall young willow, tied them securely ends to butts, but left the far end with stiff curving prongs. We collected the open-water fowl first. Then, while I paddled, Horace worked the long pole out across the ice, hooked the ducks one by one, and raked them in. And many's the time since then I have applied that lesson in game salvage across ice and too-deep mud and water.

In the gathering murk many flocks all but lit on us. In every direction the ice field was a black carpet. But all afternoon not a coot had we sighted.

Memphis, Tenn. OCT 24 1906 190....

Beaver Dam Club House Keeper

WILL EXTEND COURTESIES
OF CLUB TO

Mr. ....

AS THE GUEST OF

Mr. ...N. T. Buckingham....................................

GOOD FOR 24 HOURS ONLY.

J. G. Handwerker
Secretary.

M. L. SELDEN,
President.

Horace Miller, Enoch Brown, and Nash. This photograph appeared in Tattered Coat *to illustrate his famous story,* "Great Day in the Morning*!" set at the Beaver Dam Club.*

Nash on one of his last hunts at Beaver Dam.

Horace Miller, as "Ho'ace," the star of Nash's immortal De shootinest Gent'man. *The caption reads, "Horace at author's houseboat, O. K. Landing, Mississippi, 1915." Very near this location was the O. K. Sandbar where Nash enjoyed and recorded many great goose hunts.*

Nash and Horace approach a covey of quail the dogs have pinned. Nash, who was a friend of the late Robert Churchill of England, is here assuming the Churchill "ready" position, something he did naturally. Note that the gun is pointed high enough so the dogs are not endangered, yet low enough that the muzzles won't interfere with vision. The photo is undated, but is probably in the mid 1920's.

Homeward through the channel, we merely moved the ducks aside to let us pass. The sleet ceased as abruptly as it had begun. It was dark when we beached. We had fifty-four ducks, mostly mallards canvasbacks and redheads, so Horace, who had a license, had "house meat" for the oven. He said, "Ducks don't like to roost in woods when an ice glaze starts. Trees get to poppin' and limbs fall. They leaves out for the open. They know what the weather's fixin' to' do before we do."

Next morning my binoculars failed to reveal a duck on the ice or in the air. I gave train conductor Lawrence one sack of twenty-five ducks for the train crew and our office force divided the other. Our home handled the geese. Three years later I saw Beaver Dam, low at the time, so frozen that when the thaw came, two dead gar-fish, probably trapped and asphyxiated, floated in to the dock. One was almost nine feet long, the other more than seven. Mother Nature is quite a paymistress. Years slip past, and for duck hunters there's always ice to battle. For iced duck hunting the gunner's theme is, "You've got to keep pushing."

I n 1915 another frigid forenoon found my two gunning comrades, the lates Ceylon Frazer and Enoch Ensley, standing on Beaver Dam's boat platform dejectedly scouring the landscape with those same old binoculars. Just a frozen expanse. A mile south across the lake I spotted an open hole black with ducks. The same distance northward, a similar opening. Ducks were trading back and forth along the timber-lined shore. We were ready to hunt, but that ice was just too thick to battle.

I walked from the beach out to the dock's end and the ice held me without a crackle. Two ideas arrived. I slid a Dan Kidney duck boat onto the ice, gave it a push with my foot, and watched it slide ahead as smoothly as an iron-shod sled. We climbed aboard, and no bad symptoms. "Put in the guns and shells and half a dozen decoys and I'll return pronto," I told Enoch. I ran up to the decoy shed and found half a dozen cane poles with frog-gigs on their butts. I sawed them off to three foot handles and hurried back. Horace, sensing something afoot, had put another duck boat on the ice. "Now," I said, "As payment for this brilliant idea, you and Mr. Frazer give Mr. Ensley and me ten minutes headstart for the North End Hole. Then you set off for the South End Hole. We'll have sent ducks your way so you send 'em back. They'll keep trading."

A frog-gig pusher in each hand, Enoch and I took seats. We pointed our prow at the distant ice-hole, jabbed the gigs' firmly into the ice, and heaved ahead. We glided smooth as silk and picked up speed. Half way to the ice-hole it began to empty of ducks. We looked back and saw Horace and Mr. Frazer making good progress. We slid off into the pond, picked up paddles, and drove the duck boat into sawgrassed shoreline. Decoys riding behind us, we awaited customers.

A magnificent shoot ensued. In two hours we had Federal limits of twenty-five ducks each. Enoch asked, "How are we going to climb back onto the ice?" That was easy, "We'll both paddle fast from aft, raise the prow, and jump onto the ice." It worked, the frog-gigs were renewed, and we reached the dock just as Horace and Mr. Frazer came in with his limit. All hands returned to the city next morning and the binoculars revealed that both ice holes were packed with ducks. Where did the migration stay with the mid-South under ice? There was corn along the Mississippi River then; there isn't now; hardly a shadow of it. There are soybeans now, but the migration is a mere shadow to what it was then. The result? One mallard allowed in the daily bag limit of three ducks and thirty-day seasons of 1968-69.

My diary tells of how in December 1916, Mrs Buckingham, and I, acting as chaperones (a practically obsolete word and custom today) for three lads and three lassies at Beaver Dam, left home of a rainy Sunday afternoon via train. Mary and 'Gene, Anne and Sam, Mary and Hal. Post the merry evening meal a bleak Norther blew in. Next morning the lake was in the process of icing, but the fowl flew. High limits of twenty-five ducks. 'Gene and Mary, with a dinner party date, left on the afternoon train laden with mallards. Next day we fought ice but again "limited" and sent Sam and Anne to the city with sacks for distribution. Hal and Mary, with Irma and me, stuck it out just to see what would happen. I even got out the frog gigs but didn't need them. You could have crossed an army.

We put the girls into duck boats with two live decoys each. Horace Miller and Ed Joyner pulled guide ropes, and with long push poles, Hal and I walked behind to merely steer. It was like strolling down the avenue. But we raised no ducks. In the far South End, we imbedded the boats in a clump of sawgrass and tied out a live decoy at each corner of the perfect blind. Mary needed no one to help her bag ducks, and my Irma was the best woman wildfowler I've ever seen handle a gun. Dawn was long coming and still no movement of the flight. Horace and Ed lit their pipes and strolled off for the South End's forest. Horace had taken his gun for squirrels. After a spell three shots sounded.

Instantly, from the lower woods, spouted clouds of ducks. Later Horace and Ed related coming upon two or three acres of water kept open by masses of energetic coots. For the next two hours we had perfect shooting. Making pictures and retrieving kept us busy and warm. We were home for lunch with limits, but it took us a awhile to rest up from three strenuous days. That was fifty-eight years ago. The Federal bag limit was twenty-five ducks and eight geese a day; we so-called sportsmen didn't have to be petty thieves or wildfowl bootleggers. But there were such and still are. It took nearly threescore years (until 1960) to even get duck bootlegging made a felony, and an effort then to get excess bag limits made the same was rejected Congressionally. The answer? Scan vacant skies for vanished migrations; yield to alibis for unnecessary drainages; and stand passively for mockeries of enforcement. Worse, continue turning our inviolate wildlife and wildfowl refuges into looted areas masquerading as "recreation."

Only an ancient diary and ancient volumes of Kodak pictures tell a true story of fighting duck-shooting ice for seventy-eight years. About 1912-13 came the first one-lung outboard motors. Our wooden duck boats were tinned fore and aft against and cut through medium ice faster and more safely. Outboards' horsepowers were escalated and then came all-metal boats, bespeaking less dangerous contacts with heavier ice.

We have battled frozen backwaters in the Mississippi and banged through flooded woods in Arkansas' ricelands that would have defeated us a few years before. We come upon Kodaked scenes from fighting ice along the Potomac River below Washington, D. C., when we used to gun canvasbacks and black ducks with the late Henry Bartholomew from his shore-blind between Swan and Broad creeks. And what a string of huge, fearless, faultlessly broken Chesapeake Bay retrievers Henry Bartholomew worked and loved.

Out front there would be between two and three hundred wooden canvasback decoys in strings of twenty-five each with sash-cord weights at one end to swing up or downriver with the tide. All the strings were hitched together so that in bitter weather when heavy winds sent heavy ice in to take out our decoys, we'd hitch a powerful windlass on shore to the decoys and hustle them ashore. In those days, the Potomac held good feeding in wild celery until the Japanese beetle cleaned it out.

I'll never forget daybreak of New Year's Day 1930. The river was full of ice floes and a northwest wind was shoving a lot of it our way. Henry lowered his binoculars and said to his Manager, Ira, "There's two fellows in a motorboat upriver – looks like they're trying to salvage their decoys. Maybe you better crank up and go see if you can help them." Ira returned after a bit and said, "When they saw me coming they turned around and beat it for shore." After more prying with the glasses Henry said, "I think I see their decoys on a big sheet of ice – the wind's sweeping it in on us, too."

That floe crashed on the beach of a little cove below our blind, and we were right there to secure it, along with 186 dead canvasbacks, black ducks, and quite a few other varieties. There wasn't but one thing to do, so we did it. We notified the U.S. Fish & Wildlife Service and they rushed for the contraband.

What happened? Oh! Nothing in particular. Except a theory that market hunters made a "Big Shot" that midnight or thereabouts when there was all the celebration noise for New Year's. The grapevine held rumors of a "Big Gun" with seven muzzle-loading tubes mounted four below and three above on a frame set to throw first as the flock fed and then as it flushed. The operator reportedly lay in a small craft and used two short heart-shaped paddles to ease into the midst of a feeding raft of fowl. Then – BOOM-BOOM!

In this case, the "follow-up" boat lost the ducks in the darkness and probably worked the rest of the night trying to recapture the fugitive ice floe carrying them. I recall that nothing came of the violation, except the comment of a farmer-boatman in reply to a query as what the game agent had accomplished in the case. "Who," he snorted, "them Federal dicks?" He cudded a moment and continued, "Why, they couldn't ketch a elephant in a five-acre fenced field if there was two foot of snow on the ground and the elephant had its throat cut."

I resented that, having at one time been a "dick" myself and having known many of them as brave, intelligent, hardworking men with difficult and dangerous jobs. Without them, we wouldn't be shooting ducks today. But we heard that those 186 contraband ducks served a fine charitable purpose.

Y̲ou can relive a lot of ice battles through the years. The week that the late Ira Richards of New York, superb sportsman and shot and the "Fastest Human" at Yale in his class of 1900, as I recall, put in at

Dewitt, Arkansas, shooting mallards in Elmer LaCott's flooded woods on Mill Bayou. A freeze tied up the area as tight as Dick's hatband. We'd dawdle around until noon, cook up a picnic lunch, tramp out an iced opening, and wait for the flight started by commercialists on the prairies. With Elmer and Foy Dinsmore calling, we could have loaded a boat.

Firewood got scarce around our luncheon site one day, so I pushed over a towering snag that broke up when it crashed. Out hopped a huge fighting coon with bared teeth. He challenged our mob and took off across the ice amid cheers for his character and daring. I also found a lizard about a foot long with sunken eyes, and frozen stiff as a poker. Suspecting hibernation, I put it down in the fireside's warm ashes and stroked its belly with a rag. After a bit its sunken eyes pushed up and opened, its color changed, and it stirred. We had unknowingly served its long sleep an ill turn. So, we hunted up another dead tree opening, wrapped the lizard in sawdust and leaves with a bed of ash dust, and stored him away for a refreeze and the long nap.

Came years when wooden boats for fighting ice were put in mothballs by metal crafts. That was a tough dawn when the coved marina at Section 16 Duck Club on Bayou Lagrue, Arkansas, adjoining the Queeny preserve and Peckerwood Lake, was tightly iced by near-zero weather. But there was current in the bayou above the spillway, so George and Eddie Hackleton, the club's guards, opened passageway to the bayou with a metal fourteen-footer and powerful outboard. That gave entry to the Johnson blind for Roy Witt, Hugh Vanderventer, Bob Anderson, and me, with Eddie Hackleton along with his boat and motor. Deep cold and no flight.

Eddie and I volunteered to run up the bayou to see what was holding up the ducks' detail. We got as far as a U-turn known as Jack's Elbow that commanded a pool. It was so cold we went ashore on the point and started a fire with a bottle of gasoline Eddie produced. We heard shooting from Queeny's and flocks of mallards streamed down the bayou. The bag limit, as I recall 1944, was ten ducks daily. Eddie and I unlimbered our calls.

As "callers," neither Eddie nor I rate with the top professionals or amateurs of that fine art in wildfowl deception. But here's no duck gunner who ever blew a call but what secretly considers himself just about the best caller in the world. It didn't take long for Eddie and me to finish our limits, and from the sound down the bayou, we knew our companions were having a fine time.

There was the time, too, at Beaver Dam when we drove all the way around its North End, across the ramp, and along frozen dirt roads to a point opposite the club's old site. We took along a metal boat and motor but didn't have to use it, just walked out through the iced timber to where the coots had kept a long, narrow passageway open.

The trick was to wait until arriving big ducks circled to the call and were over the ice from which we were shooting and could be dropped for retrieving. What were all those ducks and a stray flock of Canada geese feeding on to stay in the area? Soybeans! We used to watch them early and late for filming as they flocked in to feed on hundreds of acres of the Owen plantation.

The answer to the future of American wildfowling has several grand divisions. The immediate-crash acquisition and continuing development of both Canadian and American (U.S.A.) wetlands. American wetlands allegedly produce at least 25% of the Continental population; isn't 25% worth saving? Next, the continuance of breeding stock depends wholly upon the maintenance of wintering grounds protected by tremendously escalated penalties for illegal shooting. This summarizes into far more sportsmen backing warmed by moral support and cold cash. As I write this, none is sufficiently in evidence for the job.

But, here it is again of a witheringly cold pre-dawn morning at old Beaver Dam in December, 1966. Stoked with poached eggs, sausages, grits, toast, marmalade, and very black java, P. W. Alderson (resident manager), Dr. William F. Andrews, and I make shivery way down the centuried path to the boat landing. "P. W." guards all wildlife at Beaver Dam. Dr. "Chubby" Andrews, who as a lad shot his first duck at Beaver Dam in closing years of the old club, is now a renowned surgeon and international hunter and angler. He rates straight "A's" in gunning, duck-calling, and sportsmanship. We've battled wind and wave and ice together for many years.

Those two lofty cypress trees framing the dock look as gigantic to me as they did seventy-eight years ago. They are legended, too, site of canoe crossings when the lake was Chickasaw Indian country and a howling but magnificent wilderness. No metal boats around then. Even passenger service on the friendly Yazoo & Mississippi Valley Railroad has disappeared.

On Beaver Dam during wildfowl seasons outboard motors are taboo unless there is heavy ice to force. And there seems plenty of it out yonder this morning. A binocular survey reveals ice-holes at either end. Across from us behind a sawgrass point coots are working. There'll be ducks mixed with them, too. We must get across that half-mile of ice somehow. Bunches of mallards, gadwall, widgeon, and lesser fry are trading back and forth. P. W. and Chubby, with post-hole diggers, clear a two-boats-length launching space and warm up the Evinrude.

Chub and I knew what we faced. Against tough ice, the trick is to sit a bit aft, raise the prow, jump atop the ice with a heavy lunge, do some "rocking and rolling," and smash on through. It's hard work, but you'll get there eventually if you stay in one piece. P. W. chuckled and waved adieu. He was off to his trapline.

Half-way across, with scads of ducks flushing from the woods behind the sawgrass point, Lady Luck suddenly turned upon us with a snarl. The motor gave a loud *Pop*, jumped from probably a weak transom, and disappeared in about three feet of water. Chub yelled despairingly but kept his cool and shoved down a long paddle to mark the spot. Crisis stared grimly. Back to land quickly. Fetch retrieving tackle and attempt salvage. Experience to the rescue. I once dealt in outboards and have seen many a one take French leave from a boat's stern, and spent days trolling with grappling gear. In shallow water, the best recovery tool I've ever used is a long-handled, long-toothed garden rake. I knew P.W. had one in his toolshed.

Back at the disaster scene, Chub felt around and suddenly shouted joyfully. The rake's tines engaged the motor's carrying-bar and held. A tense moment until it was lifted dripping into the boat. Back to P.W.'s on the double. The motor was ungassed, taken down, dried out, warmed by an electric heater, reassembled, gassed, and yanked. Mute as a mummy!

Into the station wagon with the corpse and off to hunt a motor mortician at Tunica, the county seat. A friendly auto mechanic, a duck hunter himself, takes pity on two woebegone Nimrods and gives the patient his personal attention. He has the equipment and the know-how as to outboards. Half an hour later, dry as a bone and with new sparkplugs, the job roars into action.

Triumphant return to P.W.'s for lunch. He has two mink, a huge beaver, a bobcat, and two coons to show for his trapline. Big-fixings by Mrs. P.W. Tender pork roast, mashed spuds and succulent gravy, greens and fat meat, crackling bread and angelic pie. A toast in java is drunk to the rake and the motor mortician. We're fighting time and ice again.

One o'clock! We chain the motor to Old Ironsides and slash through a refreezing channel. Ducks roar and coots scramble from the willow-flats ahead. We sprinkle a dozen mallard decoys in open water off the sawgrass point and a few in the pool behind it. We drive the boat full tilt into the sedges – west to east. Firm footing – flawless hide. We are hunting big ducks, good pictures, and as few pick-ups as possible out on the tough ice. From this very spot we've shot bag limits of fifty ducks a day many a time. Now the four-duck daily bag limit can contain but two mallards.

Chubby's glasses reveal considerable movement over South End timber. He unlimbers the movie camera. A tremendous cluster of scaup darts past the outer decoys. They lift, whip into a half circle, and splash among the inside pool's spread. Chub has them in focus all the while. An outfit of shy widgeons slides overhead. Chub grins at me and his lips frame, "Shoot only big ducks." He resumes the binoculars. "Here comes a bunch of mallards – they'll cross us low – are you set?"

I know his autoloader and my Model 21 Magnum Winchester pack the same Western Mark 5 plastic 3-inch loads with 4 drams of powder and an ounce and three eighths of #4's coppered. There they hang, at least a dozen mallards against a dull sky. Four hit the pool as dead as hammers. "Well," says Chub, "We're all set on mallards; let's hope for a visitation by some fat gadwalls." He resumes the glasses. "Big movement headed this way – those four shots started something – they're going to cover us up – pick gadwalls." Four more shots and four gads. Chub consults his watch.

"It's time to go picture-making," says Chub, "The light's improving a bit; I'll face the stern; you paddle slowly along the outer rim of the buckbrush – hug it close – those outlying coots will betray us anyhow." By the time we round a cypress point, regiments of coots swim out across the channel and climb onto the ice field. Comes a roar from the willow flats and back timber. Out sweeps a fifty-foot curtain of jumbled species. One burst of vivid colors is so close we look into startled, straining eyes of gorgeous wood ducks. Chub's camera swings from mass to mass of escaping hues.

Having identified eight species on film, we swing and paddle along the ice rim with its fluttery grandstand of myriad coots. Their close-up looks say plainly, "We're sure glad to see you two guys leaving us." Chub's film runs out. He yanks the motor, we regain the lake crossing passageway to the landing. It was barely three pm. "What was the feature of the show?" asks P.W. "The punch-line," replies Chub, "is that the rake stole the show." My vote is cast for Mrs. Alderson's pork-roast. "The radio says we are due a thaw and if so the jump shooting should be wonderful."

"We'll be here for early breakfast day after tomorrow," replies Chub.

"Suppose," asks Chub, tooling the big car from blacktop to highway, "Suppose we had made it across the lake early this morning; we could have limited in jig time and been home in a jiffy. Suppose, too, we had just continued shooting? How many illegal ducks could we have bagged?"

I said more than enough to get us thrown in jail with life sentences. I added that we have been shooting four-duck daily bag limits since 1947. Chub resumed ruminatively.

"I began gunning ducks here at Beaver Dam about 1931 when I was ten years old. You began when you were ten in 1890. How do you compare Continental wildfowl populations of 1890 with today's?" I replied that today's migrations seem but a pathetic remnant. Chub studies awhile before resuming.

"Conservation has many facets and problems." I agree and add that it seems almost impossible amid global frustrations and national violence to enact wildlife programs carrying any vestige of practical common sense, common honesty, or common decency. "Worse," agrees Chub, "I find it difficult to get information other than bureaucratic gobbledygook. To whom shall we turn for leadership to wildlife's Promised Land?" He brightens. "Perhaps," he adds, "we'd best write Ann Landers, Dear Abby, or Inez Robb. They may not have the answers, but they'll keep their punches up and give our wildlife resources the clean break they deserve but are *not* getting."

I said a silent Amen!

THE
FAMOUS "GIN SQUAD"
By Old Timer

Nash often wrote under the pen name "Old Timer" when the story he was relating involved himself. (From the Memphis Commercial Appeal, *March 25, 1917.)*

About the spring of 1907 came quite a revival of local trapshooting interest and with its regeneration the existence of the once famous "Gin Squad," destined to be a potent factor therein for many seasons.

A volume entitled the "Life and Battles of the Gin Squad" could be written of its travels and conquests. Its inception dates from a period when Bayard Snowden and Bright Goodbar, who had been shooting for a season or so, induced B. H. Finley, Nash Buckingham, Hugh R. Wynne and Fontaine Martin to take up the "sport alluring."

Small beginnings with large endings is an adage proved on that first April afternoon ten years agone when the neophytes faced the barrier for the initial call. It is a matter of pride with Finley that he missed 47 before effecting a consolidation. A few runs, however, and the new shooters, fascinated with the sport and fellowship, caught the fever, and the fun began.

The bunch shot together a great deal, but those pioneer days are the ones of real endearing memory. To quote a grand old member gone bone dry, "Them was *not* the days when a fish made a dust swimming upstream – neither!" And so, you see, what with one thing and another the fame of these brave fellows was heralded until that moment when all hard riders and drinkers met together and acknowledged them entitled to said grant with all tithe and title thereunto appertaining, sloe or Gordon.

Just who first bestowed this alcoholic *nom de fusee* which clung so tenaciously has never been accurately fixed, its origin being credited to general seepage. But there is a pretty little legend extant to the effect that one hot summer afternoon when the squad was showing on the small time circuit in old Nitro Dell at Dryersburg, manager Fred Schmidt has acquired a bad

109

GEO. LIVERMORE
PRESIDENT

L.P. SMITH
VICE-PRESIDENT

CLAUDE H. SMITH
SECRETARY

PAUL S. LIVERMORE
TREASURER

1917 WINNER

1918 WINNER

Ithacas Won
The Grand American Handicap
Two Years In Succession
1917 —— 1918

ITHACA GUN COMPANY
ITHACA, N.Y.

CHARLES LARSON

JOHN D. HENRY

April 14, 1921.

Mr. T. N. Buckingham,
Memphis, Tenn.

Dear Sir:-
        P. C. Hooker a Western man - tells us you did it
again last Saturday by breaking 50 x 50 with an Ithaca Single.
May you continue to trim the bunch a little more often than
the bunch trims you.

                        Very truly yours,
                        ITHACA GUN COMPANY
                        By- L. P. S.

LPS/B

A congratulatory note to Nash from L. P. Smith of the Ithaca Gun Company, on a trapshooting win in which Nash broke 50 X 50 with an Ithaca. A noted target shooter, Nash was a member of the famous "Gin Squad" of Memphis that competed and won throughout the mid-South.

attack of tonsillitis hollering for his boys to toe the scratch – they being somewhat loath to comply owing to distressing shortage of ice and limes just at the unfortunate moment. At this juncture Squire West Hawkins, napping in the tall green grass with his faithful dog, arose in great wrath at the delay and, raising his voice to high C, registered a demand for the "Gin Squad!" The name stuck.

With a year's experience the Gin Squad, collectively and individually, became a well-advertised bunch and a hard proposition to beat. Once in a great while some opposing squad was lucky enough to get a tie at the trap, but once a contest was staged on a gin basis – all bets were off. It was the custom of the squad to plan its campaign before the first shot was fired.

Mr. Finley, Capt. Finley, a strategist of great natural capacity, compiled the tactics. Each man was given an opponent to "cool" – an order would read something after this fashion:

"Snowdy will cool Prophet Cocke; Slim (Fontaine Martin), you carry Charlie Spencer to the three-quarters and make him back up; you other boys, just shoot your regular clip, and I'll cool Bill Herr and Tom Marshall!"

On a regular shooting, basis, however, outside the fun, the Gin Squad usually took away a fair share of the money and prizes. The boys shot well up at most of the big handicaps, Bright Goodbar winning a Grand American Handicap preliminary at St. Louis, and, if memory isn't wrong, Bayard Snowden and Nash Buckingham wriggled into a slice of the spending change at Denver during the Western in '09, at the Southern in Nashville, same year, and the G. A. H., Chicago, the following season. Trophies, plates and merchandise came their way, too, and many a reminiscent seance is held over good times that went on around the circuit. Woodstock, Covington, Dryersburg, Union City, Pine Bluff, Helena, and many another little city has extended hospitable sittings to the old Gin Squad.

In recent years the devastating effect of matrimony, the full dinner pail, and the high cost of shells has somewhat retarded concerted action upon the part of the squad, but a get-together day is planned at the first matinee this season. Capt. Finley, sole survivor as the target of Cupid's pattern, has sounded a recall, and the veterans again will line up and level their old gas pipes over the little green house.

It is planned to make the afternoon a reminder of old times and faces when Fritz Gilbert, Bill Herr, Bill Crosby, Tom Marshall, and Harold Money were familiar figures on the home grounds. Our own Jake Gibbs was an amateur in those halcyon days, and George Lyon as good a one as ever smashed the sharp angles of life, were always at home with the Gin Squad.

Gibbs is now a leading and very popular professional for the Remington-

111

Nash apparently shooting live pigeons, date and place unknown. The lines in the foreground were used to release birds from the traps.

112

U.M.C. Company; Herr has retired from the game, but Fritz Gilbert Heikes and Crosby are still hammering away at the barrier.

But alas, for Lyon, Long, and Money. There will always be a warm, green spot in every shooter's heart for them – George the most popular lad the game ever knew; good old Billy, and Harold, an English gentleman every inch of him, reported "missing" somewhere in France!

THE BIRTH OF "SKY-BUSTING"!

*An Old Shotgunner's Meditations Upon Man's Efforts
to Crash the Barriers of Ballistic Space Afield and Afloat!*

I n 1965, I read in a young outdoor writer's column that, "While over the years drainage and droughts in international breeding grounds for wildfowl have severely damaged continental populations thereof, they have not, over a similar period, hurt any worse than 'sky-busting,' game-hogging, duck bootlegging, enforcement that has become pallid pretense, indifferent court support throughout the flyways, and bureaucratic mismanagement of the Migratory Bird Law."

I highly commend that chap's forthright comprehension and journalistic innards. It's been a long time since I've heard an outdoor writer swing from his typewriter's shoe-tops like that; we could use more of his ilk.

But that word "sky-busting" intrigued me. It told me that the youngster meant well but hadn't exactly thought the business through as to the actual small cumulative position so-called sky-busting may occupy as to being in the police lineup of wildlife's predators. And again, before getting my text as to sky-busting off my launching pad, here's a November 23, 1960, quote from my friend, the late and great J. N. "Ding" Darling, along supportive lines: "Tragic stupidity are the only words which adequately express the misguided governmental agencies and predatory game butchers, to heed admonitions against the decimation of our game species."

So, let's operate on sky-busting – guinea pig or defendant? But what is written here is neither recrimination nor diatribe against brave, honorable, and hard-working game agents (state and Federal) who have, through the years, fought an untiring and oftimes financially handicapped rear-guard action against emboldened wildlife thieves, selfish political pressures, and the inhumanities of men's greed. For the future of wildfowling it is now a matter of the chips being down, improved and unarrogant leadership, hard-bitten enforcement, and an honest effort to demonstrate that the freight-paying sportsmen of this nation will demand and get "sportsmanship" worth more than mere social kidding such as raiding watermelon patches.

As of now, waterfowl stocks, especially the mallards, are the lowest in history. Chickens have at last come home to roost and the bank examiners are at the door. In 1963-'64, 1,856,860 Duck Stamps were sold, not all to duck hunters. As against a previous "High" of TWO MILLION, THREE HUNDRED AND SIXTY NINE THOUSAND.

Provisions of the Migratory Bird Law are now a politically punctured football. The national flyways system, established in 1948, has witnessed controversy as to bag limits, seasons, and shooting hours ever since. As a result, since 1947, the Mississippi Valley flyway, largest in duck stamp sales of the quartet, has seen bag limits shrink from four to one mallard in '65-'66. There have been "bonuses" here and there in scaup, shorter seasons when closure was deemed better by many, a sunrise shooting hour installed over earlier firing, and after a thirty-year battle by conservationists, duck bootlegging was made a felony. But probably the most salutary possible step toward salvaging mallard stocks was ignored – to wit, "half-day shooting" – as begged for by many of the most experienced and knowing wildfowl managers of the lower Mississippi Valley flyway.

Meanwhile, through the years since 1947 and due to the impairment of national moral and crime increase, sportsmanship and law observance became a by-word. It is known that when duck-bootlegging at last became a felony in 1960, Interior reportedly did ask Congress to include "excess bag limit violations," so grave had the practice become, but were told, in effect, "We don't think we are ready for that just yet." But five years later, we find United States Senators suggesting closed seasons, and a distinct feeling and predictions by many seasoned wildfowlers that the season of '65-'66 in the Mississippi Valley flyway may, in unpunished crime against bag-limits, put the mallards past the point of no return.

So let's talk about the young outdoor writer's inclusion of sky-busting as among the factors of wildfowl decline.

Since the year 1890, when I shot my first wild duck (a mallard drake) on Wapanoca (now the Federal Wapanoca Wildlife Refuge with whose acquisition by the government I was concerned), I have contacted three separate and distinct periods of what we can correctly term "longer range-shooting," or sky-busting. I was ten years of age in 1890. My armament consisted of two twelve-gauge shotguns – a lever-action Winchester repeater, and that rabbit-eared double hammer Bonehill. Shortly thereafter I became

On the back of this 1937 photograph, Nash notes: "Typical Arkansas timber shooting in the ricelands reservoir bottoms country. Left to right, Edgar M. Queeny, Elmer LaCotts, Foy Dinsmore, and the famous Labrador 'Grouse of Arden' in the LaCotts woods on Mills Bayou near Dewitt. Easy country in which to judge yardage by tree heights." Queeny was the author of Prairie Wings.

117

the proud possessor of the first twelve-gauge, solid-frame Winchester pump-gun to reach the state of Tennessee, a gift of the late Irby Bennett of Memphis, Tennessee, then district manager for the Winchester Repeating Arms Company. I still have it. Through the decades, when Wapanoca's more than five thousand acres were virgin timber and cane-braked about the great lake and its migrational myriads, that old Winchester took toll of bear, wolves, "painters," wild turkey and hogs, squirrel, dove, quail, and all the fur of the expansive wetlands.

But my first "long-range firing," as such, came from the use of several double-tubed, heavy, English-made, 8-bore double guns owned by club members who let me use them. I was fifteen years old by then and a husky hundred and eighty-five pounder, and one to whom the big guns' "push" meant nothing compared to seeing swans, geese, and ducks fall from flocks farther away than I dared fire at them with my twelve bore and the lighter handloads of that day.

In those times of go and come, migrants curtained the skies. Neither the states nor the government took any notice of wildfowl as to "laws." Market hunting was legal and the sale of game a matter of course, as hotel menus of the period reveal. Duck clubs of our area, however, put on a bag-limit of fifty ducks a day, with no limits on swans and geese. These bag-limits were gradually reduced through the years. I can still vividly recall how suddenly the swans seemed to disappear.

Improvements doubled and redoubled in both magazine guns and "doubles," to say nothing of factory-loaded ammunition. Our youthful Friday night assembly-lines of hand-loaders became unnecessary. From 1890 until 1912, I had witnessed – unknowingly – a tremendous era in both ballistic betterments and some handwriting on the walls of wildfowling conservation.

The Migratory Bird Law and Treaty Act with Great Britain moved all wildfowl under Federal protection. My old buddies the 8-gauges were banned. Autoloading shotguns had appeared about 1905. Federal bag-limits were placed at twenty-five ducks a day and eight geese. Don't smile – ruefully. There were so many wildfowl in those days that while market hunters resented and legally fought being put out of business, the so-called "sportsmen" left with twenty-five ducks and eight geese per day to bag and didn't have to become today's vandalistic scum seeking new ways to chisel, cheat, and even apply wanton waste in the marshes.

Although Federal law had silenced the 8-gauges, enforcement authorities still had them and even larger batteries and punt-guns with which to deal, plus trapping, netting, and even the cruel baited trot-lining. The trademark of all those years heard no talk of long-range shooting or crippling. The trademark of the period was "shoot faster, shoot more, and kill more." Waterfowl resources were strictly a commodity.

But the period itself had produced the world's first sky-buster with a shotgun. For away back yonder, Mr. Fred Kimble of Illinois had settled all that by proving it with his discovery (along with Mr. Greener's of England) of how to choke-bore a gun's tube to secure tighter pellet constrictions and consequent density of absorbed energy upon the quarry. Mr. Kimble's memoirs of his choke-boring discovery and market-hunting days along the Illinois and Mississippi rivers make wonderful reading. He writes that he bored out and tested many heavy muzzle-loading gun barrels, but it was a discouraging way. One day, while tooling along, he gave the cutter one turn too many and figured he had ruined the barrel. So, he loaded it up anyway, with about five drams and an ounce and a half of St. Louis 3's, and cut loose at the foot-square paper 40 yards away. To his amazement, the whole load went into the square. Offhand, I would describe Mr. Kimble as the emancipator of all sky-busters, as to choke boring. But it takes a propellant to supply the punch, so we are not interested in paternity suits.

I enjoyed a delightful correspondence with the old gentleman in the late 1920's. He had long since removed from Illinois to California and his market-hunting days with his famous muzzle-loading, hand-choked, 6-gauge, single-tubed piece. With that ponderous "near-cannon," he reports straight kills of fifty or more ducks at sixty and seventy yards. He learned shooting "yardages" by stepping off estimated paces along the streets until he got them down pat. He learned "lead" as markers or "forward allowance" for high overhead or pass-shooting by swinging so-many of a fowl's own lengths ahead: three duck-lengths at forty yards, four at fifty, and five at sixty. But, highly important, he didn't forget to keep the big gun moving ahead or "following through" meanwhile. He writes that, "I learned by trial and error," which means, probably, that he missed a lot of ducks and crippled a good many, too. But wildfowling had no "outdoor press" in those days.

Mr. Kimble was our first long-range specialist and proved to the world that the only way to learn how to shoot a shotgun better is to simply shoot a lot – intelligently, because there is a definite link between today's sky-busting and intelligence. That he was a remarkable shot at even an advanced age was related to me by my lifelong friend, the late Hugh Poston, a tremendous professional shotgunner himself and for many years Pacific Coast Manager for Remington Arms. Hugh enjoyed several duck shoots with the veteran Kimble and watched him score rights and left with almost monotonous ease. An inventor of note, Mr. Kimble wrote me not long before his passing (and in a beautiful copper-plate hand) how he made his own powder by "cooking it up on the kitchen stove with ingredients costing only a few cents a pound."

Thus, with Mr. Kimble spearheading an era of longer-range shotgunnery, we pass on through an ensuing period of comparative calm, ballistically. In those days, the ammunition companies were most accommodating and enterprising in the loading of shotgun shells to suit the fancies of duck hunters of famous and intensively gunned areas and clubs. A favorite twelve-gauge combination here and there might be three and a quarter dram with only one ounce of shot ahead of it; at another, three and a quarter with an ounce and an eighth. These handled most satisfactorily in the blossoming and destructive pumps and autoloaders.

It was about 1908 that I saw the first "step-up" in twelve-gauge wildfowling ammunition. Loads of twenty-eight grains of Ballistite and Infallible (dense) powders appeared, along with three and a half drams (bulk) powder measurement, shoving an ounce and a quarter of chilled shot. But such more-power innovations created little or no furor as to range extensions. There was no middle ground to duck shooting in those days. It was either all business or all fun. Migrational ceilings were still curtained with waterfowl, but there were whisperings of inevitable decline unless the killing pace slackened. The Migratory Bird Law moved in and there was a six-year struggle through to 1918 before the Supreme Court confirmed the act. The Federal daily bag limit set at twenty-five ducks and eight geese, was, of course, overly generous, and the fifteen ensuing years (1916-1931) witnessed possibly the most abysmal protection of the resource.

In 1931, the Federal bag limit was cut to fifteen ducks a day and four geese. Live decoys were banned about then, and the two national conservation outfits had declared war on the use of magazine guns holding more than three shots. "Sky-busting" as a term hadn't as yet appeared in wildfowling's nomenclature. But when progress and genius mate – anything can happen, for better or worse. And thereby hangs a tale. Actually, there is no telling when, where, or by whom the slangy moniker of "sky-busting" was first applied to shooting at wildfowl out of range for either effective results or common sense.

Nash shooting at high doves. The gun is the second Becker Magnum.

I so well remember the first time I ever heard the expression. Our sporting goods firm in Memphis jobbed, wholesaled, and retailed guns and ammunition of such industries as Winchester, Remington, Peters, U.S., and the Western Cartridge Company. In 1921, I was sent some unmarked and unnamed twelve-gauge shotgun shells by the Western Cartridge Company of East Alton, Illinois and was asked to test them on wildfowl for better killing power at longer ranges. They were loaded with #4 chilled shot. At Wapanoca and Beaver Dam, I had perfect testing sites. Having been asked to keep the experiments to myself and report in detail, I put the shells through their paces for the "test-gun" which accompanied them, a 9¾ pound double, twelve bore, two-triggered Fox Magnum, the first Askins-Sweeley boring by the late master-borer Burt Becker. I also shot the shells from my own 34-inch double Parker. The Fox was the gun used by Western for factory testing.

In those years, be it remembered, the use of wooden decoys had declined in favor of live mallards. Guides, commercialists, and club members used mostly troupes of well-trained drakes and susies. It was an era of accumulation, disposition, and unlimited baiting. The big idea as to range being (as Ben Tyler reports of his shooting days with One-Eyed Nick Gerno at Big Lake, Arkansas) "to call 'em in and let 'em pull their boots off." After disposing of a couple of cases of those strange new shells, I reported that I could lower ducks and geese with them from heights (and dead) at ranges of fifteen to twenty yards higher than I had attempted previously. I returned the big Fox, and sent in my report.

In the season of 1922, those new loads came on the market, the first appearance of the then Western Cartridge Company's famous and still dominant brand *Super-X*. No one had ever christened Mr. Kimble's choke-boring discovery as "sky-busting," but I'm sure I was present at its christening with Super-X.

It was of a Monday morning after the wildfowling season began (1922), and, as usual, a group of weekend gunners held post-mortems against the honkers. It was, I'm sure, my young friend the late John Lauranson who said, in describing his and the late Ben Tyler's goose safari – "We were pitted on the lower end of Norfolk Sandbar and we'd have done a lot better but for a bunch of sky-busters on the upper end. They hurt us; never gave anything a chance to get within range. We were just lucky with a couple of bunches from the south. I guess those *sky-busters* figured that all they had to do was just point these new-fangled, longer-range Super-X shells in the general direction of the honkers and cut loose and they'd fall dead. These new loads will undoubtedly do a better job at increased ranges, but you've also got to use some common sense."

Thrust is thrust whether at game or the moon. As far as I was personally concerned, I had discovered that Super-X would do the job claimed for it. That is, if properly directed, as Mr. Fred Kimble had discovered, with due allowance for some trial and error. And I didn't realize, at the moment, that the word "sky-buster" from Johnny Lauranson's highly imaginative and sprightly vocabulary would become a word renowned in ballistic controversy and a practice despised in national wildfowling circles. It hasn't made our library's biggest dictionary yet – but give it time.

Necessity is allegedly the mother of Invention. Wildfowl populations lessen and populations explode to augment selfish, wasteful bombardments and vandalistic thievery along the flyways. Life seems to have become largely a matter of whose guns will shoot the farthest. Who remembers when our fathers (as stout-hearted, patriotic Americans) brought home rockets and firecrackers and Roman-candles and set them off from our lawns at dusk – dim of the glorious Fourth of July? We kiddies stood back and ready to scamper when Dad applied the match to a rocket and ducked. There was a hiss, a swooshing roar, and high and far above the forest tops went a streak of fire and then a soft thuddy sploosh that burst and reburst into myriad fire stars – again and again. That was the birth of today's "thrust" and has carried us to the moon and Mars.

Mr. Fred Kimble writes that he figured to shoot a long way would take a cannon, so he set out to get the closest thing to one in a shoulder gun. Well, those rockets of our childhoods now have highest priorities in an increasingly war-torn, godless, and unholy world. We've managed to hit the moon amidships and shot cameras past Mars. Neither sky-busting of wildfowl, nor "space-busting" makes sense to a lot of us. But about the best we can do, like the declining ducks, is to "wiggle with 'em." Anyway, Johnny Lauranson's work – "sky-busting" – spread like Asian flu, and now, forty-three years since I first heard it, the practice is still going strong.

Basically, the term is more one of opprobrium than substance. And Super-X, a tremendous advance in shotgun ballistics, just happened to come along in time to become a benefactor suddenly named in a ballistic paternity suit for malpractice included. There are undoubtedly far more inept and churlish wildfowlers today than when Super-X emerged from the lab. And since that long-gone day, many competitive brands of extra-long-range ammo have come upon the market. The birth and nursing days even of Super-X were fraught with birth pains.

An industrial pillow-fight followed production of Super-X. No other trade-name with which I've had dealings in the sporting goods business or conservational squabbles remotely compares in praise, abuse, guess-work, mystery, pro and con publicity, and plain, unadulterated "knocking." Ere long, Super-X became a witch's broomstick.It reportedly struck wildfowl dead at uncanny ranges. It allegedly burst gun barrels and wrecked the mechanisms of autoloaders. Competition screamed its head off and lost valuable time by not recognizing worth and becoming joiners. There were a few lawsuits about twelve-gauge gun tubes being blown up by the mysterious Super-X powder. But micro-photography soon revealed the imprint of the heads of twenty-gauge shells that careless hunters managed somehow to drop in ahead of the twelve-bore hulls, so that ended.

In 1925, having for three years observed the upsurge of Super-X and its furthered advancements in components and copper-coated pellets, I became associated with the Western Cartridge Company of East Alton, Illinois (now Olin Mathison Chemical Corporation, Incorporated) as director of its new Department of Game Restoration, doubling in brass, so to speak, in sales, advertising, trap-shooting, and pushing contacts with Federal and state wildlife agencies and the growing cult known as "organized conservation." There wasn't a doubt by then but what Super-X actually saved more game by knocking it dead in the guns of good shots and those seriously interested in becoming such, than was lost by the thoughtless sky-busters. And by then, too, Super-X had opposing long-range Richmonds in the fields. For quite a spell, overly enthusiastic advertising agencies splurged in blue sky copy that had fantastic gunning yardages dancing through gunners' heads like visions of sugar-plums for kids at Yuletide. You might call it a period of over-glorification of the Fred Kimble theory of trial by error. There was also a period during which hunters were urged by some gun editors to substitute power for skill afield, in all gauges and combinations.

But, gradually, as clouds thickened on the wildfowl resources horizons, the pendulum swung back to common sense. In fact, swung a bit too far back just about then. Gun and ammunition manufacturers urged sensible ranges, improved hunting skills, and – highly important – bettered gunning ethics. Eradication of sky-busters has been, of course, impossible. We'll always have them with us. And not all of today's sky-busters are even shooting at ducks at excessive ranges, for forests have fallen and ranges have changed. It takes a high tree in the bottoms of today to rise thirty yards. And again, not all ducks that return northward with some shot in their anatomies (as shown by fluoroscoping) are fired at by sky-busters. Factually, the geese are today more set upon by the sky-busters than any wildfowl species. Both commercialists and state public shooting grounds for geese have sweat blood over that problem. Technicians have recorded triangulations of sky-busters firing at flocks from eighty-five to 105 yards high!

All sorts of measures to abate the nuisance have been employed; the best seemingly to date being at the new state grounds at Blythe's Perry in middle-east Tennessee. There, the gunners are allowed only eight shotgun shells with which to bag their limits. So, though agreeing 100% with the young outdoor writer's indictment of sky-busting as a highly undesirable practice among others in today's beset field, we find other phases of wildfowling malpractice far above it.

We can safely conclude, I think, that so-called sky-busting is no "villain-of-the-piece" in the decline of continental wildfowl resources. But I'm sure the young outdoor columnist meant well, because I've seen too many boorish sky-busters at work, and (having worn the badge of a Deputy Federal Game Agent) I have looked into too many public and commercial goose pits with bottoms covered by empty cartridges and empty whiskey bottles. So, having explored Mr. Kimble's great advance in sky-busting with choke-boring, and the mystery of Super-X, let's give a gander at a phase of decline in wildfowl which all hands have apparently overlooked. The complete antithesis of sky-busting, a system for duck slaughter which began development just about the same time that sky-busting burst upon the national flyways.

I refer to "duck-calling." From its enormous expansion sprang a system of calculated destruction without parallel, beside which sky-busting pales into insignificance. And yet, duck-calling is high and legal art. Birds and beasts have had their calls imitated by man almost since recorded history. The best goose-caller I have ever heard was Osborn, paddler at old Wapanoca who used his natural, throaty voice. You couldn't tell where the honkers took in or he left off. And one year, as I recall, a gentleman who blew through his own fingers and fist won a national calling title. Like musicians, some duck-callers achieve greatness, but few if any have it thrust upon them. Cynics complain that duck calls aid conservation in driving off circling mallards.

At world's-end, duck hunters will go down probably still arguing as to whether they'd prefer finding themselves with an ample supply of decoys but no call, or just a call with which to advertise and attract. I have said it before and repeat here, however, that regardless of advertising and imitative supremacy with charm and potential in cadence, every fellow who blows a duck call retains the secret belief that he is really the best duck caller in the whole world. But there are days when ducks will simply not respond to even the calling of champions. I have sat in a duck blind with three national champions when they couldn't buy a duck. But there come days when ducks will cover up even the most blaring novice. A novice becomes a champion and goes home walking on air.

Some callers can blow a certain type of rubber or metal reed well, but completely fail with another. It depends wholly on the blower's lungs as to a "hard" or "soft-blowing" reed. But there are definitely no "self-blowing" calls. The only call I could ever use without incurring abuse and skepticism from a blind-mate is the little, soft-blowing cane call of the 'Cajun country in Louisiana. Our superintendent at Section 16 Duck Club on Bayou LaGrue in Arkansas used to put it this way, "I know I've got a funny call. Mr. Buck and I hunt together a lot. Mr. Buck has got a funny call, too. I guess them ducks must hear the racket and one says to another, 'Do you hear that? What on earth do you suppose it is?' The other duck says, 'I dunno, les' fly over there and see.' Then they come on over an' git killed."

Just as the words "choke-boring," "sky-busting," and "Super-X" are, so to speak, dated, duck calling has a really comparative early birth date. Those small cane-calls of the Louisiana coastals were undoubtedly around in the long ago. In my boyhood days I remember a split-ended call with a horn loudspeaker end, the reed of which almost invariably got cussed out by my elders because it got full of tobacco or cracker crumbs. Just before turn of the century there was a wood-and-metal call by Allen that did very well. And the goose call of that period was the Fuller. At such market-hunting centers as Big Lake, Arkansas and Reelfoot Lake (Kentucky-Tennessee), handmade calls were in their heyday a long way back. Highly prized at Big Lake were the Beckhart calls. At Reelfoot a noted pioneer was an old Frenchman-guide named Glodo who came to the end of his rope as a famous market-hunter. My old and valued friend Guy Ward of the famous market hunting family of Reelfoot and champion trap shot of the professionals, gave me a hand-made Glodo call which I later presented to John Olin. Past turn-of-the-century use of wooden decoys declined sharply in favor of live mallards. About 1922 I wrote an article for *Field & Stream* entitled "The Neglected Duck Call." It is carried in later editions of my *De Shootinest Gent'man*. In the next five years I must have received at least a thousand letters about that article. Seemingly, from there on, a new "system" of duck shooting began in the wintering grounds of the lower Mississippi Valley flyway of today. Assisted by recurring exhibitions of what Ding Darling refers to as "tragic stupidity" in management, we may well find the answer to a requiem now tolling for today's mallard resources.

Before World War I, I had come to know and hunt with a remarkable young chap named P.C. "Perry" Hooker, chief electrician at our Memphis Union Depot. He held licenses as master electrician, engineer, mechanic, and service in the Air Corps. Reared in a farming and market-hunting family of Kansas, he was undoubtedly, in my book and those of many others such as the late and great turkey and duck call maker, Tom Turpin, the finest all-around caller that profession and art has ever known. A magnificent shot, he left all the licenses behind him upon return from overseas to become a salesman for the Western Cartridge Company. He could build a shotgun or win a high-average at targets. He was with Western during World War II. He held the confidence and respect of its executives. And with his passing left an impact upon the duck calling advances of the nation that probably set the system to work, for there have been few commercial frenzies in the world of waterfowling and sporting goods to equal the spread of duck calling and the manufacture of its instruments.

Promotional duck-calling contests overrun the flyways from local and state levels to national and world titles. And the end is not yet in sight. Young legend has it that in some regions, babes cut their teeth on duck calls rather than rattles. There are duck call collectors, and sporting goods establishments offer free lessons in duck calling as seasons approach. There are hot arguments as to when and when not to blow. There are even "species calls." It got so bad a few seasons ago that electricity crept into the act. Electrically octaned goose calls that could be heard for miles hiked the annual kill to such proportions that they were Federally banned. An electric duck call appeared just in time to be banished. I happened to sit in on a board that tested for the government on that one. But it proved ineffective; one good human blower could drown it out completely. Nevertheless, it was at this point that sky-busting went into reverse when it came to the abuses heaped upon the migrations in the club and commercialized areas.

The "system" meant just one thing: Professional guides and club or unattached amateurs in "calling" were recognized and given standing by their abilities to light ducks. The paying guests mopped up the lit fowl with magazine-gun blasts, on the water and as they jumped.

In those days, the government usually permitted shooting from half an hour before sunrise until sunset, which meant – *in the dark*. Cripples began clogging the rapidly appearing reservoirs and slaughter pens. Limits secured, relays of new customers entered blinds. Lots of money changed hands. Why not? It was legal – strictly. Around the clubs, limits were thieved ad lib. Vast rings of strictly criminal duck murderers and sellers took all the time the government had to spare to even attempt control – and that with really only one undercover operator whose name should go down in history as a tremendous performer.

It was a long time before the commercialists got wise to the fact that they had better slow down. Ducks were diminishing everywhere. Sky-busting by drunken louts was discouraged. Some private preserves were run clean but needed machine-gun protection from invading "public hunters." When rivers rose and flooded the wintered woods, the mallards received an awful beating. Deep-freezes had arrived; thousands of ducks were stored in private homes of small towns and surreptitiously peddled by school children.

But when "lessening ducks" were mentioned, it was always the fault of some *drought* "up North!" I could fill a book with slaughterous activities coming under my reportorial observation, some of them enough to gag a buzzard. But they bounced off Washington. In 1931, however, bag limits were cut to fifteen ducks a day and four geese. By 1934-'35, continental supplies were reported the lowest in history. The government appointed an Emergency Waterfowl Committee. Two of its members that I recall were the late Ding Darling and Aldo Leopold, wildfowlers and men of high honor and experience. Their first act was to clap on shooting hours of from 7 am until 4 pm. This held for six or seven years and the mallards staged a noticeable comeback. Then came World War II; hunting pressures slackened and shotgun shells became scarce. By 1943, the killers had regained shooting hours of "half an hour before sunrise until set," which practically immunizes duck thieves and bag-limit violators. The ducks had come back in such strength that an extra five big ducks were allowed. And that just about did it. By 1947, bag limits in the Mississippi Valley Flyway had shrunk to four. That was eighteen years ago and since 1947, limits, as to mallards, have shrunk to one mallard in a bag limit of four assorted fowl.

Meanwhile, however, conservationists had been able to get shooting hours of from sunrise until sunset established. Meanwhile, too, over the lower Mississippi Valley flyway petitions appeared seeking half-day duck shooting. They were completely ignored, and worse, individuals seeking to appear before committees and officials to discuss shooting hours known to have saved the migratory doves were refused. Droughts in the breeding grounds were, of course, blamed for shortages, but excesses in the flyways were kept farther than far in the background. Thus, since

1931, despite Federal and state efforts against organized rings of duck bootleggers and studied efforts by unattached hunters and so-called club members and commercial shootings, the flyways from California to Maine, and Minnesota to Louisiana have been looted. There is no other word to express the type of such wildfowling disaster areas.

It was not until 1960, as noted, that duck bootlegging became a felony. Even then, Congress reportedly ignored even worse stealage by wildfowlers. Factually, the amateurs have for long been out-stealing the pros. Call it what you like, unpunished crimes against the migrations have caused as much if not more damage than drought. The young outdoor writer is right. Cynicism may connote all this as mere decline in national morale. But applied locally and broadly, whatever remains of official authority at Washington with an ounce of pity in its heart will heed the hopes of practical conservationists fighting that same rear-guard action on behalf of U.S.A., manhood, and sound industrialism. The prestige of sportsmanship has been so horribly mutilated as to outdoor ethics and judicial recognitions by supremely arrogant legal officialdom in high places as to test the stoutest hearts among men who love guns and dogs and rods and reels and the beauties of God-made sanctuaries in the wild. As a sample of the frustration that quells hope among decent sportsmen, I quote from a letter recently received form a gentleman of the national press whose contacts with enforcement have been many. He has seen both ends of wildfowling's candle burning at the same time for years:

"You are completely right as to present day looting of the flyways. The trouble is, it is getting worse and those who should be doing something about it are not. And little, if anything, will be done about it until the last mallard falls. They will continue to slaughter the birds so long as they can find one in their gunsights, in or out of these so-called experimental teal seasons. At times, discouraged, decent hunters are tempted to join them, feeling it as their only chance before the mallards, quail, squirrels, and doves are gone. Many duck hunters hate to admit it and keep talking about being up or on a level with previous ones. But even I have been able to see during the past eight years that the struggle between decency afield and crime and dishonor is unequal. The end approaches – and fast."

Now couple that thinking with the viewpoint of the forthright column of the young outdoor writer, and you begin to get a picture of what's in store for the mallards and, for that matter, the rest of the ducks and geese exposed to processes of physical illegalities afield and intellectual, biological, and political dishonesties administrationally. One thing seems certain: It has taken eighteen years (since 1947) to get from a four-duck limit down to one mallard in the daily bag in the Mississippi Valley flyway. Probably several million illegal.

To a Birch Bark Horn!

By T. N. BUCKINGHAM

From Nature man's hand stripped thee from a parent
    tree
And fashioning to shapeliness his horn of choice,
Gave back through thee from human throat to Nature's
    heart
A luring call! A poisoned love note of the cow moose
    voice!
Ah! hear it rise and wail and float across yon darkening
    bog!
Renewed! O'er dawning glory of some ice-skimmed
    pond,
To where the weird, seductive summons finds its antlered
    Knight,
King Bull Moose, listening in a "blow-down" far beyond!
Stay, Hand o' Man! Dear Mother Nature, by thy
    kindred blood forefend,
Proclaim the siren false! Prevent this monstrous thing!
A shot! A blow that racks the stricken monarch to his
    end,
The voice of Time chants on—"The King is dead! Long
    live the King!"

Rich Man—Poor Man

By T. N. BUCKINGHAM

Rich man! Poor man! Fields are flashing,
  Frosty dawn calls golden clear—
Claim your share of life that's waiting,
  Rich in brave autumnal cheer!
See! Cattle ponds glint diamonds!
  Forest choirs pipe cheery lay,
From the distance Bob White lures you—
  Seek the Valley Come-What-May!

Rich man! Poor man! Up and at them!
  Trusty gun and comrade dog,
And tuck away that snack o' grub
  You'll munch astride some log.
Hie on, Pointer! rustle cornfields—
  Go it, Setter! Split the sedge!
And you lose—and find them—Statues,
  By the woodland's thicket hedge.

Wow! A leaping w-h-i-i-i-r o' Brownies,
  Up swings the old pal gun,
A wilting p-o-u-u-f-f to right and left,
  And your heart sings out "well done!"
Then each sentinel knoll flies signal
  To its swale across the way,
"We've won him now—he's headed—
  For our Valley Come-What-May!"

Rich man! Poor man! Gold the gloaming,
  Emptying purse of autumn day,
And star dust lowers her mantle—
  Hunter's Moon! Come, Light the way!
Tramp you home, oh, rich man, poor man!
  From the Valley Come-What-May
To treasure trove of Home Sweet Home,
  Crown jewel of hunter's day!

Lived there e'er a Croesus richer,
  Or king upon his throne,
Sharing days of joy as carefree
  As those hours you've called your own?
For yours held more of sky than theirs,
  Nor hoard of silvery moon
Could lure your gun and dog in trade,
  For gems or their last doubloon!

Ah, when embers frame your memories,
  Rich man, poor man, this hold true—
That to dwell in the Valley Come-What-May,
  Makes equal men—of YOU!

THE
FIELD TRIAL YEARS

"Remarks I made at a meeting of the Memphis, Tennessee Rotary Club, Sheraton-Peabody Hotel, Memphis, Tennessee – March 1, 1966. The event was the showing of the Tennessee Game & Fish Commission's color film 'Bird Dog Champion,' with the National Field Trial Champion Association's runnings still in progress at Ames Plantation, Grand Junction, Tennessee. Introduction by Mr. Robert Milner."

M r. Milner, members of Rotary: I am grateful for this opportunity, not because of anything of interest or value I bring, but because of my sincere appreciation for your invitation. The brilliantly photographed color film you are about to enjoy properly begins in October, 1874 at the then Greenlawn Plantation, later known as "The Messiack Place." It is now owned by Mr. Scott, its considerable acreage and the original antebellum home is situated at Old Poplar Pike at Kirby Road, extending east and southward.

There, in 1874, under auspices of the Tennessee Sportsmen's Association, was held the first field trial for pointers and setters ever run in the United States. It was won by a Gordon setter – Knight – and the top trophy was donated by the duPont Powder Company.

Twenty-two years and in the vicinity of twenty-eight continental field trials later (1896), the first National Field Trial Championship was held at West Point, Mississippi. That first National was the brain-child of a dedicated and beloved field-trialer, W. W. "Uncle Billy" Titus of West Point, Mississippi. He conceived the idea in 1895, and with the help of the late Mr. Edward Dexter of Buzzard's Bay, Massachusetts, the great classic was born a year later under title of "The Field Trial Champion Association." Its first President was Mr. Dexter. The names of Adams, Phelps, Norvin T. Harris, Mr. Stafford, George Gould, Pierre Lorillard, Theo. Sturges, C. E. Buckle, and James M. Avent come back to me as founders.

In viewing this film, let's keep in mind what Uncle Billy Titus meant when he proposed, "Let's promote a championship through which that great quality of *stamina*, so useful to a field dog, can be encouraged."

Heats in the National have always been three hours. To Judges that third hour is when the chips really go down. The stake's first winner was a white setter with black head and neck trimmings – Count Gladstone IV, owned by Mr. Hitchcock and handled by Mr. Charles Tucker. The first championship was run at West Point, Mississippi, New Albany next, then back to West Point and for three seasons thereafter on the Grand Junction, Tennessee, course, south of town, that curved southeast toward Rogers Springs and the famous old Avent Hotel.

It was run on the by-then expanding Ames Plantation for the first time in 1902. Hobart Ames, of North Easton, Massachusetts had come rapidly to the fore in field trialing, and he told me he had put up some "earnest money" to buy a shooting preserve near New Albany when he received a telegram from Mr. Jim Avent at Hickory Valley, Tennessee inviting him and Mrs. Ames up for some quail shooting and to look at a piece of property that might be acquired.

They went, enjoyed wonderful sport, and Mr. Ames forfeited his earnest-money and bought the multi-acred plantation and lovely old Manse built in 1847 by the late Captain John Wiley Jones – Mrs. Buckingham's great-grandfather. That telegram "Uncle Jim" Avent sent Hobart Ames changed history for a lot of dogs, people, and the University of Tennessee, and still has history ahead of it. Hobart Ames passed away in 1945 at that plantation home he loved so well, right at 80. I had known him since 1907, hunted with him, and judged with him from 1934 until 1941, when he retired from the judicial saddle and was replaced by Mr. Reuben Scott, his plantation director who has, in turn, but just retired, although retaining the Presidency of the National Field Trial Champion Association

I began riding Nationals just past the turn of the century, have seen field trial history made from Canada to the Gulf, and gotten stories behind the stories. Field trials are absolutely unique in the American sporting saga. No scandals and no bonus puppies. Field trial judges rarely escape criticism, just or unjust. Our philosophy there being, "If you can't take it, don't start." The dominant thought running through this motion picture like a golden thread should be of that cultured, generous, and Christian woman, Mrs. Julia Colony Ames, who left this magnificent device for benefit of the University of Tennessee through an administering Ames Foundation. This enormous, multiple-use compound of agriculture, animal husbandry, forestry, advanced game management, and the noble sport of field trialing, is, indeed, in sacred trust to the future.

Mrs. Ames passed on in 1950. In 1956, the West Tennessee Sportsmens' Association presented to the Trustees of the University of Tennessee a resolution calling for the establishment of a Chair of Forestry & Game

Management, where holders of earned degrees by our young people will guarantee trained minds and steady hands upon the futures of our great state's lands, waters, and wildlife resources. It took awhile, but the battle was won, and for several years now a Department of Forestry & Game Management has been functioning ably and ambitiously at the University of Tennessee. As this picture unfolds, give thanks to Hobart and Julia Colony Ames for having faith in us of Tennessee to keep an immeasurably greater one.

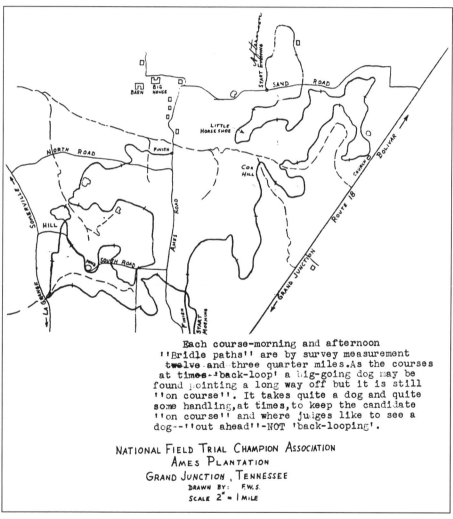

Each course—morning and afternoon
''Bridle paths'' are by survey measurement
twelve and three quarter miles. As the courses
at times--'back-loop' a big-going dog may be
found pointing a long way off but it is still
''on course''. It takes quite a dog and quite
some handling, at times, to keep the candidate
''on course'' and where judges like to see a
dog--''out ahead''-NOT 'back-looping'.

NATIONAL FIELD TRIAL CHAMPION ASSOCIATION
AMES PLANTATION
GRAND JUNCTION, TENNESSEE
DRAWN BY: F.W.S.
SCALE 2" = 1 MILE

Nash's personal map of the grounds of the Ames Plantation, site of his years of judging the "National." Nash's typed comments about the course are at right.

106 AMES BUILDING
BOSTON, MASSACHUSETTS

Dec. 28, 1933.

Nash Buckingham, Esq.,
Box 720,
Memphis, Tenn.

Dear Mr. Buckingham:

Mr. Henry P. Davis and I are going to judge the National Championship Trials this year to be held at Grand Junction, Tennessee Feb. 26, 1934, and we are wondering if we could persuade you to act with us.

As one of the judges, I should expect you to stay at my house and would try to make you as comfortable, as possible.

We hope nothing will prevent you from accepting.

I am leaving for Grand Junction on the 2nd of January, so please reply to me there instead of here as your answer would not have time to get here before I leave.

Mr. Davis and I hope very much you will be able to accept.

Sincerely yours,

The beginning of a long, satisfying relationship between Nash Buckingham and the National Field Trial Championship held at Grand Junction, Tennessee on the grounds of the Ames Plantation. Nash enjoyed his judging duties tremendously, and was honored as an inductee into the Field Trial Hall of Fame once his judging career was over in his later years. The National Field Trial Champion Association's classic originated in West Point, Mississippi in 1896, but moved to the Ames Plantation in 1902.

The late Hobart Ames outside the Ames Plantation house, Grand Junction, Tennessee, the site of the National Field Trial that Nash judged for seventeen years.

137

Lippincott Colket of Philadelphia, Pa., and Nash Buckingham of Memphis, Tenn., debate "Vest in show" while judging a luncheon-hour "Bench Show" during the Plantation Owners Field Trial near Estill, S.C. Jan. 1941, where they also Judged, while Guests of Mr & Mrs Fitz Eugene Dixon of White Hall Plantation.

Nash's writing on the photograph at left is self-explanatory. Nash's reputation as a dog man made calls for such judging, both bench shows and field trials, common duty for him, but one of which he never tired. Above, judging the trial itself.

Nash, far front, right, at the head of the gallery as a judge at the National.

An Episode
In
Dog-Trading

My field trial judging experience and hunting as much as I did and still do put me in touch with a number of canine characters and their two-footed compadres. Dog-trading is a national endeavor of folk of this ilk. As to top-flight salesmanship and transactions with material benefit on both sides, I vividly recall the trade my old friend and grand sportsman, the late R. M. Carrier (known to his intimates as "The Squire" and "The Little Giant") got into through the good offices of an old gentleman engaged by the then Mud Lake Duck Club to act as combination Majordomo and game warden for their lodge and lands – a man we'll call "The Colonel."

The Colonel might have stepped out of Dickens, a corpulent esquire, aged in the wood and woods and given to flounce-fronted shirts invariably scented with the delicate, mingling odors of mignonette and high-octane bourbon. But he did the club a grand job and was highly respected in the countryside. Bob Carrier had just opened his magnificent 30,000 acre "Barnacre" shooting preserve – west of Sardis, Mississippi. And, thanks to the supervisions of Henry P. Davis and Earl and May Bufkin had accumulated just about the finest kennel of shooting dogs and heavily populated quail fields in the U.S. When the Squire tackled any project, he saw it through. But he confided to Henry and me that what he also needed at Barnacre Lodge for his guests' night-entertainment was a real, bang-up coon dog.

One night, at Mud Lake, the Colonel heard us discussing this problem and volunteered the information that he knew a Mississippi River trapper and shanty-boatman who had a coon dog famed the country over. But he needed a sure but slow bird dog he could break to double on squirrels, quail, and rabbits

141

and thus enrich his bachelor's table. Maybe Bob Carrier had such a dog and they might get up a trade?

The Colonel was told to negotiate, and if successful, to fetch the trapper's candidate to the club the following week. "Brownie" turned out to be an extremely handsome, eighty-five pound collie-and-bloodhound cross. Powerful, cold-eyed, but – according to the Colonel – sunny-natured except with varmints and intruders. He possessed incredible scenting powers and fighting prowess not unmixed with all but human intelligence.

This called for a dissertation by Bob Carrier as to the multifold talents of an amiable and aging setter he had brought along. Both tradees, Brownie and "Ben" (party of the second part) were on the clubhouse front steps but well separated and restrained (as to canine amenities) into an obviously strained peace by rope about their necks. The Colonel (in a lowered voice) said to Mike (a club pusher who held Brownie's cord), "Lead Brownie off yonder a piece. He understands everything that everybody says, an' if he figgers he's gonna be traded away from home, he'll try to light out – right now. Bob Carrier afterward admitted that that was the greatest sales talk punchline he ever heard and it sold him.

Brownie returned to Barnacre Lodge in Bob Carrier's Lincoln Sedan and the Colonel took Ben to the trapper's shanty-boat in his Model A Ford. Brownie, kept aloof from the Barnacre kennels of enormously valuable pointers and Bob's famed Labrador retriever, "Barnacre Boy" (a British titlist in retriever trials), proved everything claimed for him as a coon-destroyer. Coons began to grow scarce and off-limits in the vicinity of the lodge.

But one day, through some mischance, Brownie and Barnacre Boy (a burly type himself) met up and tied in hip-and-thigh with no holds barred. Brownie bounced Boy around like a dribbled basketball, but fortunately help arrived. It was a T. K. O. for Brownie in the first round, but his fate was sealed.

"That dog," said Bob Carrier, "is a specialist in coon and canine destruction but he is a liability to our social order at Barnacre, so I am going to farm him out to a fine home I know of down in the Big Woods Bottoms; Curt Swango has a man down there he'll make a fortune for, but I intend to keep title. He can lick any bobcat in the delta, but he ain't gonna keep in practice eatin' my bird dogs and retrievers."

Bob's next inquiry at Mud Lake was as to how the trapper was coming along with the old setter, Ben. The Colonel said, "Mist' Bob, he has done broke that dawg t' where he can read a coon's mind an' tell his Boss which limb of a tree a squirrel's layin' on. He can find all th' pottiges in the' county, retrieves 'em by th' head, an' lays 'em in yo' pocket. And he's a natural born rabbit-agent – cotton-ails or swampers. But he can't and won't fight like Brownie could." Bob Carrier said, "Ben's got sense." Henry Davis was listening and he said, "Both you and the trapper are apparently satisfied with the transaction; something very unusual in a dog-swap." The Colonel who had been sort of dozing by the big fireplace, roused up and says, "Yes, it was a fine trade but I would sure hate for that Brownie to have acted on *my* case."

Nash at age 76. His note on the back of the photograph: "Nash Buckingham duck hunting with John P. Bailey, Coffeyville, Miss. 1956. The gun is the second Burt Becker 3-inch 12 magnum."

BO-WHOOP

Burt Becker built for Nash the famous Fox magnum "Bo-Whoop" in the early 1920's and a second, nearly identical gun in 1950.

Nash sent a series of questions to Burt Becker some time in 1956. Nash planned an article based upon Becker's answers, but no such article appeared in Gun Digest where Nash indicated he wanted to publish it. Becker's handwritten responses are nearly illegible in places, and certain questions were unanswered.

Further research by Fox Gun Company expert Michael McIntosh reveals that Becker was never listed as an employee of the Fox Gun Company, and was probably an independent, doing contract work, most likely custom barrel–boring, starting in 1915.

TO BE FILLED IN BY BURT BECKER

1. *Born:* 1871
   At: Phoenix Oswego County (New York)
2. *Early schooling:*
   Went to school until I was 14 years old.
3. *Where and under whom did you learn gun trade?*
   Syracuse. I went to work for Dan LeFever and worked for him 4 years and learned my trade.
4. *First employment:*
   1889 I went to work for Batavia Gun Works.
5. *Didn't you build those find Remington double guns exhibited at St. Louis World's Fair in 1904?*
   1900 I went to work for the Remington Arms Company. Made the double barrel shotgun and went to work and built those fine Remington double guns [referred to in Nash's question]. I made six of them to go to St. Louis World Fair in 1904.
6. *When did you go with Fox?*

I went with Fox and made some good guns for him in 1915.

7. *Didn't you bore out the first Askins-Sweeley Magnum 12?* [the forerunner of the Super-Fox, of which "Bo-Whoop" was the prime example]
[No answer given, although research indicates that the year the gun was made was 1922 and Becker indeed built the gun.]

8. *How long were you with Fox?*
[No answer given.]

9. *How long with Savage Stevens?*
I was with Savage Stevens less than 1 year.

10. *How long in business for yourself?*
15 years.

11. *Send your opinions on magnum boring, the process you used to get best results from different size shot – like best boring for 4's.*
[Answer illegible.]

12. *What's your opinion as to copper coated shot over regular shot?*
Give me the regular shot, it will not crowd or jam the load. My best shooting was at Long Branch, when I broke 190 out of 200 with the Remington. It was the gun I made myself; that gun I could shoot.

13. *Didn't you build the first 20-ga. magnum (3-inch) for Mr. Bartholomew? I still have the one you built for me in 1927.*
I built the first 20 gauge magnum and shell for Mr. Bartholomew. (Since you still have the one I built for you), keep it as you never will get another. I don't have any guns now, they all went west to California.

14. *Please send any photograph of yourself, or photographs of famous guns for a story about you for the next "Gun Digest."*

A newspaper classified advertisement asking for the return, "No questions asked," of the famous Burt Becker Fox 12-gauge magnum that was Nash's favorite waterfowl gun. The gun was nicknamed "Bo-Whoop" by Nash's friend Col. H. P. Sheldon for its distinctive sound. It was modeled after the Askins-Sweeley magnum made in 1921 and used by Nash to test John Olin's new Super-X shotshells. Nash, after testing the gun and load, liked the combination so much, he had one built for himself by the famous barrel-borer and gunmaker Burt Becker in 1921 or early 1922. But after a morning hunt on December 1, 1948, Nash and his companion, Cliff Green, were checked by conservation officers on routine patrol, and the gun was placed on a fender of the hunters' car. They drove away, and the gun evidently fell off and was never seen again. To replace this gun, George Warner and Berry Brooks commissioned Becker to build another such gun for Nash. But it was not exactly the same, sporting a pistol grip, for example, instead of the straight grip Nash favored. But in his hands, it performed as well as the original magnum.

BURT BECKER

CUSTOM MADE LONG RANGE MAGNUM - 12 GAUGE SHOT GUNS MADE TO ORDER 8 1-2 TO 10 LB.

4531 N. GRATZ STREET
PHILADELPHIA 40, PA.
MICHIGAN 7337

Sept; 27-1950

H.A.Bartholomew
Continental.Bldg;
Washington.5 D.C

Dear. Wr. Bartholomew

Just a line" for old time sake.
I have bin wourering how you are geting along.i hope
this letter findes you in good health and will abe-
able to put the old gat" on your shoulder and be your
self once again.Nothing like it" ill tell you.
Mr.B I dont know if i will be able to go hunting this
fall or not.you see its this way" my legs are goeing
bad.some times i feal good" then again i feal rotan.
Well old age comeing on with all of os.
by the way that magnum gun i sold to Mr.Brooks and

Georg.Warner is goeing to be a presont to my good old
Friend Nas.Buckingham.one thing i will say" its a
nice Gun.and i think Nas" will like it.you would like
it to if you ever see it.Well" i think its veary kind
in the two Gents" to give Nas that fine Gun.

Mr.B. let me tell you. i could not make a Gun like
it for less then 750.00 the Wood thats in the stock
and Forend. i would not be able to get at this time.

With Very.Good Helth

Burt Becker

P.S let me Hear From you

A letter from Burt Becker to Henry Bartholomew that mentions the second magnum he built for Nash at the request of George Warner and Berry Brooks. Brooks was a long-time friend of Nash's, while Warner was a Captain in the U. S. Army Corps of Engineers who had at the time never met Nash personally, but was an ardent admirer of his writings.

"MY DOG—JIM"

One of five from his royal line, one of four, then three—
One with the strength to carry on, and "Jim" was spared to me!
Puppy days! Oh! puppy days! Potlicker, rabbits and fun,
From dewy dawn to locusts' song, nothing to do but run!
'Member your first school days, Jim, your first keen bird scent thrill
When you spotted the Colonel's pet covey, over the cedar hill?
And how you chased that "cotton-tail," that led you thru the ditch
And how you took your medicine—when I came—with the switch?
Didn't the years pass happily, while we hunted on together
Across the hills and dales of life, in any old kind of weather!
I can see you sprawling in the hall of the old plantation home
With its vista of golden acres that were kingly yours, to roam.
Sure no monarch ever bore a plume with prouder caste of grace
Nor champion's heart bore cleaner mark, upon a real friend's face!
Ah! How you leaped at sight of gun and my tattered hunting coat
Then flashed out far beyond my horse, with the joy note in your
            throat!
No day too long, no way too hard, nor toil nor ice too thin
For you to work your heart out—and always work—and win!
Sundown days! Sundown days! Brave hunting thews grown old
But your noble blood still urging—and your champion's heart still
            bold.
When I've found my life's last covey—and my horse turns back to
            where
They count life's bag and pay you in specie of your share—
If they hunt thru fields Out Yonder and on thru regions dim—
Why you'll hear my old time whistle—and then I'll see—"Old Jim"!
                                    —T. N. Buckingham.

PART III

CONSERVATION

The late John M. Olin in the main room of his house at Nilo Farms, East Alton, Illinois. Olin was supportive of Nash's effort to limit the kill on waterfowl, even though it would, by necessity, limit the shotshells expended and reduce profits to his Winchester-Western division. Their friendship lasted over fifty years.

THE
CONSERVATION
WARS

$\mathbb{A}$fter eight years in the jobbing wholesale and retail business in Memphis, we had built the biggest operation of its kind south of the Ohio River, were traveling several men, and prospering. But during all that period I began to notice, and write about, the inevitability of game's decline under pressure, and that the gun and ammo industry had better take steps to do something about it. I had become a member of the Sporting Goods Dealer's five-man National Council. We were also selling a lot of ammunition for the Western Cartridge Company of Alton, Illinois, while occupying places on the jobbing lists of their rivals, Winchester and Remington.

One day I got a letter from Western asking me to pay their factory a visit; Mr. John Olin had been reading my articles in the *Sporting Goods Dealer* and wanted to talk about them. I went, and after several months' negotiations, they established a Department of Game Restoration (which name I coined). I sold my interest in the sporting goods firm and went to Alton, remaining there three years (as per contract) and getting the industry organized. I also ran trap shooting for them in '26 and built up what is today known as general public relations and publicity. It was a great experience and no one ever did business with finer folks. I met all the great industrial and conservation figures of the time.

Meanwhile, duPont had a department headed by my old friend Brigadier General L. W. T. Waller, a noted Marine and captain of the Olympic Rifle Team. I had known him since childhood – he was of a noted Virginia family. We got a lot done.

The Industry became organized under title of Sporting Arms and Ammunition Manufacturers Institute (SAAMI) and has only just been changed to the National Shooting Sports Foundation (NSSF). I wrote many, many articles and stories for outdoor and trade publications and duPont received excellent reactions.

Country-wide travel and a reporter's powers of observation pretty soon gave the national situation an answer – political game administration both state and Federal, plus tremendous pressure by the arms and ammunition industry. The original "conservationist" was a man around turn of the century known as G. O. Shields, "Coquino," who published a little outdoor magazine called *Recreation*. He wrote fearlessly, taking on the "game hogs" and the new repeating and autoloading shotguns. What arms and ammo did to that poor chap was awful and he reportedly died broke and of a broken heart.

In the earliest 1920's, my old friend E. F. Warner, former owner and publisher of *Field & Stream* magazine (for whom I wrote for many years) decided to crusade against autoloaders. Although I was on the jobbing list of Winchester and Remington, I helped him. What they did to Warner was aplenty, and I was threatened with removal from their "lists." Warner told me it cost him fifty thousand bucks before he could turn around; they almost drove him off the newsstands. He had made the mistake of tackling only the autoloaders, when his crusade should have been against *all* magazine guns.

But he got back on the reservation and I kept on to make my connection with Western. But I remember my own experience. To me, from ring days, the dignitaries in my field were just a lot of ballplayers and all I asked was for them to keep their punches up.

So, after I went with Western, I soon got to know not only the entire field of the industry, but also the main figures of the then U.S. Bureau of Biological Survey, now the U.S. Fish & Wildlife Service – Interior. In September 1925, at Denver, Colorado an international conservation group – fraternally based – was formed with seven founders. I am not permitted here to go into more detail.

I also met my good friend Henry P. Davis, later public relations director for Remington-duPont. Henry, probably the most noted field trial judge in the country, is now retired.

As my Western contract was expiring, I got a letter from Dr. John C. Phillips of Beacon Street, Boston, noted ornithologist and president of the Massachusetts Game & Fish Protective Association. He said a new waterfowl foundation was forming and asked if I'd be interested in the post of executive secretary, with GHQ at Washington, D.C.

Dr. Phillips had always had the idea of improving droughted Canadian breeding grounds, and there were other reforms needed. We had several meetings in Boston at the Tavern Inn and his home at Wenham. I talked the matter over with John Olin, and, as the Industry was now organized, I wanted to get a closer look at the nation's waterfowl situation.

At the Game Conference in New York, December 1927, the ammunition industry offered me the job of making a national game survey and writing a book thereon, but after deliberation I chose the waterfowl position and embarked on that in April 1928. I recommended Dr. Aldo Leopold for the ammunition and gun industry's job; he got it, and went ahead to great honors in a wonderful career, including the writing of his classic book *A Sand County Almanac*. The history of the American Wildfowlers has been published in James Trefethen's book, *Crusade for Wildlife* – Stackpole. It lasted but four years, but in that length of time it accomplished more than anything before or since, and its results are on the books today.

The Chairman of the Wildfowler's Executive Committee was Mr. Charles Sheldon, the great big-game hunter and father of Mt. McKinley National Park, a truly wonderful man of action with a head full of common sense and ample guts. He and Dr. Phillips made a wonderful team. We didn't have much money but there were no strings on us. Dr. Phillips was the first man to ever conceive water-restoration possibilities on the breeding grounds of Canada, so, we turned to that. Charles Sheldon was the father of the stalled "Game Refuge Bill" so that went on the immediate agenda. We got off an expedition to Alberta to study conditions across Canada, and I took a box-look at the Game Refuge matter.

I had, by now, formed a great friendship with the late Col. Harold P. Sheldon, then Chief Conservation Officer of the U.S.A., and later author of the wonderful *Tranquility* stories. One of my first jobs was to go to the office of Mr. Thomas Cochran of J. P. Morgan & Co. and return a check for $15,000 he had given us to help get the Game Refuge Bill passed. Figuring I would have a hard time getting in to see Mr. Cochran (he was a benefactor to Andover School in Massachusetts), I reached J. P. Morgan and Co.'s Wall Street office early and asked a big Irish policeman if I could see Mr. Cochran. He turned to a young fellow sitting nearby and asked, "Has Mr. Tommy come in yet?" The chap replied – pointing – "Just go on down to the end of the hall, sir, and you'll find him readin' th' mawnin' paper." I did, and we passed a pleasant hour talking duck shooting and plans for the good of the order. I told him that we could not pass the Game Refuge Bill in its present form, but I'd be thinking.

I knew that the International Game meeting would be in Seattle in

September, and that if a new group butted in with proposals, its fate would be sealed – oldtimers don't like Johnnies-Come-Lately. So I want to Hal Sheldon and said, "You go out to Seattle and propose the formation of a committee to be known as the American Waterfowl Committee, whose explicit duty will be to rewrite the Game Refuge Bill and get it before the Congress immediately if not sooner. We'll get you the funds necessary for the campaign." We then surveyed guys for the committee, and I had a chairman in mind.

We got hold of the late (and great) Dr. T. Gilbert Pearson, the President of the National Association of Audubon Societies and took him to lunch at a little restaurant on upper Broadway. After hearing our story, he said, "Gentlemen, nothing would give more pleasure than to become the chairman of such a committee." That did it. I contacted Dr. Phillips, who was shooting in Ireland, and Mr. Charles Sheldon – and they gave me the green light. Unfortunately, Mr. Sheldon died of a heart attack within the month. But Dr. Phillips came home, got together a little fund for the campaign, and we went to work on Capitol Hill. In February of '29, President Coolidge signed the new bill, and it has been working ever since.

D r. Phillips had begun writing his text on water restoration for the Canadian breeding grounds, and he and I began discussion of a crusade against magazine guns on migrants – and even upland game. The first thing I did after we decided to tackle the magazine-gun campaign was to write a brief on their known and proven nationwide destructiveness to wildlife resources. The evidence was compounded by wide-open conditions and declines. The idea among conservation groups was that if you offended, your job went. But what the hell. The bigger they come, the harder they fall, and these guys were right down John's and my alley.

I sent the brief to my old and valued friend Ding Darling, who was just beginning his fruitful conservation career. He approved. I talked to officials of duPont, Remington, and Winchester. John Phillips let fall guarded hints that a bill might be put in to curtail magazine gun capacities to three shots, and outlaw .410 shotguns on migrants. My friends around the circuits wrote and came to try to draw me off the conflict. My old employers, the Olins, were only in the shell and cartridge business and wisely kept aloof.

After nearly two years of this (I had a three-year contract with the Wildfowlers), a meeting was held at 25 Broadway, New York, at Remington's office. There were about twenty gun tycoons on hand, including my friend M. Hartley Dodge, Chairman of Remington's board. I had taken him and Felix duPont and Hal Sheldon on a tour of Arkansas' commercial gunning circuits to show them the ill-effects of magazine gunfire on wildfowl. Dr. Phillips' and my position was that unless magazine gun capacities were curtailed to three shots and the industry given time to gradually retire, while recommending the idea themselves, that pretty soon, or even more so, we'd be out of ducks.

Sitting in a rear-row was a grey-haired gentleman who said nothing and appeared about half asleep. Finally, however, he arose and said, "Gentlemen, I have listened attentively. These two men, Dr. Phillips and Mr. Buckingham, are, in my opinion, telling the truth and giving us sound advice. We can fight 'em off for awhile, but they will win and we will lose, anyway you look at it – in the end. I vote in favor of their idea." Then he sat down. It was Mr. Samp Pryor, of Remington.

That did it. Through the magazine-gun campaign, thus far, John Phillips and I had been somewhat wryly amused by the ominous predictions of conservation groups and friends as to what was in store for me. I remember one night during a game conference in New York at the Pennsylvania Hotel that I was slated to appear before an arms and ammunition committee, and in my pocket I had a letter from the executive secretary of a national group approving our crusade and wishing us luck. This chap, all but white-faced, got hold of me and asked me to not read his letter before the committee. "Why not?" I asked, "Are you afraid of retaliation? You should have thought of that when you wrote me – but – if you're afraid of your job, why okay, I won't read it." That fellow was a great broken-field runner and was around for quite awhile.

Not too long thereafter, I had a telephone call from Mr. M. Hartley Dodge of Remington Arms asking me and Hal Sheldon to meet him at the Roosevelt Hotel in New York to see and suggest ideas for Remington's new three-shot 20-gauge autoloader to be called "The Sportsman." Colonel Sheldon and I spent two days with Mr. Dodge and an assistant or two, and several of our suggestions were embodied into the new product. Both the Colonel and I told "Marcy" Dodge that eventually we would like to see the model changed to the smooth-framed weapon in use today. Later, I was given guns numbered 7 and 8 by which to remember the "battle of the autoloaders," as Marcy put it. They are around yet.

I also want to add that in that battle we got a deal of quiet help from the late U. S. Senator Harry Hawes of Missouri, an able, courageous, and fair fighter for conservation.

So, other autoloading gunmakers took a hint and the battle dragged along until Ding Darling gave up $100,000 a year as an Iowa cartoonist to become chief of the Bureau of Biological Survey at Washington. And it wasn't long before Ding, to his eternal credit, went to President Franklin Delano Roosevelt's office (Ding was a Republican, as I recall), explained details of the magazine gun situation's baneful influence upon national wildlife resources, and asked for an Executive Order banning all magazine-gun shotguns for more than three shots. And to Roosevelt's eternal credit, *he signed the order* – and that's how that happened.

Thereafter, through the years, many so-called sportsmen followed their usual course in such matters by evading the ruling whenever possible. But states soon began passing enabling acts that also forbade the use of such weapons on upland game for more than three shots. It was the fashion, for quite awhile, for scofflaws and marsh goons to get in a "hot corner" and remove their gun plugs, so the regulation was amended to cover that. Even today, however, there are chiselers and cheats who pull their plugs in some way, if they can get away with it. And it is well to note that before the American Wildfowlers pulled their David and Goliath as to magazine guns, that there were actually magazine extensions on the market and in heavy use by the organized rings of duck bootleggers that permitted nine shots instead of five.

I was in a pit one morning on a Mississippi river sandbar when two market hunters jumped into my hide (at my request – for geese were a-wing), and both their autoloaders were equipped with extensions and tinned-in over the ejector vent. Magazine gunmakers have long since admitted that had this curtailment of rapid firepower not come about, that we might not be shooting wildfowl today. You doubt that? Well, you should have watched outlaws at work and heard their confessions to district attorneys. You should have watched wire pens full of live goose decoys, enfiladed by concrete pits full of hunters firing, a dozen at a time, into lit flocks of honkers come to feast on shelled corn tossed onto wheat fields for bait. Or watched in horror atrocities of commercialism that would turn an enforcer's stomach, stuff the government could and should have stopped had it the guts of a zombie.

In that period I met all the great Congressional figures, saw the Game Refuge Bill passed, worked on national committees, instigated the winning battle against pump and autoloading shotgun capacities, and, with Ding Darling, cleaned up a lot of bad spots in the duck bootlegging areas. I saw 95% of the nation's and Canada's waterfowling grounds, served as a Federal game agent, and watched the wheels go round generally. And I saw a lot of odd sights.

In addition to the major projects of the American Wildfowlers, unusual incidents of cooperation with other groups aided conservation progress. Dr. Phillips had completed quite a manuscript, with the most authoritative legal aid available, entitled: *Game: Its Legal Status.* I still have a copy and there are others in existence. I took the manuscript over to Wilmington, Delaware, to my friend the aforementioned General Waller, at duPont's game department, and told him that the American Wildfowlers didn't have the funds to get the job done as it should be, but that here was a wonderful opportunity to aid Federal and state agencies and conservation groups by condensing the manuscript and printing it for nationwide distribution. General Waller got duPont's approval, the job was done, and *Game: Its Legal Status* became for years one of duPont's most valuable contributions to the conservation scene.

The American Wildfowlers had hardly gotten going in Washington before several wealthy contributors called attention to a situation existing down in Currituck Sound (North Carolina-Virginia) where, for decades, wildfowling and fishing had sustained communities and millionaires had "shooting lodges" and some of them killed a hell of a lot too many ducks sometimes and had to send their lawyers down to Washington to perjure them out of trouble.

It seems that during World War I, the U. S. Engineers had removed the locks and dams from the Elizabeth River at Norfolk, Virginia "for experimental purposes." Salinity had crept into lush Currituck, all but K.O.'d the hunting and fishing, and reportedly bankrupted three counties. We were asked to contact the comptroller, Mr. Warren, (a very fine man he was, too) and say that if the government would get busy and repair the damage, that two or three of the "wealthies" would advance the funds to get going. So I made the offer and then began really looking into the situation's background.

It seems that one choleric and angered "wealthy" had made a crack to the effect (and I was to contact that same old guy later on) that he would pay for the job himself provided he was permitted to install a bronze marker on the locks and dams in which he expressed his personal opinion of the United States Engineers. The crack got back to them and years had elapsed with nothing done.

I turned for aid to my old friend Seth Gordon, then directing the fortunes of the Izaak Walton League of America. Like the corn, Seth was all ears. He was also the best detail man I ever saw around conservation. The League had a fine magazine for publicity, so Seth got the U. S. Senator (I think his name was Simmons) of North Carolina to write a long article on the situation and need for economic restitution and restoration to the area. Then we discovered that there were several other interests in on

159

the deal: navigation, shipping, and goodness only knows what.

It took us a couple of months to sort all that out, and finally we got a three-day hearing before several commissions at Norfolk, Virginia. Eventually it was decreed to restore the locks and dams, and after so long a time, they were. But, even so, the "wealthies" had to finally advance a lot of money to get the job started, and Seth and I always hoped they got their money back. I made a couple of shooting trips to Currituck to look the situation over; it was different from things I'd seen there many years before.

It was along here, too, that Illinois contributors to the American Wildfowlers began asking that we begin looking into duck bootlegging activities along the Illinois river, a long stretch of clubs and commercials with an increasingly evil reputation. I had been all through there shooting when I was with Western, so our Executive Committee said go ahead and give the government as much help as you can. We hired an undercover operator; I'll not give his name in case he might still be alive. But suffice to say he was a good one and worked hard and well.

Nor was the government inactive. I knew one of their men who actually lived with one ring of duck bootleggers for nearly two years, posing as a drug addict known as "Dopey." John Perry was his name and he passed on some years back in retirement in Nashville, Tennessee. He was located in my home town of Memphis for years and was known as a shrewd, fearless, sensible, loyal, and resourceful agent.

I recall one bit of John's work that stood out. At Memphis in Shelby County, Tennessee, the 5000-acre Penal Farm has for many years proven a spectacular institution, a tremendous farming and cattle exhibit. Naturally, planting and feeding operations attracted mourning doves in quantities. Pastures were "salted" for the cattle and together with combined grain fields, brought the mourners in great flights. But the only way you got to shoot at the Penal Farm was to be "right" politically when the weekly invitations were issued. Of course the doves were being shot over what amounted to baiting of purest ray serene. But both state and Federal game agents hadn't interfered – until John Perry came along.

Under the guise of an agricultural inspector, he went out there just before the season opened and made a long and careful investigation. Then he went to the front office and announced who he was and that he was padlocking the "jernt." Roars! Screams! Threats! He would be fired immediately if not sooner. John laughed and told 'em to go ahead and try to get his job and he would help them.

Several years passed in peace before John was moved up the country and a new agent sent in. It didn't take "the boys" long to get his number and reopen the farm. We recall going over it the afternoon before open season that year with an oldtimer. It was the worst baited place I ever saw and next afternoon 88 guns killed 880 doves and no telling how many cripples.

That did it. A bunch of West Tennessee Sportsmen Association's members went to the office of the late Mr. E. H. Crump, our beneficent political overlord. They said, "Mr. Crump, signs at the Penal Farm say open to the public, 'This Is Your Farm; Use It,' but we can't shoot there, and worse, the place is illegal because it is construed as shooting over a baited field. But, if it is cleaned up, we couldn't even shoot there then, because we ain't invited."

Mr. Crump said, "Gentlemen, this is all news to me; I am not a hunter, and obviously you gentlemen are known to me as friends who tell the truth. I think the best thing to do to settle all this is to turn the Penal Farm into a wildlife production center for the surrounding farms and dove breeders of the future. Let it be an object lesson to law, order, and wildlife production in the future." Mr. Crump was like that.

There has never been a dove shot at the Penal Farm since, and as of now it is the home of the Memphis Retriever Club which holds its trials there. It has been my lot to know any number of both state and Federal game agents and as we go along I'll relate stories of incidents I have seen in their dealings. But of one thing you can be very sure: Most of them try and try hard. And, oftimes, they are working with "higher ups" and "low-downs" ahead of them as tip-offs.

In 1934 I returned to Memphis; my home had always been there and I commuted to the national work. I began writing outdoor books compiled from older stories and new material. I also made outdoor motion pictures, did radio work, and contributed articles to national outdoor magazines.

OLIN MATHIESON CHEMICAL CORPORATION

EAST ALTON, ILLINOIS

April 11, 1957

Mr. Nash Buckingham
Box 720
Memphis, Tennessee

Dear Mr. Buckingham:

Your letter of March 29, 1957, to
Mr. J. M. Olin, regarding the possibility of producing a dehydrated, bomb-like, live-growing duck
food composite, has been referred to me for reply.

Based on my personal field observations
of plant communities, the law of the "survival of
the fittest" still applies. As a rule, there is
always an abundance of various types of various plant
seeds. Through ecological succession the plants that
are best fitted for the habitat persist and continue
to regenerate their species. The only method of
changing this concept is to alter the habitat by such
means as mechanical equipment, fire, floods, fertilization, etc. After there is an alteration in the
habitat, the whole cycle leading to a climax vegetation
is again repeated. This concept has been used in
establishing waterfowl areas on the coastal marshes
of Southern New Jersey; that is, the present vegetation
in the majority of this area is in cattail--a plant
with practically no food value for waterfowl. By
diking and flooding to a depth beyond the tolerance
of cattail, this species is eliminated. Afterwards
the pond is drained and the bare soil is exposed.
Without any seeding, an abundance of volunteer vegetation is produced such as smartweeds and millets,
both of which are excellent duck foods. In September
these areas are flooded and are utilized by ducks
in large numbers.

As I understand it, your thought would be
to include plant food along with seed of some
particular duck food. Although habitat can be
changed by fertilization, it usually takes a large
amount to alter the plants already established in
any given area-- this is costly, to say the least.

This letter and the one that follows show the length to which Nash was willing to go to save the waterfowl resource. The correspondence is between Nash and Dr. Ed Kozicky, director of Winchester-Western's conservation department, himself a giant in the conservation movement along with many W-W staffers such as John Madson and John Olin himself. Over the years, Kozicky and Nash became close friends and comrades-in-arms in the conservation wars.

- 2 -

One of the interesting facets of habitat management in game work is that every area is an entity and requires detailed study of the existing plants and soil conditions before one can start to recommend changes that will be beneficial to waterfowl. This is one of the reasons why many of the states have established the position of area game manager.

It is possible that your technique may work in a particular locality and may some day have wide application. However, with our present state of knowledge on plant succession and waterfowl ecology, it appears to me that we have considerable to learn before your thought of having a dehydrated, duck food composite can be materialized.

Sincerely yours,

OLIN MATHIESON CHEMICAL CORPORATION

Edward L. Kozicky, Director
Conservation Department

ELK/lp

Box 720 Memphis Tenn.
May 18th '57

Mr. E L Kozicky,Director
Department of Conservation
Olin Mathieson Chemical Corp.,Inc.
East Alton, Illinois.   Personal--Confidential.
                                                   Return letter copy
Dear Mr. Kozicky-:,
            In current release of Outdoors Unlimited (OWAA's organ,
Gillham can probably furnish) is included copy of an agreement twist Interior
and the US Airforce as to " cooperation".May I suggest your reading it? About
three weeks ago I took up with my good friend the new Assistant Secty of Interior, Hon. Ross Leffler, the possibility of Interior's making some sort of a
"purely cooperative deal " with the F B I,in an effort to cut the enormous violations of the Migratory Bird Law and the Treaty Act with Great Britain.The enclosed copy of a letter to Pink Gutermuth,tells the story.The F B I--Interior
coalition could even be mustered by an Executive Order from the President.Just
the mere announcement of such a deal,costing neither agency a dime,would as we
tell Pink,cut violations 50% the first year.
            The other night at a sportsmens' directors meeting,19 men
were asked to write on a paper,their estimate of how many "illegal ducks" cross
the Memphis-Arkansas bridge during a 70 day open season? This meant just chisel-
led ducks.The guesses averaged 250,000.What happens north and south of here,on
inter and intrastate,is something else.And,in such situation Interior has,until
now(because we hope the situation will change) refused to change shooting hours
that give these criminals(for that's what they are) all the best of the decent,
freight-paying sportsmen.The whole concept must change,or we're getting thru.
And,incidentally,the situation on the prairies,right now,is revealing apprehension that maybe D U's and the Canadian authorities' man-made water agencies will
be tested to their fullest in the face of impending drought.We hope not.But if a
decreased migration and shortened seasons are cut into--what then?I realize fully that your outfit isn't in any position to 'shove'OObut it can 'push'.Anyway,
our Association is going to call this matter to top-level attentions.Good luck
and regards.

164

Ottawa, Canada,
May 4, 1957.

Dear B. Buckingham:

PERSONAL

The Minutes of the 30th
Annual Meeting of the "B" held at Washington, D.
C., are enclosed. The meeting made an assess-
ment of $1.00 per member in support of routine
expenditure. Novitiates and those who paid at
the meeting are exempt. Others may wish to con-
tribute this amount.

Greetings to all!

Sincerely,

M. of G.

One of the mysteries of Nash's life – The "B." This group, which Nash describes as "Fraternally based," was organized with seven members who used their influence behind-the-scenes to shape the conservation movement in North America. The minutes of one of their meetings follow. In keeping with Nash's wishes, the names of members have been removed.

MINUTES OF THE 30TH ANNUAL MEETING
OF THE "B"
Statler Hotel, Washington, D. C.
March 4, 1957.

The 30th regular Annual Meeting of the "B" convened at 9.00 p.m., in the Statler Hotel in Washington, D.C., on March 4, 1957, as a delightful but unofficial part of the annual North American Wildlife Conference. The Master of Game, the Honorable   , of Canada, presided at the meeting. The following members were present:

The minutes of the 29th Annual Meeting of the organization, which was held at the Jung Hotel in New Orleans on March 5, 1956, were read and approved.

The ceremony of the breaking of the flowers for departed members who had passed away since the last meeting of the organization was performed by the Master of Game. These were:

There then followed the report of the Executive Committee read by the Master Scribe, which reviewed the present status of nominations for consideration at the present meeting. This report indicated that one nomination, Mr.   , had been received during the year, but since five are still before the "B" for action, the name of Mr.   had not been forwarded to the Membership Committee for consideration. Included as a part of the report was a list of members who could not be present, but who sent their greetings and best wishes. These included:

The report of the Treasurer was read and found correct. The balance on hand was $55.46.

The Master of Game then called for nominations for the Membership Committee for the ensuing year and it was unanimously decided that the same Committee should be continued. This consists of:

-2-

The Master of Game then called for a report of the Membership Committee, during which it was outlined that each nominee was a man of high caliber in the field of conservation. Numbers of the members present joined in the discussion of the qualifications of each. Following the taking of secret ballots on each name, all were elected, as follows:

Following the election of new members, a search of the convention was made to locate novitiates, which resulted in Mr.
and Dr.   joining the group; also Dr.
, of New York, who had been elected last year but had not yet been initiated.

There followed the usual initiation ceremony when the Master of Game instructed the novitiates in the fundamentals, principles, and background of the "B". He told them of its inception during times of strife and turmoil in earlier conservation days and how the group had been formed to overcome some of the internal strife in conservation circles for the good of all. He then read the ritual, to which they all subscribed, and they were duly inducted into the Order.

The annual lesson, prepared by   , was read by the Master of Game. Its theme was the "Power of Science". The author discussed the need for the use of science and scientific knowledge for constructive purposes and argued against the devoting of scientific talents to areas of destruction. He summarized the theme by asserting that conservation is the conscience of science but its voice is too often unheard in the over-ruling voice of power. He argued that conservationists must take a more prominent place in national life if our people are to maintain and perpetuate basic conservation principles and philosophies.

Following the reading of the lesson   took the chair for the election of officers. This resulted in the following action:

    Master of Game   Yeoman of the Hunt
    Master Hunter
    Master Forester
    Master Scribe

-3-

          Before returning the gavel to   , as re-elected Master
of Game,   took the occasion of his occupancy of the chair to
deliver to the assembled numbers, in his own inimitable style, some
of the early history and background which lead up to the organization of the Order.   was one of the very few people still
active in the conservation movement who was present and took part
in the organization meeting in Denver, in September, 1925. This was
at a time when there was considerable bitterness of feeling in the
conservation circles which was pointed up by rather bitter debate on
the floor between

          who also attended the 1925 meeting in Denver supplemented
          remarks.

          The usual annual collection of dues of $1.00 each was made,
resulting in $23.05 being collected and turned over to the Master
of Game for necessary expenses during the forthcoming year.

          The Master of Game resumed Chairmanship, called for addition-
al discussion, and there being none, he adjourned the meeting at
11.00 p.m., after announcing that a second session of the same meeting would be held on the following evening at 5.00 p.m. for the purpose of initiating the other new members that could not be located
for initiation at this session.

                              Master Scribe.

 After comments in similar vein from a few of the members, the meeting was adjourned at 5.30 p.m.

          (Additional dues collected, $4.00.)

                              Master Scribe.

William Harnden Foster, shooting friend and writing contemporary of Nash's. The note on the back of the photo in Nash's hand says: "William Harnden Foster shooting at R. M. Carrier's Barnacre Preserve." Foster was a skilled magazine editor, talented artist, and the author of the classic New England Grouse Shooting. *The gun looks like Foster's favorite 20-gauge Parker.*

THE
EVOLUTION
OF DUCKS UNLIMITED

Here is the low-down on the Wildlife Service-Ducks Unlimited "Feud." I know, because I saw it start and was mixed up in it with the American Wildfowlers. In 1929, the Wildfowlers (our office was in Washington) got the idea for a foundation composed of the then-leading groups, but old man X_____, who, with a lot of other redhanded old duck murderers with lodges down on Currituck Sound, got the same idea.

So Dr. John Phillips, president of the Wildfowlers, and I went to New York to his apartment to discuss the projects. X_____ was a beefy, high-blooded old guy, the type one just naturally dislikes right off the bat. He asked Dr. Phillips how much our group had behind it – financially – and was told. He scoffed and asked how the hell we ever expected to get anything done, whereupon I asked him what, with all the money he had, he had ever done for the ducks or anybody else except kill a lot over the limits and have to send his lawyers down to Washington to get him off the hook, excusing perjury?

I thought he was going to have a stroke, but Dr. Phillips managed to smooth things over and X_____ told us he proposed a membership of such wealth that they could really put the heat on Washington. Dr. Phillips said we want to put the heat on in Canada. It ended in a year with X_____ getting together a bunch with $100,000 a year for ten years to be called "More Game Birds In America." This was the richest gravy train that had ever rolled down the conservation Flyin' Jinny. The announcement was made in Toronto in 1930 at the Wildlife Conference.

The first president was slated to be U. S. Senator Harry B. Hawes of Missouri, a good guy; seven years at $35,000 a year. But, somehow, Harry, who was pretty cagey, got wise to some factors and turned down the offer. They then made a man named Y_____ president. To even discuss his lack of qualifications is a waste of time. Their first act was to send a Nazi-type down to Washington to literally demand bigger bag limits and longer seasons on the strength of what More Game Birds *expected* to accomplish.

Right there was where such an attempt to strong-arm went wrong. Bad blood has existed ever since, passed on from one administration to another. More Game Birds eventually absorbed the Wildfowlers, and I was offered a place in their organization, which I very promptly declined.

When our records were sent to New York after the absorption, there was a plan or "brochure" in my desk written five years before by Dr. Phillips who is really solely responsible for the plan to restore adequate water to the Canadian hatching prairies and sloughs. More Game Birds had about bogged down after some abortive publications and a plan to tax shells, when (1935) someone must have found that manuscript and they still had funds enough to start *Ducks Unlimited* – the name Dr. Phillips liked.

Thus began the first practical attempt at realistic water restoration to ever enter conservation in the U. S. A. – and the finest. For a few years there were birth pains because some of the old wealthy game hogs stayed alive and wanted increased relaxations every season, but they died off and a newer and finer set of younger men took over to handle things in a business-like way. No doubt exists that if Ducks Unlimited hadn't come on the scene, we would long ago have been through shooting wild ducks.

Nevertheless – regardless of changing administrations – one figure remained in Federal service who still hated Ducks Unlimited, and while on the surface there exists a polite situation, there is really every effort at obstruction whenever possible. It would have paid the government (Interior) to have turned the engineering and contract work over to Ducks Unlimited and actually hired them and their know-how to get the job done in both the Northern U. S. and Canada.

The Wetlands Program is about bogged down now, but Ducks Unlimited goes right ahead while Interior flounders around and plays flagrant politics and lets the vandals and game hogs steal the profits from the freight-payers. It is a damned shame.

Some
Comments
On Decency

To take my story further, I go back to 1931, when, after fifteen years administration of the Migratory Bird Law and Treaty act with Great Britain (Canada) by designated agencies of the United States Government, everything as to duck shooting in the United States ground to a temporary stop.

Daily bag limits of twenty-five ducks and eight geese, before sunrise until dark shooting, baiting, live decoys, widespread duck bootlegging, inadequate enforcement, and excessive bag-limit stealage had put unmistakable handwriting upon wildfowling's wall.

Too, in 1931, one of the worst breeding-grounds droughts in history, a searing that was to last nearly eight years and extend far down today's Mississippi Valley flyway, was already at work. In 1931, bag limits were cut to fifteen ducks and four geese, the season cut to thirty days, live decoys were banned, and baiting was on its way out. But too early and too late shooting hours remained. By 1934-35 continental wildfowl stocks reached their lowest of record. An Emergency Waterfowl Committee was appointed, composed of the lates Ding Darling, Aldo Leopold, and Thomas Beck; conservationists and gunners themselves, good and true.

That committee's first act was to fix national shooting hours from 7 am until 4 pm. Mr. Darling became Chief of the Bureau of Biological Survey. As I have said, he ended a long battle by securing from President Roosevelt an Executive Order curtailing capacities of pump and autoloading shotguns to three shells on migrants. Other benefits for wildfowl and upland game birds, conservationally sponsored, began appearing. The Pittman-Robertson Bill, still in sound condition, was passed.

That Executive Order on magazine-gun capacities and passage of the

Pittman-Robertson Bill were to mean much to Tennessee. Almost immediately thereafter, two men appeared in the Nashville office of then Director of Game Howell E. Buntin and asked his cooperation in getting two bills passed in the next Legislature. The Pittman-Robertson Bill requires that states seeking benefits must provide a percentage of the fund. Mr. Buntin's visitors sought a 3% tax on ammunition in Tennessee to cover the state's participation. They also wanted an enabling act and bill to bar magazine guns for more than three shots on Tennessee's upland game. Mr. Buntin escorted them to the office of state's Attorney General Nat Tipton and the matters fully discussed and agreed upon.

The bills were passed at the next Legislature and are on the books today. To date, the amount collected by the State of Tennessee from that ammunition tax is probably a bit in excess of $712,000. We know of two individuals who have made a cash contribution of that amount to Tennessee wildlife resources: Their names are Nash Buckingham and Henry P. Davis, the same two men who, in 1928, walked into the Chief Game Warden's office in Nashville and announced that they had come to begin putting game commissions into Tennessee and Mississippi. It took us three years in Mississippi and seven in Tennessee, and that is the answer to that.

But for us, the chances are that Tennessee might never have had a game commission, an anti-magazine gun act, and $712,000. Nor are we cognizant of any acknowledgment of thanks due them through the years. Rather – to the contrary.

More Game Birds in America, the group I mentioned earlier as a heavily endowed conservation group, came upon the scene in 1930 and after five years became Ducks Unlimited (1935). Along there, too, the great National Wildlife Federation opened for business and has become a national mainstay. The Outdoor Writers' Association of America, a conservation group organized in 1927 to mobilize a national outdoor press, the Wildlife Institute, the Audubon Society, the Izaak Walton League, and the Wilderness Society are all fighting a rear-guard action against forces of evil toward the out-of-doors in many forms. Along about that time, the picture is not a happy one.

Fortunately, however, those wise shooting hours of 7 am 'till 4 pm imposed by the Emergency Waterfowl Committee lasted six years. Right-thinking duck hunters realized their value to both sport and enforcement. But, with the advent of World War II, less hunting pressure, improved breeding grounds conditions, and an obviously resurged waterfowl population, those intimate and restive forces of evil which are never content with enough gradually brought pressures to bear that saw shooting hours lengthened. It was the beginning of the end for another era in wildfowl mischief.

By 1943, bag limits had been raised to fifteen (ten plus five big ducks). Then it sank to twelve, to ten, to seven, and then to four. We have been shooting four-duck bag limits since 1947. And then the token limit sank to two ducks in our flyway.

The "flyway system," opened in 1948, became a political football as to regulations, with California (the Pacific flyway) getting all the breaks. In the Mississippi flyway, the bag limit became two ducks, one of which could be a mallard, with a bonus of two scaup – if and when these little wildfowl became available. Many hunters racked up and quit; wildfowling had become economically unsound for them. Professional duck bootleggers, too, laid pretty well off, because duck bootlegging, thanks to Mr. Gross of Iowa, became a felony on September 30th, 1960.

But the amateurs redoubled their stealage. In fact, a new breed of wildfowling sadist developed, the thugs who just shot down ducks until sated and then picked up a limit and left. There were arrests and convictions in U.S. courts for this ghoulish operation. In 1962, the game commissions of Arkansas and Tennessee, alarmed by the previous season's economic depression, cut under the government's stupid continuance of all-day firings and shot half-days. But Washington continues to refuse breaking with tradition and do the two or three practical things necessary to protect and renew the resource while programs for wetland rehabilitation get underway in the U.S. and Canada.

Unquestionably, operators of commercial duck shooting properties have learned their lessons and turned over a new leaf by realizing that they are, after all, businessmen dealing in a free resource; that they have an investment and that their patrons must cease chiseling and getting all hands into trouble with the law. That is as it should be. It has been shamelessly abused in Arkansas. But Federal and state protective authorities would do well to watch the operations of certain duck pond owners and syndicates whose members oftimes employ light planes to fly out ten to fifteen times a daily bag limit – and get away with waterfowl murder. Much less the thieves who, dressed in civilian garb to not attract attention, ease through the lines with much contraband.

Boiled down, it is all just a part of the decline in national morale and human decency. If the decent wildfowlers of the Mississippi Valley flyway would form what amounted to a Vigilante's Association and not only refuse to hunt with thieves but openly turn them in when the opportunity offers, not only we but our sons and their sons may, too, have a chance to go duck shooting. It's up to us – strictly – for the Lord helps those who help themselves.

I realize that in writing this, I'll be taken in by wildlife pacifists and (in their own estimation) purists, the type that likes to chant, "Be as good as I am," and all that kind of buncombe. I am not after the sometimes if oftimes duck-shooting buddies who find themselves a duck or two over the bag limit, any more than I am in favor of the gimlet-eyed game agent who, to swell his number of "cases," likes nothing better than to catch some such victim or victims of circumstance and help them into some J.P. court for a fine that oftimes never reaches its proper destination.

When you've heard boasts of 200 mallards flown out; when you've stood in an airport and seen dozens of bag limits multiplied by ten fly north with no questions asked, you begin to get the Big Idea. When you've seen home deep-freezes packed with illicit ducks peddled by school children, you get it even bigger.

Thus, in perfect good humor, I am ready to defend my position on a "pistols for two and coffee for one" basis, or with the weapons with which Nature has so generously endowed us. The next five years will tell the story. And unless during that interim the Federal government, the state commissions, and the so-called duck-stamped sportsmen decide to evidence gratitude to God for His bounty to them, we deserve to be stricken from His roll.

THE
THOUGHTLESS,
TOO-GREEDY YEARS

My shooting life and my views on conservation got started in 1889, when I was nine years old. I had been afield a year with my own gun and in an atmosphere of bird dogs and retrievers, quail, squirrels, and rabbits. I hadn't been taken duck shooting yet, but I had seen many a sackful of geese, ducks, and swans brought home for neighborhood distribution by my Dad. Our bird dog kennel was just across the back fence from that of Mr. Bryson who owned the great English setter Gladstone, patriarch of the line. I would come home from kindergarten, get a lot of cookies from our cook, feed our hunters, and divide the rest with not only Gladstone, but such great setters as Bo Peep and Peep o' Day that I remember.

Somehow, however, everything seems to start from that Christmas morning of 1888 when my brother got that 16-gauge Parker double hammer gun, and I drew a set of boys' boxing gloves. Both gifts were to shape destinies. It became 1889 shortly and it wasn't long before I had lowered my first bobwhite and was taken to Arkansas where I got my first glimpse at an even-then vanishing species on the brink of extermination by a thoughtless horde of hunters spurred on by today's possible death-trap – promotional greed.

I was taken to the shooting lodge of one of father's friends on the Grand Prairie of Arkansas where they hunted prairie chickens, quail, deer, wild turkey, geese, ducks, and snipe. Rice was years away as God's gift to Arkansas. The lodge was at a hamlet called Goodwin, some fifty-odd miles west of our home in Memphis. It is there today and I pass it frequently, but the prairie chickens are long, long gone. Two-horse buckboards with hard-driving bird dogs roaming a vast unfenced prairie carried the hunters to thrilling points – a feature of which was that they rarely knew what species of game would be flushed from afront the pointers and setters. Mixed bags were prodigious.

We went to and fro from Goodwin on a railroad (the Rock Island) that hadn't been there too long itself. Particularly I remember late afternoons on the prairie, when, over distant woodlands, myriads upon myriads of ducks, geese, and swans milled in the confusion of finding food and roosts. And I recall the stories of my late father-in-law, Mr. Tom Jones, whose grandfather's plantations lay alongside the Arkansas river. As a youth in the early 1870's, to escape the yellow fever in Memphis, young Mr. Tom would ride his horse from Memphis to the plantations and remain until well after frost fell. He had a single tubed muzzle-loading shotgun and it was his job to keep the tables supplied with game. "I didn't need a bird dog," he'd relate, "I could kill more prairie chickens and ducks than I could carry, preferably spotting a bunch of the birds on the ground for the single shot I had."

I saw the prairie chicken decline of the early 1890's. Hearing our elders talk, we came to notice the increase of hunters. Then came announcement of a closed season on prairie chickens for two years. When closure was reopened, the railroads reportedly ran excursions for the grand onslaught. By turn of the century, the prairie chicken was pretty much history in Arkansas. I shot some in the Panhandle of Texas in '05. And in 1904, with my father and a party of friends from Chicago, I was taken along on a prairie chicken hunt from a private railway car in Brown County, South Dakota. We were sidetracked at a village and hunted for a week, the routine being the same as in Arkansas years before. No pheasants and Huns as today, just clouds of chickens and sharptails – and ducks – if you cared to shoot the latter. On railway station platforms, barrels of chickens were enroute to Eastern markets. You could buy all the prairie chickens you wanted from almost any produce dealer anywhere or from the bill-of-fare of almost any hotel. Market hunting was free enterprise undisguised, but it was a hideous drainage tube in wildlife resources' vitals.

Finally, common sporting decency's outcries put an end, or at least aimed a lethal blow, at market hunting. It took six years of protest, but on May 25th, 1900, Congressman John F. Lacey's bill was passed making interstate shipment of game killed in violation of state laws a Federal offense. His bill had other teeth in it and put enforcement under the Bureau of Biological Survey. Note that shipments continued during those years of Congressional debate, and longer. Even today more

"This is like they flushed at Wapanoca in the old days."

illegal wildfowl than legal are being literally stolen. Violations of waterfowl and upland game are mere misdemeanors with no more meaning than raids on a peach orchard. And the debacle continues.

To observe today's remnant waterfowl populations in contrast to those I saw starting Thanksgiving Day 1890 is but to mourn. Drainage was still for a distant future; lumbering of the South's great hardwoods and cypress brakes was in its infancy; the lakes and marshes of the lower Mississippi River states, clean to the Gulf, were but little removed from an unbelievable past. From 1890 until 1909, while there had been murmurings of apprehension as to inroads upon the migrations, not a Federal hand had been turned to slow down obvious plunderings. I gunned most of the famous duck clubs and public shooting grounds from Reelfoot and Big Lake in upper Arkansas and Tenn-Kentucky, on down the Mississippi along which Menasha, Lakeside, Mud Lake, Beaver Dam, Wapanoca, and a hundred others, clean to the famous Delta Duck Club in Louisiana were samples. I have shot Canada geese and a very very few blues and snows from practically every worthwhile sandbar from below Cairo, Illinois to the Louisiana and Texas coastals. Memories of shooting canvasbacks and redheads from the flats off Rockport, Texas and San Jacinto Bay are priceless. Then is when you really saw ducks and geese, but, even so between 1890 and 1900, I saw the swans disappear. They just seemed to evaporate. Like the prairie chickens in Arkansas, I saw them vanish from a favorite hangout – Wapanoca – until they were gone. And Wapanoca, for its size, was the finest concentration area of wildfowl of any in what is known today as the Mississippi Valley flyway.

I have camped for a week on sandbars along the Mississippi and watched early morning and late afternoon migrations that arced skies until closed off by darkness. I have sat on lakes such as Wapanoca, Beaver Dam, Mud Lake, and many another and watched their wooded flats encircled sky-high late of an afternoon with ducks and geese coming to roost. Clouds of ducks milling until moonrise, and settling for the night.

In an old diary, I have a record of a Christmas week hunt at Wapanoca in 1899. Most clubs put on a daily bag limit of their own, usually the same at fifty ducks a day and as many geese or swans as you wanted. That day at Wapanoca there were twenty-two guns, sixteen members and their sons, home from college. Every gun bagged its fifty ducks and there were thirty-eight geese bagged. Today, on that same Wapanoca (now a Federal refuge), you would be lucky to bag a modern bag limit of four ducks, two of which are permissibly mallards.

Now as to what became of the ducks killed by market hunters and club members in those days, days when drainage had no adverse effect, and only the gun and its excesses were involved: Definitely the public ate more game; it was a profound part of its regular diet. Produce merchants in the cities bought it for a comparative song and resold to hotels and restaurants. The sportsmen divided it out around their neighborhoods. Families were larger in those days, servants easily available, and a comparatively small percentage of the wildfowl fetched home was wasted.

A tremendous, old time meat and grocery house in my home city used to do an enormous business in game. I have seen as high as twenty-five deer hung in one cold-room; more than fifty wild turkeys, and all the prairie chickens, wildfowl, and quail, one could desire. Ammunition was considered, by today's standards, dirt cheap. Along the river effluents of the Mississippi, steamboats from inland had market hunters who shipped to city merchants and supplied the boats themselves with all sorts of game. And, incidentally, steamboats invariably had good cooks and we can go on from there along that line in today's gourmetized "enterprise" and add a great truism: No flesh, fish, or fowl is any better than the abilities of the cooks into whose hands it falls.

In this period (1889-1909), people appreciated being sent game. Few do today unless it arrives picked, dressed, and frozen. Nor are family meals and appetites the same. Nor are today's game cooks versed in the culinary arts of yore. There may be a few around, but they were taught by oldsters. I'll wager I could go into a dozen of the nation's finest restaurants and not find a corn-fed mallard or a plump teal prepared with the succulence bestowed by our old cook at Beaver Dam, Mollie Merrit.

By 1889 the muzzleloaders of the market hunters had given way to 8- and 10-bore double hammer and even hammerless weapons. Then came the repeaters, pump guns, and autoloaders.

I remember when there was no quail season, to speak of, in Tennessee. They were not only shot ad lib, but country folks maintained "city quail customer routes" when they wagoned their chickens, eggs, vegetables, butter, and meats to city trading posts. One such stood where the Robilio Restaurant and merchandising interests stand at Vance and East streets in Memphis.

There were shade, hitching racks, watering-troughs, and snack tables with barbecue pits handy. In-town customers were cared for and then the farmers provisioned at the post and began homeward treks to lands sprouting skyscrapers today. Nearly every country wagon had a dog or two trotting along behind or under it in case of attack. There were plenty of fights. Quail customers preferred "trapped birds" because they had no shot in them. Shotgun shells loaded with black powder were thirty-five to forty cents a box of twenty-five. The finest factory loads of smokeless powder cost sixty-five cents a box. Many hunters loaded their own ammunition.

Quail market hunters not only used traps but, with the cost of shells in mind, spotted whole bevies on the ground and wiped them out with one blast. Hotel menus listed quail (along with wild geese, swans, ducks, snipe, woodcock, turkey (wild), deer, and even bear meat). Restaurants often festooned their fronts with strings of all species.

Gradually, however, as inroads into wildlife resources became apparent, state game departments (usually headed by a "State Game Warden") were created. Alarmed sportsmen organized protective associations. Game wardens, usually county political hangers-on, were appointed at meager salaries, if any, plus a compensation out of the fines. Local magistrates gulped the costs. City hunters were preyed upon avidly and it was quite awhile before states began selling non-resident licenses.

Prior to recognition of shooting season, gunning began with the first touch of autumn. When "The Law" really began to move in, quail-shooting season usually began November 1. But, as I was to learn during Prohibition, bootlegging quail (and later ducks) lasted a long, damaging while and is still not without its black markets of sorts. I recall listening to the confession of a live-quail bootlegger in the office of a United States game agent. Using "rings" of school children as trappers, qualified state game wardens as "collectors," and two State Senators (at twenty-five cents a bird) for "protection," he stole 85,000 quail from that state. His shipping-point "hide-out" was in Memphis, and I remember two shipments totalling 17,000 bobwhites. This was just one individual; others were at work.

Later, a Memphis-born undercover investigation in the Tri-States revealed shocking conditions and led to arrests and convictions that had much to do with drying up this curse to a region's most valuable game bird resource. So deeply rooted and inefficient were state enforcement practitioners in political wildlife protection, the success of this particular drive depended almost wholly upon Federal undercover agents.

Bitter arguments have long ensued as to what constitutes proper opening and closing shooting dates in the mid-South on quail. For the record, and to outline rocky roads conservational progress has had to travel in game management problems, in 1928 , Henry P. Davis and I (then Executive Director of the American Wildfowlers) began the first actual effort to put game commissions into Tennessee and Mississippi. I mentioned this earlier.

It took us three years in Mississippi, aided by powerful, determined conservation interests and individuals, plus intelligent press and legislative support. Mississippi had been terribly abused, but scarcely worse than the beating Tennessee had taken over the years. The new Mississippi Game & Fish Commission functioned superbly for many years, adopting (after studies and consultations with summit quail biologists and decent, thoughtful hunters of the state) December 10th opening and February 10th closing. The chances are that any unselfish well-informed, well-matured bird hunter of the mid-South will agree that not only in improved wingpower, food values, flight self-preservations, better cover for dog work and field trials, lessened fire hazards, crop lay-bys, and general public gunning satisfaction are such dated better, but an improved public morale and sportsmanship were enhanced.

Mississippi has now dropped back to December 1 for quail season opening. This concurrents Arkansas, and, in the handling of increased pressures by less law-abiding populations, is not out-of-line. In fact, had the Tri-States (Arkansas, Mississippi, and Tennessee) long ago gotten together with enlightened wildlife management and concurrented the quail seasons to December 1 – February 1, they would have had more birds, improved resources, more funds, and public behaviors founded upon visible returns from common interests.

In Tennessee, however, getting a game & fish commission established was another matter. It required seven years of weary, teary, dreary, tawdry political skirmishing and legislative shenanigans to get one by 1935. But, thanks to hard pushing by Tennessee's Federated Sportsmens Association, it was finally accomplished. Several Tennessee newspapers had begun outdoor columns, the late Frank Vestal being a forceful proponent of journalistic education along such lines for the *Memphis Commercial Appeal*. But when, among conservationists and sportsmen in general it came to discussions of "open season on quail," middle and east Tennessee hunters clung tenaciously to at least a "Thanksgiving Day" traditional onslaught, while west Tennessee, gifted with larger quail populations, was willing to open later.

Popular middle and east Tennessee claims were that their quail nested and matured earlier in their "colder climates"; a biologically fallacious bit of wishful thinking that sounded good when political pressures ensued. The new Tennessee Game & Fish Commission (1935) was a five-man affair that began with commendable zeal but questionable political merit. During early World War II years, Mr. John R. Flippin of Memphis, Frank Vestal, and I, representing Memphis and Shelby County conservation and field trial interests, made an intensive study of Tennessee quail conditions and seasons, even to enlisting the services of the nation's greatest quail authority,

Mr. Herbert L. Stoddard. Weather Bureau studies of intrastate frostlines and quail hatchings and nestings were studied, along with too-young quail pulped by vicious gunners and young birds dog-caught, quail bootlegging, and license-fee losses along the long Mississippi-Tennessee state line.

Mr. Charles Poe was Tennessee's Conservation Commissioner, a gentleman and able administrator, but of unclaimed biological training and gun and field experience. We'll let the five-man Game & Fish Commission be nameless. Messrs. Flippin, Vestal, and I went to Nashville, were courteously heard, and even applauded by the commission for the scholarly thoroughness of the brief we submitted (with Mr. Stoddard's aid) and filed for consideration as to the impending quail season in Tennessee.

The Commission may have had a biologist, but he was not present for debate, discussion, or rebuttal. Mr. Poe was called to the telephone. Returning, he said, – and I quote from vivid memory – "That was a 'bunch of the boys' in Jackson, Tennessee. They say gas-rationing is about to be announced, so they want quail season opened earlier than usual so they can still buy plenty gas for quail hunting." Mr. Flippin jumped to his feet in expostulation – "Gentleman, we have traveled here on serious business, representing several conservation and sportsmen's groups protesting that, by evidence introduced, quail season already opens too soon in Tennessee; we wish it concurrented with Mississippi's – surely you would not consider such a proposal without full public hearings." An uneasy silence ensued, broken only by our departure for Memphis without the courtesy of a discussion. Next morning's paper stated that the Game Commission had voted to open quail season a week earlier than usual; obviously (but not published) as requested by "a bunch of the boys in Jackson." Fortunately, the government postponed gas rationing a week, so with credit to the Game Commission, bobwhites got a break. Pure politics.

Next year, at the Game Commission's Memphis meeting, our local committee again tried for a quail season concurrent with Mississippi's. Hemmed in by proponent witnesses, the Commission's chairman finally stammered – "Your requests are, unfortunately, illegal. Thirty days' notice has not been filed for your petition." Mr. Vestal replied – and heatedly, "We filed notice a year ago, and later – in plenty of time – here's a copy of the letter in case you don't keep records – this is the second time we've had a cheap political dodge pulled on us, not in any thirty days, but twice in thirty minutes. God help the wildlife resources of the State of Tennessee." Whereupon, our delegation again walked out.

It would be unjust and untrue to say that Tennessee, despite inevitable politically mistaken attitudes at times, has not advanced in wildlife administration, management, and educational values in public relations, especially. A tremendous impetus to such improvements has come through cooperation by the Tennessee Conservation League, the West Tennessee Sportsmens Association and, most important, a solid-front of factual exposition by the Tennessee Outdoor Writers Association. But even these forces for good have been unable to penetrate a hard core of sublimated political pressure for too early quail season opening in Tennessee.

Simply enough and however mistakenly, an element of quail shooting voters in Middle and East Tennessee still like to shoot bobwhites as of yore, meaning too early for the resource's good. And this element's influence upon "their" game commissioners causes the latter to indicate to "their" biologists that "their" voters, like the customers, are always right. So what? So the biologists have the option of either finding for the defendants (the too-early shooters) or losing their jobs. Some do – for better pay than Tennessee and with a measure of self-respect salvaged.

In turn, commissioners, squirming t'wixt conservational and political pressure, write "bed bug" letters to both proponents and opponents, reminding them that their decisions are based upon "the findings of our biologists." I yield to no man in my respect for wildlife's biology, but I have no respect whatsoever for those who distort or dodge behind its principles. And you can apply that in two directions.

We may as well face up to it: Lands are being increasingly and rightly posted by owners wearied by vandalistic invasions and bold-faced thievery. Consequently, any wildlife resource should be harvested only in a period best suited to its own self-defense by flight-power. Through the years, taking the name of biology and sane quail management in vain politically (and Tennessee is by no means a sole offender) to please game commissioner clienteles afield (like that "bunch of boys in Jackson") has wasted resources, funds, and declined human behaviors. Only massive aid from organized conservation forces has kept us shooting. And a mobilized press (state and national) has fought a telling rear-guard action around its guns – with casualties.

I look for the day that game commissions are better able to listen to the voices of comprehension and reason from their best friends, the law-observing, knowledgeable, freight-paying sportsmen and not to the blustering demands of lower-graders, who, you will note, almost invariably predominate hearings as to what's best for wildlife resources. Too, the day is long past when landowners and worthy tenants should tolerate invasion of their fields and waters by vandalistic felons. They should post, enforce, or give written permissions only. Better still, they should turn to productive and protective wild game crop productions to be sold at suitable per diems for gunning. Increasing commercial gunning preserves fill a long-felt need. Hunters of means find in them a recreational certainty according to purses. On state-owned managed areas for fees, the charges should be sufficient to enable management and enforcement of the best type.

What's the difference between a November 18th and a December 1 quail season opening? Two weeks' additional growth do wonders in wing-power and flesh to young bobwhites. Their God-given intuitions improve. As beneficiaries of Divine largess, why not give our finest game bird a better chance afield? You would think that after two-score years of going the wrong way, despite examples of betterment elsewhere, that some Tennessee hunters and their Game Commission would have had the sporting fairness to at least yield the proponents of later quail season openings a fair trial.

ALTERED

MIGRATION:

The Decline and Fall of a Great Wildfowl Resource
in the Lower Mississippi River Valley.

Early on the morning of October 31, 1919, my partner in the sporting goods business, the late Major Enoch Ensley, together with the late Perry Hooker, the late Hamilton Long, and I left Memphis in a twenty-foot metal inboard gas boat for a goose hunt down Ole Miss. The Federal season on migrants opened the next day, November 1. We decided to shoot Whitehall Bar, then run on down to the head of Rosa Lee Bar and leave the outfit at Frank Ritch's camp for the season. We had another boat and good outboard motor at Ed Williams home at O.K. Landing downriver a bit. We would return home via railroad from Beaver Dam.

We had blankets and a good tarp, four-dozen fine lightweight metal goose decoys, ample grub, water, and gas. As Hooker was a magnificent engineer (he had just come out of the Air Corps in World War I, along with Ensley), engine troubles didn't loom. By midafternoon, after a leisurely passage, we landed midway of Whitehall's bend and tied up at what we knew as "Battle-Axe Landing," merely a small shack with hay stored and used as a steamboat gangplanking for plantations inland. But it made a good overnight campsite.

Examination of the opposite bar through our binoculars revealed a low river and a very wide bar, fully a mile across to the first timber. Near the timber we spotted two ponds about half a mile apart. It was decided to cross the river, not more than three hundred yards of swift channel, and camp that night on the bar, with pits dug and in readiness for the 'morrow.

Crossing, we were fortunate in finding a nice inlet, and at its far end we left our craft well hidden from passers-by and wave-wash. Securing it with two lines tied into a big snag, we divided the decoys. Ensley and Hooker chose the lower pond and Hamp Long and I the upper one. We had water, coffee, sugar, bacon, eggs and bread, shovels, guns, shells, skillets, blankets, and Kodaks. Divided among four "huskies" the dunnage was trivial. The hugely expansive sandbar was dotted with drift-litter. It took Hamp and me a full thirty minutes to plod across the bar to where the pond seen through our glasses turned out to be a string of pools left from previous high waters. And from the nearest leaped scores of duck flocks – a propitious sign.

The bar shelved off very gradually to the pools and climbed again to the timber with sedge-grass skirting. Through our glasses we picked up Hooker and Ensley half a mile to the south, looking about them just as we were doing for a good pit location and the best place to bed down for the night. A fingered snap-log was selected for the night roost, and then with the shovel we dug a pit a couple of hundred yards away out on the sand. Made short work of it, too.

It was getting toward sundown when we finished and returned for a snack of supper before turning in alongside the log. While digging the pit we had spotted several bunches of geese traveling south and innumerable flights of ducks were pouring into the bar-pools. After supper, we spread the bedding rolls and lay quietly watching afterglow fade. And with it came geese – geese – geese. Flock after flock of gabbling, croaking honkers poured downriver, and, wheeling, wings cupped, lit all over Whitehall Bar as far south as our eyes could penetrate the night. Geese passed so low overhead we could almost reach up and grab them by their legs. And by the time darkness closed in, their hub-bub and backtalk kept us awake with only catnaps through the night.

Before daylight we could hear signals of departure and fanning wings overhead. A tiny fire, shielded behind the log, gave us hot coffee and boiled eggs. Then, in the gloom, we stole out to the pit and set up the decoys with careful placement as to the breeze that was picking up from the north – a good sign, too. Our equipment was carefully concealed behind the log. All we had were binoculars, Winchester pumpguns, the heaviest loads available in Leader shells and #4 shot, together with great expectations.

Pre-dawn on a gigantic sandbar at a wildfowl migrational peak can be a wonderful experience, and we had broken records in sightseeing as to geese the evening before. We had scarcely gotten settled in the pit before Hamp, peering through his glasses, whispered, "Between us and the river, a bunch headed this way with their wings stiff – they're talking – they've seen our decoys – they're gonna make it – get ready." It was barely coming sunrise and now I had 'em cased – swerving to come in directly upwind – a perfect light. You couldn't have tied a string to them and pulled them in any straighter. We let them hover and begin to pull their black boots off just to one side of the profiles before going into action.

"Shoot on the left," Hamp said as we arose. We had twelve shots between us, and, when the last shot died away, what with a second shot necessary here and there in the excitement, we had eight very dead honkers sanded out front. Hamp, being the lighter, was carefully boosted from the pit to check a cave-in, and soon had the victims neatly set up as decoys.

Back in the pit, we sat watching the ducks ply the ponds and then turned the glasses on Hooker and Ensley. We had arranged a set of signals back and forth between our pits by handkerchiefs tied to gun barrels and waved. It had been decided to quit the pits not later than 9 o'clock in order to reach Ritch's and have him take us downriver to where Ed Williams would carry us to the railroad in his Model T Ford, for Ensley, Long, and I had to be at the store next morning for sure.

Hamp said, "Yonder's four geese heading straight in to Perry and Enoch – watch 'em – quick." I did. Four geese sailed in and none left. "High, low, Jack, and the game," grunted Hamp. A quarter-hour sped. "Gosh," said Hamp, "Wouldn't I like to have a blind in the roots of that old snag down yonder by that pond and a bunch of decoys; you could kill a boat-load of ducks and geese in a day and not half try." Just then, from the north, a bunch of geese swung in, took a look, veered, and seven in number, they left four behind. Hamp advised leaving 'em lay because we now had a dozen; the limit was sixteen but he had little stomach for lugging eight geese each a mile or more. We glassed south. Almost simultaneously we sighted a big bunch of honkers headed upward and inward from the river.

"They've spotted the boys' spread," checked Hamp, "and here's where those lads can get even – watch close – listen." Geese began to fall from that decoying outfit before gun-raps thudded our ears faintly against the wind. "There must have been twelve or fifteen geese," said Hamp, "but only three got away. I'll bet you the boys start picking up and wig-wagging us right now." Sure enough, both Ensley and Hooker left the pit, the signal was given, and we, too, began loading up for the big trek. As it turned out, they had knocked ten geese from that last outfit, making them fourteen to our twelve.

Guns thrust across the vents in our hunting coats, and the shovel, too, and packs shouldered, that left only the six geese apiece to be considered. The geese were tied singly to a dead pole, and we each took an end of the pole and easily sledded the load across the sand. Hamps drew a sigh of relief as we reached the boat well ahead of Enoch and Perry who staggered in about pooped-out with a shouldered burden. It was 8:15 am and we were forty-five minutes ahead of schedule.

About four miles below Battle-Axe we swung into the Ritch light, by great good luck finding Frank and his wife there. Hooker gave Ritch all the boat engine's dope and mannerisms. What a game country and fur-pocket those Ritch folks had in that sequestered river wilderness. Past Hardin's Point, across from which on Ship Island Bar we had had so much fine goose and duck shooting for so many years. Ed Williams was home, and after starting Ritch on his return trip with two fat honkers, we loaded into Ed's Model T (with another pair of geese as down payment), and away we went to Beaver Dam Duck Club, lunch, and the afternoon train for Memphis. As there were several members at the club staying over, we left two more geese to save them from possible starvation. That left us five fowl each to dispose of in the city. It took an even dozen to feed all hands at the store and that left geese enough for the hunters' folks. In those days along the Mississippi, in 1919, we probably saw more Canada geese than have actually flown that same immediate locality in the past ten years.

I began shooting swans, Canada geese, and ducks at Wapanoca in 1890. There seemed to be as many swans as geese, if not more, but by 1890 they were practically gone. I recall that about 1912 a Memphis lawyer shot what proved to be two swans at the Menasha Duck Club just above Wapanoca and was fined, Federally. He didn't know what he had shot. That was the first year of the Migratory Bird Law.

At Wapanoca, then about 5,400 acres of land, timber, and 1,900 acres of water at normal shooting stages (and fishing superb), the daily bag limit was fifty ducks (put on by the club) and as many geese or swans as one could bag. There was practically no attention paid, Federal or state, to wildfowl management or laws until approximately 1903 – even mention of it – market hunting was legal. Wapanoca lay on a big bend – a peninsula – into the Mississippi, roughly two miles inland, airline. In early mornings when the boats reached the entrance to Big Lake (there was a smaller lake adjoining), rising clouds of fowl, swans, geese, and ducks would literally obscure the heavens.

My last shoot on Wapanoca was Washington's Birthday, 1901 (I became of age that year). Judge Gilham and I shot together in Trexler's Corner on the mudflats and killed 100 pintails, mostly drakes, and eighteen geese. I did not shoot Wapanoca again until 1920 when I inherited my parent's membership. But I have a close friend, just my age, who entered the club in 1904 and he would corroborate populations.

In those days I would estimate the Wapanoca Canada goose population, seasonally, at not less than 10,000. Between 1920 (when I rejoined) and 1925,

I'd say the seasonal population was around 6,000. From 1904 my friend and I shot geese and ducks from Saskatchewan on down the Platte, Missouri, Mississippi, Minnesota, to Vermillion Bay, Louisiana, and Texas coastals, San Jacinto, Rockport, *et al*.

At Wapanoca, I have witnessed some strange and magnificent flights of Canadas. In late afternoon I've watched them stream in to roost from Ole Miss, sometimes here, sometimes there, until one could easily have killed 100. One rainy morning my pusher, in going up the bayou to Little Lake, rounded a viney corner and the boat's prow actually knifed into probably 500 Canadas banked in. Wapanoca was just one wintering population center along the lower reaches. The only time Wapanoca ever went plumb dry was in 1933 (the great drought). After it, with water returned, though low, the rapid growth of usual post-drought years saw probably the last Canada goose population of any great moment. A friend relates that once he reached a point on the Big Lake and found he had forgotten his gun; all he had was a .410 and a box of light loads. He said he saw more Canada geese try to light on him than he ever saw before in any one place and shot a limit of four by watching their eyes. (1933 was six years after the establishment of the refuge at Horseshoe Lake, Illinois, in 1927.)

As Director of Game Restoration for the Western Cartridge Company and as Executive Secretary of the American Wildfowlers, I saw practically every worthwhile refuge and wildfowling center east of the Rocky Mountains. I've shot from Colorado to the Atlantic and was of the committee that first sought and obtained Mattamuskeet Lake. I have been at Horseshoe Lake, Illinois, since that first refuge (state) started in 1927. I have, as Chairman of the Outdoor Writers Association's Waterfowl Committee (1941-54), seen all the rest of Illinois, Missouri, Michigan, Wisconsin, Kentucky, and Tennessee refuges start and expand.

It is indeed a gloomy experience to look back upon the actual decimation of a region's waterfowl resource, the noble Canada goose. It was easy to see the situation approaching, but futile to attempt opposition when apathy, oil, and the almost total loss of corn crops that once lined both sides of the Mississippi from Cairo to the Gulf were assimilated by crass stupidity, not an ounce of Federal prevention or thought thereof in warning, and a like acceptance by the lower states. Oil ruined the coasts, and the departure of corn crops below Cairo did the rest. Much less when for forty years now – a lifetime – the mushrooming of Federal refuges and commercialism north of Cairo could very well terminate the mystery of the migrational urge that is nothing but goose brains to go where there's grub and for free. Apparently now, each flock has its feeding and wintering refuge and these are managed as to kill.

Starting in 1910, by December 20 of each year 95% of the Canada goose population along Ole Miss was south of Cairo, lessening in volume northward as the corn was fed out south to the Gulf coast. Their numbers were incredible. In the 1930's came the White River Refuge of Arkansas that even then built up a population of 10,000 and was doing a good commercial business when the crash came a bit later.

In those same early 1930's, the American Wildfowlers tried desperately to interest the Biological Survey in using their river fleet to throw in check dams and planting the rich mud acres exposed in corn or anything else grazeable for the migrations to use during next fall's flights. We didn't even get to first base yet, right today, as much straightened as the river has become that will be the *only* approach seemingly possible, with corn gone and public and managerial apathy at impasse. That is, unless some miracle occurs – financially and managerially – to resuscitate apathy civically and among landowners and sportsmen and their state game commissions to readjust agricultural patterns to reharbor Canada geese. Here is a clear-cut struggle between "the will to hunt," and the soybeaned agricultural "fast-buck." The Canada geese are now strictly an above-Cairo commercial asset. What habitat refurbishing could the Gulf Coast's former winterings offer? What force can reform a forty-year headstart of feeding that began north of Cairo in 1927?

For twenty years – 1910-1930 – we maintained a winter's goose camp at O. K. Landing, on the Mississippi side of the big river, in Harbert's Bend, probably then twenty-five miles above Helena, Arkansas, and seventy-five miles south of Memphis. The Harbert's Bend was some twenty-five miles around the neck, being but a couple of miles across. That neck was blown in the early 1940's and the area is now known as Tunica Cutoff. In the immediate area, probably two miles inland, airline, lies Beaver Dam Lake, the oldest fine duck club of the area, established in 1878. Below it, just a bit closer to the river, is big Flower Lake, with two smaller bodies, lying t'wixt the levee and river and flooded during rise. O.K. Landing sandbar, across from the land, was a curving bar and wild area. Above our camp, at the houseboat of Mr. Williams, was Ship Island Bar. Across and above, Rosa Lee Bar, opposite the huge White Hall Bar.

There were twenty or more such bars, older rivers, and towheads 'twixt Memphis and our camp. There were so many Canadas downriver then that it was difficult to sleep nights. I have been pitted across the river on O.K. Bar and watched literally thousands of Canadas come out of Flower and Beaver

"Canada geese feeding in refuge at Horseshoe Lake, Illinois above Cairo. This was where conditions brought about closure of two counties in '45-'46 for two years."

Dam lakes at dawn, dispersing to croplands up and downstream. I have sat in a pit on Ship Island Bar and seen interspersed acres of ducks and geese, starting about 3:30 in the afternoons and continuing flights that lasted past darkness. I have seen a rising river covered by acres of ducks, floating down in separated rafts; they'd finally rise, fly back upstream, and resume the float. But, at seemingly a signal, the thousands would suddenly come ashore along the sandbar, line up for miles (probably eating digestive sand), and then, suddenly at what appeared a signal, push back into the river, begin to spiral upward, and disappear with the downcoming hordes.

In 1915, on Ship Island Bar, immediately above O. K. Landing the bar's lower end was mud-blocked with accretion and growing two to three-foot high switch-willows. On opening day, my companion, Mr. E. C. Palmer of Winchester Company, and I went up the bar and dug two pits in the edge of the switch willows, at opposite ends about half a mile. We sat there until after lunch and never even saw a Canada goose. The weather was warm. Palmer decided to go to camp. I went to sleep and was awakened by the arrival of my hunting companion the late Hal B. Howard. He had one live goose decoy, a hybrid, and staked it out on the open mud blocks outside the willows.

Away above us, an old river took in and re-entered the river in an oxbow between us and camp. Happening to look over my shoulder, I saw a bunch of geese rise from the old river, come down it to opposite us. They saw the decoy and swung across the bar. Below us, near the land, a herd of cattle grazed. Immediately, flocks of ten, forty, or more took off from that old river, followed the first flock down upon us, and within twenty minutes there must have been 1,000 Canadas trying to light and feed on those switch willows; they hovered about and frightened the cattle into a stampede and departure. We bagged our limits in almost continuous fire, picked up the slain, and departed with geese still lighting on that willowage.

In 1922, with the late E. F. Warner of *Field & Stream* and Charles P. Williams of Greenville, Mississippi, we made a motion picture below Lake Providence, Louisiana, that stayed on the circuits twenty years. In the same type old river we found a concentration of several thousand Canadas. We sank the cameras in the outlying switch willows, then surrounded the old river and drove that concentration over and into the cameras.

Until the early 1940's, those same sights and situations prevailed all along the well-corned habitat from Cairo to the Gulf. From 1920 through 1925 at Wapanoca Lake Club, the shooting hours were from 7 am until 4 pm. I have seen thousands of Canadas pouring into lake after 4 pm. I have shot from Dog Tooth Bend, far above Memphis, downriver past Sunrise Towhead,

Brandywine, Ashley Point, Birdo (Bordeaux), clean on down. I saw and helped the White River Refuge into being and the development of a perhaps 10,000-goose population.

Now, a number of people *north* of Cairo are saying there was never much of a Canada goose population *south* of Cairo.

This is not illogical when it is remembered that it is now, to all intents and purposes, forty years since that first refuge (state) went in at Horseshoe Lake, Illinois. Since 1927, the growth of Federal refuges in Missouri and Illinois was especially rapid. The disappearance of Canada geese from the Gulf Coast and the Mississippi's lower reaches was equally swift. But absolutely no attention, Federal or state, was paid to it, though sportsmen down the river here and there made efforts to call attention to the situation, but were ignored. Having been employed as a refuge locator by the late J. N. Darling for a period in 1934-35, I made several efforts – completely futile. Later, as Chairman of the Outdoor Writers Association's Waterfowl Committee and also as of the American Waterfowl Committee, I published papers on the disappearance.

The effort did, however, result in the padlocking of two counties for two years in Illinois as the result of slaughterhouse conditions on Canadas. The situation has been better up there ever since. It might be remembered that in 1945 the Wildlife Service yielded and declared that when the kill reached 5,000 in the Horseshoe Lake area the season would end – willy-nilly. It is of record that there were 7,000 Canadas killed before the orgy could be officially stopped, and the season lasted just *22½ hours.*

It was not until 1958 that through prodding by the West Tennessee Sportsmens Association of Memphis, Tennessee, there was a meeting called at St. Louis during the conference of the National Wildlife Federation to expose the ruination of the river's lower reaches as to Canadas by the Northern refuges, and the government called a meeting (two days) at Memphis a bit later. Not long thereafter, the state of Tennessee bought land west of Dryersburg on the river and has been making efforts at habitat and other management efforts at Canada goose restoration.

About the same time, the government began negotiations for the remaining lands and waters of the famous Wapanoca Duck Club (the Wapanoca Wildlife Refuge) when negotiations were finally successfully concluded. I had a hand in the buyout of the club by Federal authorities. Much good work has been done there in five years: croplands increased, wood duck boxes installed, dove and duck and goose-banding operations launched, and a bridge and dam completed. But the major project remains untouched, to wit: wells and pumps to maintain water, and level controls so that lake can be drained and replanted from the air and turned back into the great green marsh it once was.

In those distant years, the whole countryside was a mass of corn. It is now a mass of soybeans. If it has taken five years to produce only this much, how long will it now take to not only produce water levels but to convince the surrounding landowners that geese can and will be returned southward for private recreation, commercialism, and public shooting grounds? There is an enormous public relations job ahead.

The main objective, therefore, is do the people of the ruined goose region want it restored, and, if so, will they pitch in and help get it done? The north-of-Cairo folks will fight back, and the geese themselves will have to be shown the newer and more attractive grubline – south. But to do this will require a far heftier attack on state public relations than at present. Refuges like Wapanoca can and should be remade into the vast duck marshes (and fishing lakes) they once were, if for nothing else but the mallards and other species of wildfowl. Mechanized farming, now able to turn two and even three cash crops a year, are increasingly not inclined to plant a costly corn crop on the prospects of today's goose situation. To even begin getting this goose restoration problem back into official and public scrutiny again is going to require a far, far more intensive state-by-state action study than today's status of things.

John Findlay, Bob Stoner, and Nash Buckingham at Wapanoca Lake, Arkansas October 26, 1963. Findlay was the Chief of Enforcement for the Department of the Interior. Nash was instrumental in arranging the sale of his father's old duck club to the Interior Department as part of the refuge system taking shape at that time. Nash was one of the early leaders in the call for a refuge system that has provided thousands of acres for waterfowl and other species.

LET'S
TAKE STOCK!

An Editorial by The Outdoor Writer's Association of America Waterfowl Committee: Nash Buckingham, E. Sydney Stephens, Bob Becker, Roy N. Back, Gene A. Howe, J. Hammond Brown, Col. L.B. Rock. (From Field & Stream *magazine, October 1947)*

By now most duck hunters will have digested the 1947-48 wildfowling regulations issued by the U.S. Fish and Wildlife Service August 1, after a seven-months "cry-havoc" campaign as to deterioration of basic wildfowl stacks, a 12-city tour of public hearings, a U.S. Senate "chit-chat" conference, and a last hearing very generously accorded the recently formed American Waterfowl Committee.

Awakened at long last to necessity for bolstered public relations, U.S. Fish & Wildlife Service officials wisely broke precedent, pulling waterfowl administration out of ruts into which this great natural resource seems to have slipped. It was a healthy and commendable move. The hearings got off to a late start, were not well publicized, and were poorly attended. However, experience will improve next year's routine, and let's hope there be necessity for such. If the situation gets completely out-of-hand this season, another heavy over-kill may necessitate complete closure of gunning. When that happens, states will have to cut down or close upland game shooting; stocks simply won't stand the pressure. Then the economic picture becomes really involved, as to both sales of duck stamps and state shooting licenses. This year the red light and "Watch Your Step" signs are up aplenty.

It becomes doubly imperative, therefore, that the situation be put squarely before the hunters themselves. Unless American wildfowlers awaken to the fact that as duck stamp and license buyers they are stockholders in a vast production plant run 100 per cent by whimsical nature, that same involves untold future recreational benefits plus a business side totaling billions of dollars, and that this business needs rebuilding rather than "shooting up," we are getting all ready to hang out the bankruptcy sign as to national wildlife resources.

To kid ourselves is fatuous. Group recriminations, charges and countercharges as to "lost ducks" had better cease, and be replaced by some cool, unselfish, steady thinking and concerted action by the real sportsmen who pay the freight and want, along with their children, to enjoy some sport in the future.

With its appropriation for "protection of Migratory Wildfowl" again cut to the near pitiful figure of $350,000 and with probably a net of less than a dime from each duck stamp for enforcement, the U.S. Fish and Wildlife Service may or may not be right in throwing in the sponge and admitting its inability to enforce the Federal law. It may be wrong in appealing to the "conscience" of the so-called sportsmen. If the states, given such choice, which have selected split seasons, realizing Federal inadequacy, fail to redouble energies during intervening closed periods, we are this year simply shooting on borrowed time. If we surrender to the chiselers, scofflaws and out-and-out near criminals of the marshes, we'll deserve any calamity upthrust.

Whether as many ducks come down this year as last or not, they are fewer by far – numerically. Every agency of observation so reports.

What is to be done about rebuilding the situation?

Well, the Waterfowl Committee of the Outdoor Writers' Association of America has three ideas along such lines. We are neither self-appointed Messiahs nor controversialists. We claim no corner on ideas; we look eagerly for and will support constructive ones. We bear malice toward no one; we are just trying to think straight, that's all.

Here are our three suggestions:

1. Immediate Federal and state registration requiring legal description there and vital statistics, annually and semi-annually, of every class of American duck shooting, even down to the individual duck-stamp buyer, who should be given a return post-card with his stamp and asked to send in a record of his season's bag and observations. Much talk of "managed shooting" and "harvesting wildlife crops" had been bandied about in recent years.

Three years ago, following rose-colored wildfowl inventories, we were allowed an extra five ducks per day (a total of fifteen) and told "waterfowl are no longer a problem of production, but management." And now, almost in a trice and largely because of inadequate enforcement along national flyways, we are down to the most drastic gunning curtailments in wildfowling history.

Yet, strangely, Wildlife Service officials (Washington, July 17) told the American Waterfowl Committee that '47 over-all, Continental migration would equal that of '46. According to the best observational effort, just such an unbalanced production does exist, the prairie provinces down, the vast North and Northwest up. But three of our four main flyways draw flights from the "down production areas." This maze of official and conservational bickering of recent years over "duck figures" is time, money and paper wasted, to say nothing of personal animosities, jealousies and " acrid recrimination." Autopsically, the ducks came to their deaths at the hands of guns unknown, but the whole unfortunate business does reveal an entire lack of waterfowl gunning management naturally, much less enforcement.

The amazing puzzlement of the whole business is why an inventoried system of duck shooting wasn't in force years ago. It needs no enabling legislation and will easily pay its own way through registration fees, and actually the idea was approved three years ago by former Wildlife Service Director Ira N. Gabrielson. Here's a box look:

(a) Furnish forms for immediate registration for an annual fee of say $10 for every private duck or goose shooting preserve (owner); every duck club shooting for recreation alone (owning or leasing); every guide on public waters (state or Federal) leasing blinds and giving boat and shooting service; every proprietor, company, partnership, association or irrigation project selling "memberships" or charging per diems for commercial duck shooting. At registration they must furnish to state and government legal description their shooting lands and waters, memberships, etc. Commercialists would be required at season's end to make a financial statement of their businesses for transfer to the income tax department. Let's know who, what, where, how and how much about the people who see, control, observe and kill the ducks. If restriction is a business necessity, then readjustment and improvement is even more so.

(b) At the close of each Federal shooting season, each shooting class will receive a form calling for reports on kill by species, number of guns, water, weather and duck populations in general, food conditions – in short, a true picture of "what happened there." Such are the places that really hold and see both migrations. Their records and those of the volunteers, already built up so ably by Mr. Lincoln, could be of untold value. And remember, a comparatively small registration fee, hundreds of times smaller than many of those concerned pay in bickering, fees and trouble, would pay such business management's way easily. It's just a matter of getting the job done.

2. A bill to increase the price of duck stamps from $1 to $2 failed to get under the recently recessed Congressional wire. According to thoughtful conservational opinion, the measure needed rewriting. There is grave doubt in the minds of thousands of conscientious duck hunters that a $2 stamp will see results against the odds and problems involved. The ravages of crows, drought, fire and vagaries of whimsical nature come in for increasing consideration. But the great, vital objective now is enforcement, self-admittedly prostrate. Every other issue is insignificant and lesser objectives postponed. Law enforcement should cover all classes: the wealthy sportsman who has his freeze box loaded as well as the poor violator who claims (and ofttimes with justice nowadays) that his family is hungry. Only an upped national gunning morale, born of individual and group sportsmanship, will save the ducks.

After all, increase in the price of duck stamps does not cost the American taxpayer a penny. It is strictly the duck hunters' business. It is simply a legalized request by duck hunters to be permitted to tax themselves, with funds thus secured to be spent by Federal administrators, as per earmarking on said bill's face.

Of course, there should be increased funds for sanctuaries, research and migrational studies. But until we get adequate enforcement, as low as national gunning morale has fallen, it would be foolish to put research in there against such an opponent. The average law-abiding duck hunter hasn't the faintest idea of the disgraceful over-killing, game bootlegging and chiseling now ravaging the flyways. And if the duck hunters of this country think we will ever get enough dough from Congress to put a stop to such business, we are simply kidding ourselves. It is up to us to "grab the check," and the sooner we set about it the better. For one more – just one more – drought of the severity of that of 1929-32, and we'll be just as through gunning ducks as through can be. All of which is a matter calling for ablest official and conservational leadership, plus complete acquiescence and cooperation by organized conservation and state wildlife authorities.

3. The OWAA Waterfowl Committee suggests thought as to the formation, by Presidential appointment, of an International Waterfowl Committee to study waterfowl problems of North and South America, and assist Federal authorities in final regulations and studies. Material changes are occurring not only in the heavens above but upon and beneath the earth.

In closing, your committee is pleased to note and acknowledge mention of our cooperation and that of the American Waterfowl Committee by Director A.M. Day in the June 24, 1947, Senate hearing.

We also acknowledge a profound gratitude to Sen. Willis A. Robertson of

Virginia for his continuing devotion to the cause of conservation.

May we again ask that our Outdoor Writers give as widespread publicity as possible to the thoughts suggested here and also renew their pleas for cooperation by sportsmen with the Service's regulations for 1947. The authorities have had a hard task, and we commend them for venturing into fields of fresher and perhaps more potent thought.

OWAA Waterfowl Committee

NASH BUCKINGHAM,
   author, Memphis, Tenn,. Chairman,
   OWAA Waterfowl Committee.
E. SYDNEY STEPHENS,
   conservationist-publisher, Columbia, Missouri.
BOB BECKER,
   outdoor editor, *Chicago Tribune*, Chicago, Illinois.
ROY N. BACH,
   Federal coordinator PR, Bismarck, North Dakota.
GENE A. HOWE,
   publisher, *Amarillo Globe*, Amarillo, Texas.
J. HAMMOND BROWN,
   president, OWAA, *News-Post*, Baltimore, Md.
Col. L.B. ROCK,
   publisher, Dayton *Journal-Herald*, Dayton, Ohio.

   •

```
  J. N. DARLING                                    DES MOINES, IOWA
```

September 16, 1947

Mr. Nash Buckingham
Box 720
Memphis, Tennessee

Dear Nash ---

When I got home this morning the new issue
of FIELD & STREAM was on my desk and I immediately read the
editorial.

I find no fault in it whatsoever. From a
moral and conservation standpoint it is sound as a dollar -
more sound than the Roosevelt dollar! - and you have stated
your case vigorously but by no means too brutally. I am for
the program from start to finish and having had some of the
same problems to meet during my administration I know of the
great need, not only now but in all future time, if we are
going to have any duck shooting left for the coming generations.

Now for a brief analysis of some of the suggestions which you have made in your editorial. I am a little
doubtful whether the ten-dollar license fee for registration
of commercial shooting and privately-owned or rented duck
clubs can be stretched to cover the cost of carrying out that
program. Ten dollars ought to do it from a business-man's
point of view but government costs are double or triple what a
business house would do the same thing for. When I think of the
amount of printing and mail and clerical hire necessary to
mechanize that licensing of duck clubs and commercial shooting
grounds I suspect ten dollars will not cover the costs. Those
organizations which cooperate willingly and fully will be no
problem at all but in order to make that registration program
work it will be necessary to do a large amount of sleuthing
and enforcing in order to get them all in. Anything else would
be very unfair to the willing cooperators. That will mean an
additional burden on the law enforcement staff.

I suppose you must have estimated the number
of licensed shooting clubs and based your ten-dollar fee on
the results but I feel very sure that the Fish and Wildlife
Service has no funds to cover a deficit and that matter should
be gone into carefully before the ten-dollar fee is finally decided upon.

*An example of the correspondence between J. N. "Ding" Darling and Nash, two who
felt strongly about waterfowl conservation and weren't afraid to speak out. This is
Darling's response to the October, 1947* Field & Stream *editorial authored by Nash.*

Nash Buckingham – – – – – – – #2

When I undertook the rigid enforcement in 1934 I had just twenty-one Federal Wardens to enforce the law. I added to it a few during the season and mobilized them and sent them out in squads and did a fairly effective job - much better, in fact, than had been previously done with the men sitting in their own bailiwicks and starting out alone to enforce the law among roughneck violators. Those flying squadrons did a swell job and I believe that with the number of wardens they have now an efficient job could be accomplished if it were not for the regional limitations. Wardens are assigned to the various regions and they stay pretty much in their home quarters. That is a serious mistake. Everyone knows when they start out, where they're going and the underground warns the violators ahead of time that the wardens are on the way. They should be mobilized and, above all, not restricted to a single local community where everyone recognizes them. Of course it takes the wardens away from home during the entire duck-shooting season and that was the chief howl when I tried to make the men move around across the country but it worked and it's the only scheme I know of which will work.

Ducks Unlimited are still on the optimistic side and are circulating considerable literature saying that the duck situation is not as bad as reported but I have had very direct connection with a lot of the observers up north this season and they all are a little shocked to think that their estimates have been interpreted on the liberal side rather than on the pessimistic side, even by the Fish and Wildlife Service.

I think your editorial will do a great deal of good. I think it should be copied by every sports writer in the country and published in their various columns. I think that will do more good than just the FIELD & STREAM publication which must reach only a comparatively few. I suggest that the Outdoor Writers Association petition their members to republish this editorial as a quotation from their Committee and from the FIELD & STREAM. The real sportsmen of course will observe it, as you have urged them to, but a great many of them will prefer to kid themselves and step over the line wherever they can without being caught.

It was wonderful to see you again and note your mental and physical keenness. I don't see how you can keep it up.

Best regards and good luck.

D:S

J. N. DARLING   REGISTER AND TRIBUNE   DES MOINES 4, IOWA

January 17, 1962

Nash Buckingham
198 South McLean
Memphis, Tennessee

Dear Mr. Buckingham:

You should have been there when I handed Mr. Darling your book. That really "turned on all the lights"! I haven't seen him so pleased with anything since he became ill. His eyes lit up and he said "Oh Boy! Am I glad to have that! That fellow really can write and "De Shootin'est Gent'man" was one of the best books I ever read."

He'll dictate a letter to you later after Mrs. Darling has read more of this new book to him. His days are necessarily quite short and we have to take it a little at a time to prevent his getting too tired but I assure you you have made him very happy by sending him the book....More from him later.

Sincerely,

Merle Strasser

Poor, fine Ding, he was 2 years my senior + we planned + did much well together. And some day well see what well armed as an Authority will come to pass.

A note from a close friend of Ding Darling's during the latter's final days, with Nash's handwritten eulogy for a passing friend. The "authority" he speaks of is for a waterfowl board, continent-wide, entrusted with managing the resource and the habitat that produces it.

ADVENTURES
WITH
GAME-LAW VIOLATIONS

W hen I began shooting at the age of ten, my locales were eastern Arkansas and extreme northwestern Mississippi. Nationally, in the United States and Canada, I have seen a lot of varied species of large and small wildlife and a deal of prime habitat, lands, and water unpolluted by mercury, sewer discharge, and insecticides.

For instance, I have seen the famous Wapanoca Outing Club, literally raped by neglect, turned into the finest Federal refuge in the southern Mississippi flyway. And thanks to private ownership by the Owen family and splendid cooperation by an alert and positive county protection and enforcement system, I have seen possibly the oldest duck club of them all, the Beaver Dam club of yore, an ox-bow eight miles around, still maintained for friends with an ample supply of clean water, wildfowl foods, varied fish, wild turkey, and deer. Hope springs eternal in our hunter's hearts.

I have seen tall timbered forests fall and replanted to foods for ever-increasing human populations and seen once-beautiful rivers channelized into conservational ruin and even larger streams mangled into hopeless crisscrosses of pollutioned monkey business and devastated wildlife.

I have seen the enforcement measures of many states desecrated by political shenanigans and castration of alleged sportsmen's outfits that turned the laws into mere cat's paws on a par with a lot of kids stealing watermelons or apples from farmers' orchards and vines.

And I have seen many a brave and competent game agent, Federal or state, risking their lives to beat back all this mess until the great question arises – what hope is there for alleged posterity?

It is comparatively easy for aged, experienced wildfowlers to follow the

Nash's membership card for the American Protective League, which operated under the Justice Department. Nash was able to do game enforcement work because of this affiliation; most likely he carried this card for in-the-field use in case he confronted violators and no enforcement officers were at hand.

paths of wildlife destructions down the years. First came the market hunters and unlimited havocs for livelihoods and unthinking, unorganized sportsmanship. Some few duck clubs voiced warnings and clapped on bag limits of their own. That lasted until about 1912-13 when, as I've said earlier, the Migratory Bird Law came into effect and bag limits of wildfowl were placed at twenty-five ducks a day and eight geese, a more-than-ample compromise. Even then it was six years until 1918 when the Supreme Court upheld the Federal law and turned a mumbling-grumpling bunch of violators into what became known as duck bootleggers. Prohibition had appeared and many of the market hunters merely changed their names to duck bootleggers, and strange to say the bootleggers sold most of their contraband ducks to people who didn't really need the money: shadowy restaurants, alleged "club" gatherings, swank hotels, and politically protected individuals for their "entertainments."

Once upon a time I belonged to a duck club of several thousand acres of dammed up-water amid timber. Two trails had been cut across its center, north to south and east to west, with heavily marked white and yellow paint to prevent getting lost. The two trails crossed at a point about equidistant.

The north end trail led straight across to the south end, and at the north end's high bank, game wardens used to loaf and build a fire and lie in wait for the hunters to emerge and be checked as to bag limits and any other infractions. It got so that when the hunters reached the junction, they would look down the straight-away and if any wardens were sighted, they would toss an extra duck or so overboard before risking bringing it in. The ducks thus abandoned would be eaten by predators. Reportedly the wardens got so they would wait until all the hunters were checked out and then they would run the trails and stands and pick up enough abandoned ducks to make their own limits to take home without firing a shot.

I had an odd experience there one morning. I was shooting by myself when a boat containing a professional guide-caller came alongside. I knew him well as a decent and competent chap. He said – "Mister Buck, I'm in a jam. I've got two new members over there – you must have heard all that racket – and they are both drunk and won't stop shooting. They have killed way over their limits and won't stop; they have a bet on who has killed the most ducks; won't you come over and give me a bit of help?" I knew the two new members only slightly but I went, as I had just finished my own limit.

At the trail's junction we spotted the game wardens sitting around their fire. I was not a deputy Federal game agent at the time. We went down the trail and explained the situation. They said they would follow us and stay out of sight until the situation developed; they would then come around the corner, so to speak, and take over. The guide and I joined the drunks' stand; they had been shooting all the while, but they were both about asleep and had dead ducks scattered everywhere. They were sullen and arguing about who was ahead. They rather resented my appearance. Suddenly the game agents arrived on the scene. The wardens began a check-up of the dead ducks and discovered that the two drunks were twenty-five fowl over their limits. That settled all arguments and all hands went ashore. The two violators were taken in charge and they and the wardens and the guide left the scene. I was excused, with a wink.

The two drunks were bound over, heavily fined, and almost immediately resigned from the club. The case proved a solemn warning both ways at the club and to the game agents. I don't think the club is still in existence and all the magnificent timber has become an open lake, but a lot of wildfowl still concentrate there.

At another club there was an amusing case. Two members brought over a new member for initiation. He was not a wildfowler but a clean sportsman. By ten o'clock the three of them had only seven ducks – the bag limit was four ducks apiece. The new shooter said he thought he could find a crippled duck over in the woods. He got in the boat and started along the bank so as to not get lost. It was agreed that if he heard his friends whistle, it meant they had ducks in sight and to grab a tree and hold on out of sight until the firing ceased.

When he had gone about 200 yards, he saw a man standing on the bank who proved to be a game warden and they had a chat. The new member explained that he was hunting a cripple and the warden said, "Yonder's a duck out behind that big tree, I've just seen it." Just as they picked up the duck, they heard a bombardment from their companions' blind. When they reached the blind, it was discovered that their friends had killed five ducks from a big bunch and that completed the limits. But another stranger had joined and he proved to be another game warden. With the one duck the new member had picked up, that made thirteen ducks – one over the Federal and state bag limit.

They all had a good laugh and the two wardens said, "Forget it, we'll take the extra duck home for dinner." That was a decent and common sense end of the matter. But when at home, it was discovered that the duck the new member had found was badly spoiled and it had meant that the wardens had just accidentally picked up a good fowl and the members had only eleven

Tunica, Miss. March 2nd, 1910.

Mr. T. N. Buckingham,

    c/o Chicasaw Guards Club,

        Memphis, Tennessee.

Dear Mr. Buckingham:

        Your letter of yesterday received.

        Mr. Handwerker wrote me to know when the law against shooting ducks went into effect, and I gave him the exact letter of the statute.

        However, don't let that stand in the way of your coming to Beaver Dam to shoot all the ducks you want, this month. There is no one here who will bother you. We don't pay any especial attention here as to the exact time of shooting ducks, as we even begin to shoot summer ducks in July, when the law prohibits the shooting of them until September; and I feel perfectly justified in assuring you that if you and your friends want to shoot ducks on Beaver Dam this month, you will not be molested.

        Very truly yours,

A letter to Nash from a member of the Beaver Dam club telling Nash that his concerns over the law against spring duck shooting recently enacted are ill-founded. It was this type of disregard for the law that started Nash on his lifelong fight against game-law violations. Note also the reference to "summer ducks" and their shooting. Such practices were widespread and contributed greatly to waterfowl shortages, especially when combined with habitat loss through drought and development.

good ducks. All very amusing and a good joke all around.

That was in December. The following March the hunters got a letter from a Federal bureau's attorney saying they had been filed on for breaking the Federal bag limit and to come over and pay a fine. Feeling outraged, they came to me for help. By good luck the Regional Federal Game Agent was in our town, and he was an old friend. He immediately contacted the necessary parties and a full investigation was launched.

Of course the game agent who picked up the extra duck in the woods should have known it was an "old" duck. But anyway, they admitted at once that when they explained the case originally, their district warden said he had it in for a certain member of the club (but for none of the others) and so he had insisted that the case be filed on. As a result, the agent was reprimanded and the whole matter quashed, and the two game agents came to the club and apologized. That "one duck too many" case needs reviewing all too often; it fattens an agent's records.

O n another occasion, I was in a distant state, seated in a blind before opening time on a well-known river famous for its duck shooting, bag limit violations, and a good measure of duck bootlegging. There were four of us, all armed, two civilians and two highly placed Federal officials.

Just as shooting time arrived, over a hundred mallards swung by and sprinkled down into the decoys. All hands erupted. When the dead were picked up – there were six of them – the bag contained two wood ducks, and wood ducks were "off limits" at that time. There wasn't a chance, due to the dim light, of knowing who killed which, a problem of no small discrepancy with confrontations of conscience in the offing. At any rate, nothing ever happened so I guess those two wood ducks just got "et up." As a matter of record, it was never even mentioned.

The late Captain Ben Tyler, a friend of long years and a top shot and keen sportsman, and I have hunted together in many fields. Once we were shooting in a good-sized woods pond surrounded by tall timber and cypress just off a broad river noted for its wildfowling. We came downriver well before daylight, walked through the timber, and took station behind a giant cypress. Suddenly, in the dark from behind us a couple of hundred yards came a burst of gunfire. We yelled at the shooters to stop shooting in the dark – using exceedingly hard words. The firing ceased, and daylight sifted down into shooting time. Ben was an exceptionally fine caller and it wasn't but a short time before we were about through with our limits of ten mallards each.

Just then five men walked into our blind behind the big cypress: two dudes in blue overcoats and fedora hats, and three roughly clad guides (as the matter developed) armed with autoloading shotguns. And in that day and time, licensed guides were not permitted to carry guns. They were en route to another lake about a mile north of us. One of the dudes suggested that they remain with Ben Tyler and me and added that we could shoot some additional ducks on "their credit." But their pals prevailed and their whole party left. Our flight sort of slowed and ere long came a terrific firing from the direction of the other lake. It seems they had come down the river originally, gotten lost in the dark, and left their boat upriver and walked downriver to where they started shooting in the dark.

When Ben and I had finished our limits, we sat around for a while drinking hot java and eating good cheese and crackers. Then we processed our ten mallards, walked through the beautiful sunlit woods, got in our boat, and started to our houseboat. The firing upriver had increased.

We went around a big bend in the river and spotted another boat coming downriver well upstream. On the riverbank we spotted the motorboat in which the five other hunters had originally come downstream. In the other boat we met an old friend, the district state game agent. I had known and coached him as a prep-school football captain in our home city. We mentioned what had happened and he said, "Let's land and look into that boat and see what is happening."

We did, and by turning back a canvas over the front deck of the dudes' boat we uncovered fifty mallards! So we continued to the lake and when our game warden friend took over, the five violators had thirty-nine mallards too many. Our game agent friend took the whole bunch on downriver to town and put the screws to them aplenty, including shooting too soon and the guides-with-guns matter. All hands were unlicensed. Of course, all the ducks were confiscated.

One of the strangest episodes in my experience concerns the wholly accidental. Five of us were touring the area of a noted duck-shooting mecca in the southern Mississippi flyway. One member of our outfit was a man I've mentioned before, Col. Harold P. Sheldon, the Chief Game Warden of the United States. We were looking around for refuge locations and also laying the foundations for reducing the five shots in magazine guns to a three-shot basis, and doing some shooting in the process.

Another member of our party was the sporting editor of a great Southern newspaper. The other member was the public relations director of a tremendous explosives dynasty, and the last member a civilian who knew his way around in the conservation field.

At our hotel one evening, I met two men with whom I had done considerable trap shooting around the circuits. They were headed for a place that *guaranteed* a legal limit of fifteen ducks. They suggested our joining them and said they could make arrangements by telephone. We met them next morning just before daybreak in the timbered river bottoms. A barbed-wire fence surrounded a sloping ground with a man at the gate. Our friends talked to him privately, and we were admitted.

Beyond the slope to the bottoms, we saw a dirt dam about fifteen feet high and behind it a black mass of ducks resembling a solid carpet. Our usher said, "You fellows scatter out around the base of the dam; my brother is around behind the dam, and when he shoots, the ducks will come directly out over the dam; there is another pond over beyond this one with a connecting neck."

By this time, the Colonel and I had had our suspicions aroused that something unusual was on tap and that we had better keep an eye on the proceedings. When five of our group were in their places, the Colonel and I backed off up the field a bit to watch what happened. We heard three shots over beyond the dam, and out over the pond and dam came a smothering scatter of mallards. The gunners opened up and the ducks fell like rain. There were some cripples among them.

It took about fifteen minutes to empty the pond, and a halt was called. The Colonel and I hadn't fired a shot. The usher opened a gate and in rushed a troop of hogs that were obviously trained. They caught and ate the cripples, fighting over their prey like wolves.

The five shooters picked up an even fifty dead mallards. Our party was entitled to fifteen ducks each at ten dollars per limit. The usher said as we gathered at the dam's base, "Last week there were forty shooters at once behind that dam, including the Governor."

At the dam's base we met the usher's brother. He had thirty-five mallards he had killed with those first three starting shots by firing into them on the water. And there he stood totally unaware that he was in the presence of the Chief Game Warden of the United States. Out on the pond were men dumping rice sweepings into the water from a truck for bait. At fifteen ducks per limit, our five hunters were now entitled to seventy-five mallards, but with the two fellows who had invited us to join them, the entitlement was 105 ducks. With the thirty-five the brother had shot on the water, we had eighty-five, so the proprietor went around a neck in the woods into the other pond and scared out enough for the balance.

Meanwhile the public relations man and the sporting editor were busy taking pictures not only of a big heap of dead ducks, but of the proprietors and the baiters. Not a word had been spoken, but they realized that there was something in the wind.

We paid off and after securing our ducks, the two chaps who had invited us along borrowed all our leftover shells as they were expecting to shoot again that afternoon with a large party. It developed that about a mile away there was a big lake from which an enormous concentration of ducks fed into the baited ponds.

Well, what ensued is dim history. The sporting editor wrote an article and so did the public relations man. Colonel Sheldon also took action. The entire plant was padlocked, and deep trouble ensued for the proprietor.

I belonged to a duck club with just twelve members only twenty miles from Memphis and it was a honey. It held a fine stock of bass, crappie, and bream that made it an all-year attraction. We built a good clubhouse with our own hands as one of our members was a noted mill builder.

Bag limits were ample, fifteen ducks a day, and our members were handpicked for sportsmanship. But eventually two of them somehow fell from grace. It was customary for the members to spread their ducks on the broad screened front porch to cool off. One day, a member came in and spread his limit along with several others and figured all hands had finished. He was standing there counting when he turned around and saw another boat coming in with a limit. That necessitated a recount and he concluded sorrowfully that there was one too many limits. He was counting again when another member confided that he and his companion had just gotten excited and killed too many ducks and to please keep still.

The discovering member refused to keep mum. He called a meeting of the executive committee of the club and they reached a verdict, with options: The offenders could write a personal letter of apology to each member and stay away from the club for a week; or, they could sell their memberships and resign; or, they could take their chances of being informed on and face prosecution. Well, you can decipher which route they took. They wrote the letter and took a week's vacation. There was never another violation at that club and the two offenders were invited to a "make-up" luncheon and life-long friendships remained intact. This is an example of fine sportsmanship by all hands in resolving a situation, of shooters standing up for the resource and others "seeing the light."

Gradually, thanks to what became known as "conservation," authorities met shrinkage in wildfowl populations head-on. Bag limits, Federal and state, were lowered to fifteen ducks a day and two geese. Federal and state game agents, taking great risks, broke up duck bootlegging in several of the more notorious states. The risks had become too great for bootleggers, even though there was an equal reduction in sportsmanship. Incidentally, that last named attribute – sportsmanship – had and has become tainted. It has become a struggle between the "decents" and the "indecents." And any time you think the "indecents" haven't been a huge factor in the reduction of wildfowl populations, you are just badly mistaken. Again meeting the enforcement proposition head-on, inadequate funds play a leading role. But staring starkly is the fact mere violations of game laws are completely overshadowed by the enormous and hideous increase of crime in all its major aspects in our society.

But I want to make one statement that circumvents any "holier-than-thou" involvement. I sincerely doubt if there is a man or woman around who has not, at some time in his or her career, intentionally or unintentionally fractured the Federal or state bag limit regulations or some minor infraction. I have two such cases personally in mind.

It's been nearly sixty years ago when the bag limit was twenty-five ducks. I was accompanied by my great old Chesapeake Bay dog, "Baltimore." Shooting in the timber, I had by late afternoon bagged twenty-four "big ducks." I wanted a teal for my wife, so in my duck boat we drifted down a flooded trail hoping to jump one. And sure enough, I spotted a teal swimming along at about the same instant it spied me and took off.

I snatched up my gun and swung ahead of the teal when it was about two feet off the water and nearly forty yards away. At the same instant, an enormous bunch of teal jumped from the woods and swung across in front of my trigger-pull that killed the victim. The dog and I waded over and, to my amazement, I saw some flutterings beyond. My shot had knocked ten teal from the other bunch. So there I was and with a "what-to-do" staring me in the face. Well, there wasn't anything to do but what I did. I gave the club keeper, Horace Miller, ten mallards and told him to take them up to the home of our landlord as a present. Horace, of course, had a license.

Now you figure the right or wrong of that one.

Another time, Bob Anderson and I were shooting under a bag limit of four ducks each a day. Bob had his four down and I needed one. A gadwall swung out over and across the pond, and I prepared for a reasonably high shot. I had mounted the gun and swung for the lead. From the corner of an eye, I saw another gadwall swing across with the speed of a hawk to join my chance. I couldn't stop the trigger pull, and down they both came. Many of you have had a similar experience. What to do with an extra duck? Leave it to be eaten by predators or put it to some good use? Many a game agent has struggled with conscience against common sense in such cases. We gave that extra duck to a nearby grateful tenant farmer.

ONE WAY
TO SALVAGE
A WATERFOWL SPECIES

It was in the early 1950's. I recall the date approximately because my fine friend, John D. Findlay, former Director of the Tennessee Game and Fish Commission, had left that outfit and gone with the U. S. Fish & Wildlife Service of the Department of the Interior at Washington. His title was Chief of Enforcement & Game Management, and he was a courageous man of his word and ability.

Along there, my shooting companion for many years, Bob Anderson, magnificent shot and duck caller, and I were invited to the lodge of a friend at Reelfoot Lake (Tennessee-Kentucky) for several days' wildfowling, my first visit to the lake since the 1908. Our host said to bring plenty of shells and when asked why when the bag limit on ducks was only four, he replied, "After you shoot your limit of big ducks you can shoot all the fish-ducks (mergansers) you want to and it is fine sport because, as you know, they are fast-flying targets."

We asked what was done with them. "Oh!" he replied, "We just leave 'em for the coons and turtles and I guess most of 'em rot." I asked if there were no Federal bag limit on them and he said "No." This I doubted, but anyway, the proposal didn't attract us. I had shot many fish-ducks and when well-cooked they ate just as well as a lot of higher-class ducks ruined by incompetent cooks. Of course I wouldn't trade you a teal for a merganser, but I've seen the time when the latter tasted awfully good when steamed and stuffed with onion gravy on the side as old Aunt Molly sometimes worked on them at Beaver Dam. And, as our prospective host further explained, it was common practice, at Reelfoot and for that matter at other wildfowling centers, to massacre mergansers just to see 'em fall.

We went to Reelfoot for several days, had a most delightful time eating fried crappie and hush-puppies and besides bagging our four mallards a day, we learned a lot about what was going on around the lake and most of our information, while true, was not good.

But I had decided to investigate the real status of the embattled mergansers – hooded, American, and red-breasted. So I wrote John Findlay and asked for the low-down on the mergansers' legal status, asking if it were possible that so beautiful, edible, and inoffensive species (other than their taste as fish eaters when they got real hungry) were actually allowed to be shot down to rot and for turtle food, ad lib. I added, too, that in not too many years, the so-called duck hunters were in a fair way to be glad to even see a merganser to get a shot. Even as I wrote, however, I had a suspicion of what I'd hear.

Ere long, John wrote that the hooded merganser (one of the most beautiful ducks awing) had protection but the American and red-breasts were legal at twenty-five in the bag opening day, and no limit thereafter. I wrote back that this was one of the most incredible insults to wildlife management and a lovely species, much less to sportsmanship and economic principles, that I had ever heard of, and that as Chairman of the Waterfowl Committee of the Outdoor Writers Association of America, I was going to try to get a great wrong corrected. John concurred. So I wrote immediately to four national conservation groups, including the then-head of the Audubon Society, my old friend John Baker, explaining the injustice of the situation, and frankly asking for aid to get it corrected at once.

Three of the groups pulled their fright-wigs and went in the tank (as usual), but the Audubon came out fighting. Publicity through the Outdoor Writers widened and became demanding. It took a year, but when the smoke cleared away, the hooded merganser had become a "big duck" and on the same footing with the mallard, while the wretched American and red-breasted were cut to *one in the bag*. The abominable thing about the whole business was that such a nauseous situation had been tolerated for so long. Since then, mergansers have eased back up to five in a bag limit; an incredible yielding to political pressures.

Now the point in this recital of species salvage is that it came as the result of sheer luck. A friend just happens to tell someone engaged in waterfowl protection about a situation that has been going on, unheeded by the Federal authorities pledged to protect migrants. If he hadn't intervened and had behind him a potentially powerful and mobilized outdoor press and the Audubon Society, there would probably be a minimum of mergansers in existence today.

And a good question is, how many million mergansers, through such decades of terrible slaughter and waste, have been needlessly shot down to rot and for turtle food? What kind of thinking – if any – has prevailed in the supposed sanctum of national protection? And I still carry with me the contempt one can hardly help feeling for the conservation groups that did not even acknowledge a plea for aid to a species in crisis.

GOODWIN J. KNIGHT
GOVERNOR

SETH GORDON
DIRECTOR

STATE OF CALIFORNIA

Department of Fish and Game

Sacramento, California
August 24, 1954

This is how I settled the California Magnum deal — Olin's letter.

Mr. Nash Buckingham
Box 720
Memphis, Tennessee

Dear Nash:

In response to yours of the 20th, the most our Commission is willing to do at this time is to prohibit the use of 10-gauge guns on our public waterfowl hunting areas. The regulation is very simple. It reads as follows:

"Sub-section (k). Shotgun Limitations. No shot guns larger than 12-gauge shall be possessed or fired on any of said waterfowl shooting areas."

Since Mr. Wente had the material you sent him in July, I gave the President of our Commission, William J. Silva, my file copy to take along on the train to Washington in the hope that he might persuade the Federal authorities to handle both the too big and too small fire arms on a nation-wide basis. After he returned, he told me that they were unwilling to tackle it at this time. Therefore, the Commission decided to take care of the 10-gauge question only. This is probably the first instance in the whole country where a Commission has had courage enough to act in a matter which apparently frightened the Federal boys.

All the other information contained in yours of the 20th would be most amusing were it not for the fact that some of it is tragic. I just can't understand people serving on commissions who are inclined to be so selfish. Much as I hate to admit it, I think your size-up of the Washington situation is correct. Choking the limit down too small is just as dangerous as being too liberal.

I am returning John's letter of May 12 to you herewith.

Sincerely yours,

State manager

Seth Gordon
Director

Nash very much favored the elimination of the 10-gauge and .410-bore as legal waterfowl guns. Even though Federal law allowed the use of the 10 (and still does), Nash was instrumental in getting it banned in California because commission members there valued his opinion. The push for a ban on the use of the .410 was evidently dropped as a compromise. Nash felt that the small bore contributed to crippling losses, and the 10-gauge encouraged skybusting and overbagging, as well as crippling at extreme ranges. The reference in Nash's hand to "Olin's letter" probably meant that John Olin of Winchester-Western was kept apprised of the situation and was in agreement with Nash's position.

PART IV

AWARDS
&
RECOGNITION

Nash at his induction into the Field Trial Hall of Fame, 1963.

My Speech To The Field Trial Hall Of Fame, Upon Induction, 1963

Beholden as I am to so many thoughtful friends for my being here this evening, I welcome this opportunity to acknowledge the deep obligation. Would that the late Louis Bobbitt could be with us; although he is, I'm sure, in spirit. In memory I see Louie riding along ahead of the late Hobart Ames, Henry P. Davis, and me in 1934, up and down and across the sunlit sedges, weathered hills, and wintered dales of the National's course behind Sandy, his Sports Peerless. Louie's mellow calls reflected the moods of every moment: pride – hope – concern – confidence – encouragement – but always love and eternal vigilance. I see his Sports Peerless Pride, National Champion of 1939, whom I judged on chickens, sharptails and Huns in Saskatchewan, pheasants in New York state, and bobwhites here at Grand Junction. Yes, I'm sure Louie Bobbitt and his champions are with us tonight.

And there will be old Mike, too, the one and only Eugene's Ghost. And thank goodness his old boss is here, in person. I saw the Ghost in his finest hours of the shooting field and championship petitions. In my book he has always been the greatest of his breed to ever spoor an upland. Just as Luminary has always been the same to me among pointers. Mere opinion, of course, because, when you have seen and get to discussing great setters like Gladstone, Sioux, Pioneer, Citation, Beau Essig Don, and Mississippi Zev, to name a few, you are out on the thin ice of disagreement, a pertinent component of the field trial saga. But I'm sure we loved them all.

I am particularly grateful for having judged Fast Delivery in many of his races at the Continentals and Nationals. A truly great fellow who took the tough with the good and was a champion, every inch and pound of him. And I pay tribute here to the finest sportsmanship of his handler, Mr. Paul Walker. Standing here this evening, a curtain rolls up. The stage is Grand Junction at turn of the century – sixty-four years ago – when coal and even wood-burning engines hauled freight and passengers and bird dogs north, south, east, and west from the sagging old depot-hotel. The National was in its salad years and not as yet in a permanent home. We bird hunted on land the late Hobart Ames was yet to see and own. And we have heard his own story of how he came to locate here in the home built in 1847 by Mrs. Buckingham's great grandfather, the late John Wiley Jones.

The wonderful thing is that we are together tonight, in flesh and spirit, a still free people and ready to battle for it when the chips go down. We are here, too, to prosper the cause of American field trials, given us here, in this, the greatest of titular runnings, through the generosity of the late Hobart and Julia Colony Ames. Few states in the United have been so befriended. Let Tennessee and field trials keep their memories forever green. So, my friends, permit me and Mrs. Buckingham, who rode the old courses out from Rogers Springs and hunted on the lands of her forefathers with Mr. and Mrs. Ames, in thanking you again, pray that some of you – and more of yours – will gather here sixty-four years from tonight, with more birds and even better bird dogs than we judged – dogs whose bloodlines flow proudly back to every last National Field Trial Champion. God grant that you are still free and with the flags of field trials nailed to the mast. In saying goodnight, let me repeat and wish for you the thoughts of Moses as he turned back from Nebo and Pisgah and the Promised Land, "May the Eternal God Be Your Refuge, and Beneath You, the Everlasting Arms."

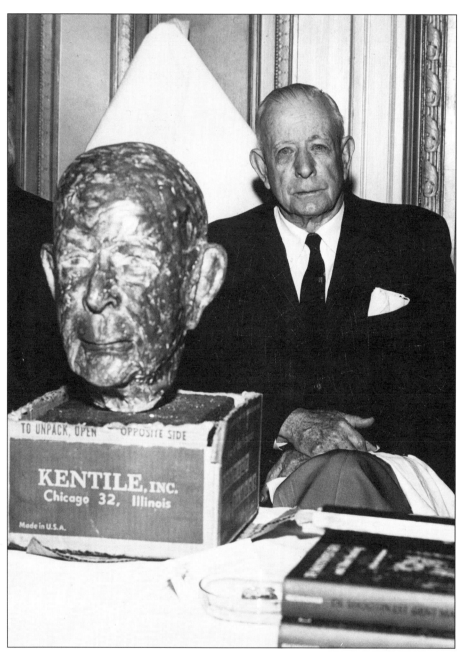

Nash Buckingham at the Greenhouse Party in his honor, November, 1961. Nash was honored on the release of his book De Shootinest Gent'man and Other Stories. *The Greenhouse was a popular column Nash contributed to in the* Memphis Commercial Appeal *newspaper.*

THE BEOWULF
OF THE BAYOU

"Richard Watson Owen gave this address on Sunday, November 12, 1961, upon release of the new edition of my De Shootinest Gent'man. *Mr. Owen and his brother own Beaver Dam and 14,000 acres, from their grandfather. A wonderful family. This was read at the Greenhouse Party at the Hotel Peabody in Memphis – 400 present."*

I n 1600, those lands lying between the Ohio and Mississippi Rivers were fabulous in their flora and fauna, and even a civilization which we today can scarcely comprehend. More specifically, in the language of Audubon, the Yonconnah Bottoms "teemed with the greatest abundance of wild game that I have ever encountered." This section by corruption we now call the Nonconnah, which begins just south of Memphis and ranges southward through Mississippi and even beyond the still uncharted wilds of the Vicksburg Bottoms.

As they occurred in history, we find that Marquette, LaSalle, and Joliet drifted downward on the breast of the Mississippi, but due to the boggy swamplands along her banks did not venture inland into this vastness to any appreciable degree. Until the intrepid DeSoto pressed back the cat claw briar and came in 1541, we have no detail as to the personality of this country. This was the land of the Indian: the Chickasaw, the Cherokee, the Tunica. From the chronicles of DeSoto, "the Governor," until the first waves of colonization came to this country, there is an unfortunate lapse in written history. As the timber cutter, the trapper, and the early farmers began to carve out an empire in this wilderness, there began the stories and legends which we must accept today in lieu of a more accurate written history.

Strangely enough, it was not until early 1900 that the spokesman for this wilderness should feel a compulsion to sink his taproots into this mellow earth, to call it his heritage and to dedicate his life into translating the spirit of this primeval into the captured romance of the written page. This man as you have rightly guessed was Nash Buckingham. He came here to Memphis with laurels still fresh from the athletic fields of the University of Tennessee.

Here begins, in my mind, the first paradox in the life of this man. With such a background, one might properly think that here should be another Grantland Rice, a Paul Gallico, another Bob Neyland; but somehow I know the Almighty intervened and a soft voice whispered and the legacy for generations still unborn was begun.

This was a big story, and a big man had to write it – big in stature, rugged in frame, keen-eyed, keen-scented, and more of the spirit than the flesh. Nash became permeated with all that nature offered and unto him all of her secrets were made known. He sunk his teeth deep into the flesh of a raw wilderness and what he tasted and saw and felt, he has written. He has captured with the rapier thrusts of his pen the wood smoke of a campfire, the smell of well-oiled boots, the sting of sleet in his face, the sweet scent of dust in the rain, the patter of fresh snow or, maybe, just the simple beauty of a wild rose by the roadside.

He was wedded to this country while they both were still young. The cry of the panther could still be heard in the bottoms, the black bear still slept in the cane. The stumps were still white behind the woodsman, the roots still bit at the plow in the new ground.

Here was a land of intrigue, of wonder, of promises unspoken, and among the first hunters to taste this virgin sweetness was Nash. He found his affinity along the sleepy banks of an oxbow lake called Beaver Dam. Here was to begin a lifetime of devotion and into these quiet waters he has dipped his pen to spin into history the enchantment of yesterday. Here he became a part of a group of sportsmen who called themselves the Beaver Dam Club. Most of these were Memphis men and each in his own right was a gentleman.

How many times have I wondered at the sights that met their eyes. I have seen through the pen of Mr. Nash and feel in a way that I was there. I have seen the dawn break. I have seen the fog lift her cool garments, I have seen the first rays of sunlight on the riot of waterfowl that covered the lake. Overhead the platoons of wild geese, and even wild swan, have hovered above the quiet waters, and between the tall cypress, the mallard has called. Here stood Mr. Nash as nerve raw to nature as salt to a wound and he has written as he has remembered and what he has written is his bequest to posterity. With seven-league boots he has followed nature as her pulse beat and as he held her, his fingers were kind. He has become a legend in his life-time and for this I think of him as the *Beowulf of the Bayou.*

Today as I talk to him, his eyes twinkle with stories still untold and as he chuckles and rubs his hands, I realize that he is more than just a man – he is a breed. He is a breed because he belongs more to the wild things he has loved than to us. And yet he belongs to us too because he has lived in the house by the side of the road. He is not bitter toward those who have destroyed the green forest, for from some depth in his soul he seems to understand. As much as he loved the sharp crack of his old "sky-buster," today he has a new love. Because he sees and fears for the future of the thin flights of ducks that come southward, he has dedicated himself to conservation. Only a man with seven-league boots could do this, but today he hunts with a camera. Years still unborn will add this to the even richer legends that belong to the *Beowulf of the Bayou*.

Nash with still another recognition. The plaque reads: "We the members of the Tennessee Outdoor Writers Association present this award as a symbol of lifetime membership to Nash Buckingham who has contributed so much by pioneering conservation publicity." Nash often jousted with and challenged his fellow writers in various organizations to be better journalists and watchdogs of the public trust where conservation matters were concerned.

REMINGTON ARMS COMPANY, INC.

MANUFACTURERS OF
SPORTING FIREARMS, AMMUNITION
TRAPS   TARGETS

ARMS WORKS, ILION, N.Y.
AMMUNITION WORKS, BRIDGEPORT, CONN.
BRIMSDOWN, MIDDLESEX, ENG.
CABLE—HARTLEY, BRIDGEPORT—ALL CODES

PETERS CARTRIDGE DIVISION
BRIDGEPORT, CONN.
TRAP AND TARGET WORKS
FINDLAY, OHIO

BRIDGEPORT 2, CONN.

October 30, 1947

Mr. E. F. Warner, Publisher
FIELD & STREAM
515 Madison Avenue
New York 22, New York

Dear Elt:

Here I go again butting in where I have no business but I am sure that our long-standing friendship will cause you to understand this letter.

For the past several years you have been awarding recognition to the individual who has made the most outstanding contribution to conservation during the year. These awards are, I know, highly appreciated and the recipient has every reason to feel extremely proud.

I don't know, of course, how the selection is made, whether or not you have a committee, or what the procedure is, and I may be offside offering any suggestion whatever. But I would like to call your attention to the work which our mutual friend, Nash Buckingham, has done in the last year as chairman of the Waterfowl Committee of the Outdoor Writers Association. I know that you are entirely familiar with the activities of that group and the effectiveness of its work.

As a former member of the Committee, I want to add that Buck has been the sparkplug all the way through on it, and in many instances has carried the ball alone through a sometimes rough and rugged field, this at a considerable sacrifice to his personal funds, as well as giving a great deal of his valuable time which could have otherwise been spent in profitable writing.

Personally, I know of no individual who has made as great a contribution to conservation as Nash has during the last year, to say nothing of the torch he has carried so valiantly in the past. Often times, his has been a "lone voice crying in the wilderness" but later events have proved that he has been right in practically every instance. Insofar as conservation thought is concerned, he has been, and still is, far ahead of the parade.

Recognition for Nash's part in saving a waterfowl resource. Henry P. Davis, Nash's lifelong friend, nominated Nash, and Field & Stream *agreed. Nash was honored on March 9, 1947. Without his help, the Mississippi Flyway population of Canada geese would have surely been decimated by overgunning at Horseshoe Lake.*

233

E. F. Warner   -2-   10/30/47

       I hope you will not deem me presumptuous in making this earnest suggestion -- that your committee give full consideration to his work of the past year. Your award will not only be a fitting tribute to the splendid accomplishments he has made in 1947, but would also be a just recognition of an illustrious career in game restoration which has extended for more than three decades.

       Again hoping you will accept this suggestion in the spirit in which it is offered, I am, with kindest regards

                             Cordially yours,

                             Henry P. Davis
HPD:JV   Public Relations Division

"FIELD and STREAM" HONORS NASH BUCKINGHAM

Eltinge F. Warner, through his well-known magazine "Field and Stream",
of which he is the publisher, honored our own Nash Buckingham at the
annual dinner of the International Wildlife Conference held in St. Louis
the evening of March 9 last.

Before the largest number of conservations from all over the Continent,
Nash was awarded the Field and Stream Trophy for "the Outstanding
Achievement in Conservation for the Year".

In the absence of Mr. Warner, who had been called to California on
important personal business, the award was made by Harold Titus, of the
Michigan Conservation Commission, who is the Conservation Editor of
the magazine.

The award according to Mr. Warner was given to Nash for his untiring
fight for decency in the ancient sport of wildfowling, which culminated
during the past year, when he as chairman of the OWAA Waterfowl Committee was instrumental in exposing the harrowing conditions existing
in the surrounding territory of the Horseshow Lake Canada goose preserve
in Southern Illinois.

Nash's fight led to the final closing of all of Alexander county in
Illenois to goose shooting and the dramatization of this event in the
press of the country has led to a quickening of interest in all enforcement problems connected with wildfowling.

Nash richly deserved the honor and through him the OWAA itself can feel
satisfaction in the knowledge that his and its work has not been in vain.

It is nice to know that once again it is demonstrated that a man is not
without honor even among his own people, friends and fellow crusaders.

                                                    --J.H.B.

SPORTSMAN'S
HALL
OF
FAME

October 24, 1969

Mr. Nash Buckingham
198 S. McLean Avenue
Memphis, Tennessee   38104

Dear Mr. Buck:

At the OWAA Convention in Deluth, Minnesota last June, much
informal discussion was had about forming a non profit organization called "Sportsman's Hall of Fame."

The purpose of the Foundation would be to honor the outstanding sportsman in the various fields of outdoor sports, including the field of conservation.

Members will be nominated by members of the board of directors
and, after proper investigation, they will be voted into "The
Sportsman's Hall of Fame," and with proper ceremony they will
be inducted into the organization. Publicity will be given to
their local newspaper and they will be the recipients of a
handsome wall plaque, a bronze lapel button and an attractive
jacket patch.

After receiving this honor, the new member of the "Sportsman's
Hall of Fame" will be given the opportunity to make a contribution to the Foundation. The suggested endowment, which is
tax deductible, will be in the amount of $100.00 and up
depending on the wishes of the donor. This money will go
into the Foundation and will be used to finance the business
of the Foundation and to promote conservation projects recommended by the board of directors.

I have been asked to serve as Executive Director in order to
get the legal status of the Foundation established and I am
most anxious for you to be the first charter member of "The
Sportsman's Hall of Fame" and to serve as Honorary Chairman
of the board of directors. I have already deposited a check
in the amount of $250.00 as your endowment of the Foundation.
All I want you to do is to say that you will accept.

You are the first person I have written because I felt that
your presence on the board of directors would give the

*One of the last honors Nash received was induction into the Sportsman's Hall of Fame
as its Charter Member. So that there would be no basis for refusal of this honor, voted
by members of the Outdoor Writers Association of America, Fred J. Moses, Jr., the
Hall's executive director, deposited the endowment all inductees were asked to make.*

SPORTSMAN'S
HALL
OF
FAME

Mr. Nash Buckingham
Page 2
October 24, 1969

Foundation a great deal of prestige. I assure you that your
fellow directors will be men of high caliber in the outdoor
field and I am sure you will personally know most of them.

Please do us the honor of accepting.

Yours sincerely,

Fred J. Moses Jr.

Fred J. Moses, Jr.

FJMjr:s

P.S.   Erma tells me that Mrs. Buckingham is doing poorly.
I know it keeps you confined. I'll think of you these beautiful October days along the trout streams and as the
streaking doves race into the cut corn, kicking their rudders
around and making impossible targets.

198 S McLean Memphis Tenn 38104
October 27th '69

Mr. Fred Moses,
Sportsman's Hall of Fame
4602 Kingston Pike
Knoxville, Tennessee 37919

Dear Fred-:,
        Thanks for the very great Honor extended me re the
Sportsman's Hall of Fame.Do I understand this is a subsidiary of
OWAA,or a separate NATIONAL entity? At any rate,I'm convinced that
unless some sportsmen's ORGANIZATION arises in this country to face
the impending downfall of not only wildfowling,but the spirit of decency afield and enforcement judicially reestablished both State and
Federal,the end is definitely in sight.I would be unfaithful to the
trusts left me by such dear friends and coworkers as the lates E. Sydney
Stephens of Missouri,J.N. 'Ding' Darling,Harold Sheldon,and many another who labored in the vineyard.Last year,I became Honorary President of
Wetlands for Wildlife,the 9 year old organization that has worked desperately to salvage the being-wrecked wildfowl producing of our northern US
belt.My old friend, Ben Boalt,President of the group,nationally knownre-
triever figure,for whom I used to judge,asked me to help and now the battle rages anew,but is being won.Go ahead with your plans and if my help
will salvage even a setting of mallard eggs,I'll be glad to try.My Irma
is not well;we hope to be in Knoxville ere long to make our home there.
        With every appreciation for your kindness,

                        Nash Buckingham

Nash's acceptance note for induction into the Sportsman's Hall of Fame.

FEBRUARY, 1963
50 CENTS

Nash Buckingham Receives Honors

1962 OUTDOORSMAN OF THE YEAR AWARD

LONG BEACH, TUCSON SHOOTS

OFFICIAL A.T.A. MAGAZINE

The February, 1963 issue of Trap & Field *magazine that carried a story about Nash's Outdoorsman of the Year Award, and a further honor. The cover photograph information says: "Nash Buckingham, noted author and conservationist, was honored recently by a trapshooter who has admired his writings and accomplishments for years. Lyman McLallen III, (standing right) presented Buckingham with a complete set of duck stamps the government has issued since 1934. Mrs. Irma Buckingham is seated on the left."*

Outdoorsman
Of The Year

Press Release from Olin recounting the Winchester-Western Outdoorsman of the Year Banquet January 18, 1963. Nash regarded this as his highest honor and the "getting-off place" in his conservation battle.

The 1962 Outdoorsman of the Year Award was presented to Nash Buckingham, the "grand old man of American conservation," during the Fourth Annual Winchester-Western Seminar on Firearms and Ammunition Development, Alton, Illinois.

Mr. Buckingham, a resident of Memphis, Tennessee, who has spent most of his 82 years at the forefront of the nation's major conservation battles, was honored at a special banquet on January 18 at the Lockhaven Country Club attended by some of the country's leading conservationists, game management specialists and outdoor writers.

In addition to his award scroll, Mr. Buckingham was presented with a custom-made Winchester Model 21 shotgun with an inscription designating the recipient and the occasion of the award.

Colonel Forrest V. Durrand, Director of the Tennessee Game and Fish Commission and Dru Pippin, Commissioner, Missouri Conservation Commission, were among those honoring Mr. Buckingham.

The Outdoorsman of the Year is selected by a national poll of some 4,000 outdoor writers and conservationists, and the award is donated by the Winchester-Western Division, Olin Mathieson Chemical Corporation. Former recipients include General Curtis LeMay, the late Dr. Logan Bennett, Walter Alston and Robert Taylor.

In making the 1962 award, John M. Olin, Chairman of the Executive Committee, Olin Mathieson Chemical Corporation, stated that Mr. Buckingham's entire life has been an example for the nation's conservationists and sportsmen. He said Olin was particularly pleased with this year's award because Mr. Buckingham had been the company's first Director of Game

Restoration back in 1925. Mr. Buckingham held this position with the old Western Cartridge Company for three years.

An outstanding contributor of articles and stories on outdoor subjects to national magazines, Nash Buckingham was one of the founders of the Outdoor Writers Association of America and has received their coveted "Jade of Chiefs" award. In 1928, he helped found the American Wildfowlers, a foundation devoted to the study of waterfowl conditions in this country and Canada, subsequently absorbed by More Game Birds in America, and later to become Ducks Unlimited.

Mr. Buckingham, a lifelong hunter and conservationist, was the first individual to receive the *Field & Stream* trophy for "outstanding service to conservation" in 1947. At that time the magazine noted Nash Buckingham was "one of America's greatest shots, one of its foremost field trial judges."

A graduate of Harvard, Mr. Buckingham was later an all-round athlete at the University of Tennessee where he took his degree in law. He earned varsity letters in baseball and early professional football. His athletic background was put to good use when he became a sportswriter for the *Memphis Commercial Appeal.*

Mr. Buckingham is the author of many books on hunting, fishing and the outdoors. His latest, *De Shootinest Gent'man*, was published recently by Thomas Nelson & Sons.

The annual Winchester-Western Seminar on Firearms and Ammunition Development is attended by the firearms editors of national magazines. Among those present for Mr. Buckingham's award were: Jack O'Connor, *Outdoor Life*; Warren Page, *Field & Stream*; Pete Brown, *Sports Afield*; Pete Kuhlhoff, *Argosy*; Bert Darga, *True*; John Amber, *Gun Digest*; Elmer Keith and Tom Siatos, *Guns & Ammo*; Milton Shapiro, *GUNsport*; Larry Koller, *Guns & Hunting*; Ted Hecht, *Guns & Game*; Duncan Barnes, *Sports Illustrated*; Sid Latham, *Popular Science*; Jack Lewis, *Gun World*; Bev Mann, *Guns*; and Dave Wolfe, *Shooting Times.*

GUESTS

COLONEL FORREST DURAND
Director of the Tennessee Game and Fish Commission

WILLIAM LODGE
Director of the Illinois Conservation Department

WILLIAM TOWELL
Director of the Missouri Conservation Commission

JOHN AMBER — *Editor,* Gun Digest
DUNCAN BARNES — *Outdoor Reporter,* Sports Illustrated
HAROLD BRAND — *Outdoor Editor,* Alton Evening Telegraph
PETE BROWN — *Arms Editor,* Sports Afield
GEORGE CARSON — *Outdoor Editor,* St. Louis Globe-Democrat
BERT DARGA — *Associate Editor,* True
TED HECHT — *Editor,* Guns & Game
JAMES KEARNES — *Outdoor Editor,* St. Louis Post-Dispatch
ELMER KEITH — *Shooting Editor,* Guns & Ammo
LARRY KOLLER — *Supervising Editor,* Guns & Hunting
PETE KUHLHOFF — *Gun Editor,* Argosy
SID LATHAM — *Gun Consultant,* Popular Science
JACK LEWIS — *Publisher and Editorial Director,* Gun World
BEV MANN — *Editor,* Guns
WERNER NAGEL — *Missouri Conservation Commission*
JACK O'CONNOR — *Shooting Editor,* Outdoor Life
WARREN PAGE — *Shooting Editor,* Field & Stream
DRU PIPPIN — *Missouri Conservation Commission*
MILT SHAPIRO — *Editor,* GUNsport
TOM SIATOS — *Editor,* Guns & Ammo
DAVE WOLFE — *Executive Director,* Shooting Times

PRESENTATION

and

BANQUET

in honor of the

OUTDOORSMAN OF THE YEAR

1962

———

Given by

the

WINCHESTER-WESTERN DIVISION

OLIN MATHIESON CHEMICAL CORPORATION

During the

Fourth Annual Seminar on Firearms

and Ammunition Development

LOCKHAVEN COUNTRY CLUB, ALTON, ILLINOIS

JANUARY 18, 1963

PROGRAM

Toastmaster:
WILLIAM R. KELTY, JR.
Vice President for Marketing, Winchester-Western Division
Olin Mathieson Chemical Corporation

Presentation of 1962 Outdoorsman of the Year Award:
JOHN M. OLIN
Chairman, Executive Committee
Olin Mathieson Chemical Corporation

1962 Outdoorsman of the Year:
NASH BUCKINGHAM

An Appreciation:
RUSSELL R. CASTEEL
Vice President — East Alton
Olin Mathieson Chemical Corporation

Introduction of Special Guest:
EDWARD L. KOZICKY
Director of Conservation
Olin Mathieson Chemical Corporation

Special Guest:
FRANK P. BRIGGS
Assistant Secretary of the Interior

Speaker:
LOWELL E. KRIEG
Vice President and General Manager
Winchester-Western Division
Olin Mathieson Chemical Corporation

MENU

Hors D'Oeuvres

☙

Shrimp Cocktail Supreme

☙

Caesar Salad

☙

Broiled Sirloin Steak, Sauce Bordelaise

☙

Grilled Mushrooms

☙

New Green Asparagus Spears, Hollandaise Sauce

☙

Oven Browned Potatoes

☙

Lemon Ice with Creme de Menthe

☙

Cake

☙

Coffee

The program from the 1962 Outdoorsman of the Year dinner and award presentation, including the list of speakers and invited dignitaries. Nash always considered this his highest achievement: recognition by the industry for his contributions to conservation.

The presentation of the scroll and gun as Outdoorsman of the Year for 1962 at the banquet honoring Nash January 18, 1963. The gun, held by Jim Rikhoff, Winchester's Director of Public Relations, is the famous Model 21 "Award Gun." The presentation of the gun and scroll was made by John M. Olin.

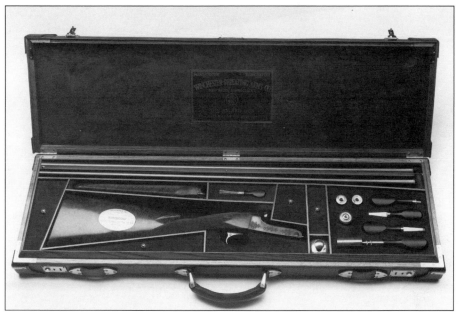

The "Award Gun." Now owned by Mr. William R. Ireland of Birmingham, Alabama (photos courtesy of Mr. Hal Hamilton).

OUTDOORSMAN OF THE YEAR
TRIBUTE BY FRANK P. BRIGGS
Asst. Secty. Fish & Wildlife Service
Dept. of the Interior

Ordinarily when one is called upon to make a speech, a definite subject is assigned to him – by that I mean a limiting subject – and he is told to stay pretty well within the bounds in presenting the subject matter before any group.

When Ed Kozicky asked me to be here tonight to express, on behalf of the Fish & Wildlife Service, our appreciation and our regards for the guest of honor, he merely said to say a few words – and may I emphasize, he said, "*Say a few words.*" I have searched through various publications we have at Washington to find just what I thought would be appropriate to say on this occasion.

The search revealed that instead of there being a dearth of material, there is really a wealth of material that one could weave into a speech, giving the guest of honor some of the acclaim he so readily deserves.

For instance, I found that I could spend much time, if I were of such a mind, discussing his athletic abilities – he was an athlete of the finest sort – being a four-letter man – an all-Southern on the University of Tennessee Vols – a professional baseball player – an AAU of America boxing champion. Our guest of honor proved his athletic ability and his competitive spirit early in his life.

If I were of such a mind I could make quite a speech telling of his work in national field trials where he has officiated at so many conservation and -hunting events where true sportsmen meet to exchange ideas – to watch favorite dogs – to talk guns – to talk hunting – to do all of those things so familiar to you.

And then I found that Nash Buckingham, early in his life, found out that to be one of the top men in 1963 he must attend Harvard – this he did!

Of course, being a newspaperman, I was more than intrigued with his ability to use the English language to express true situations, to point out pictures for everyone to see where certain conservation programs were meeting with resistance, or where wildlife was losing a battle, just where wildlife needed help – he is a newspaper writer – an editor of no mean renown!

He wrote for and he edited many magazines – he has authored many of our best books on wildlife and out-of-doors.

Anyone could talk for many hours about our guest of honor's writing ability, about the things he has written about, about the accomplishments his writing has brought – I can even talk about his record in business, pointing out to you how he managed his own sporting goods store and he has filled many positions of trust with the Western Cartridge Company.

I could spend an hour discussing the awards he has received for his merit in writing and for his activities in conservation, telling you, of course, that he is the recipient of the Jade of Chiefs award, *The Field & Stream* trophy, and many, many others. I could talk longer and longer upon his love of hunting, his keen shooting eye, his knowledge of guns that led to the development of the magnum gun and the magnum ammunition.

I might relate to you a story that I was told about Nash Buckingham entering a blind early one morning, firing seventeen shots and coming out with fifteen ducks – that, in my book, is good shooting, but I understand that Nash was very disturbed because he had missed two shots.

I could tell you how he worked long and hard to bring about a regulation limiting to three shells the number any gun could carry when in use for waterfowl hunting.

Our annals at Washington are fairly well filled with writings of Nash Buckingham. Many, many of them critical indeed of some of the actions taken by this administration and by previous administrations in carrying out laws and setting up of regulations.

Mr. Buckingham has been consistent throughout the years in insisting that any shooting excess or any illegal slaughter must be stopped and the offenders must be summarily punished.

I think that I might bring to you two quotations which I found in studying the life of Nash Buckingham – one of them from Henry Davis, whom most of you know, a former public relations director for Remington Arms, and I quote, "Nash is the finest field shot I ever knew."

And then "Ding" Darling, a man with whom Nash Buckingham worked long and faithfully, had this to say, "A great sportsman and with all a writer of classic distinction, Nash Buckingham stands with the great torchbearers in the history of conservation in the United States of America."

Most of us well realize that in presenting this Outdoorsman-of-the-Year tonight I am speaking of a man who has held that position in the hearts of sportsmen everywhere for more decades than most of us here have been associated with conservation and outdoor sports.

Nash Buckingham was born 82 years ago at a time when much of our country still had almost the original abundance of many wildlife species. This was especially true of waterfowl in the wintering grounds of the lower Mississippi. Mr. Buckingham grew up in the midst of this abundance, beginning his hunting career when he was first large enough to carry a gun. Though he has hunted almost every species of American game in almost every part of the country, waterfowl hunting and waterfowl have always remained his first love.

Furthermore, when their numbers began to dwindle before the early, almost uncontrolled slaughter of lesser men and by the destruction of habitat from land use, he demonstrated his concern by becoming one of the first and foremost effective fighters for waterfowl preservation this country has every known.

His was one of the first minds to conceive the Federal Migratory Bird Stamp. You know the sale of this stamp has brought in sadly needed funds and has been practically the only method we have had to build waterfowl research and provide for waterfowl management.

He spearheaded many of the hunting regulations needed to restrict the excessive kill of species needing protection.

To the public at large, Nash is probably best known as a writer of outdoor tales of fact and fancy which have delighted readers since he first began writing for outdoor magazines early in the 1900's. Since then he has written countless articles and stories and several unique books which have given him an enviable reputation among the writers of the great outdoors.

Nash knew the value of an informed and active outdoor press and was one of the founders of the Outdoor Writers Association of America, an organization which is comprised of most of the great names in outdoor writing, and is today one of the largest writers' organizations in the country. In recognition of his status both as a writer and as a conservationist, Outdoor Writers Association of America accorded him a life membership, and in 1960 they gave him their top award – The Jade of Chiefs Award for distinguished service to conservation.

All of these things have been very important, but the thing, Mr. Chairman, the one thing that really motivated me to come to Alton tonight to speak for the Fish & Wildlife Service in appraisal of this good man was the fact that back in 1936 when a small, but determined, group of Missouri sportsmen under the leadership of the late E. Sydney Stephens wished to put the State's wildlife administration on a sound effective basis, they sought the services of Nash Buckingham to plan and organize the course of action. As you know, he planned well.

Missouri electors were so thoroughly electrified by the campaign to pass this constitutional amendment that they turned out en masse to vote for it and they have consistently, through the twenty-seven intervening years, beaten down all attempts to change the amendment – yes, any word of it.

The Missouri Conservation Commission established thereunder has become the model of game, fish, and forest commissions.

Personally, I would have never been called to Washington on this job I am now trying to fill had it not been for the high reputation the Missouri Conservation Commission established. And the Missouri Conservation Commission probably would not have been in existence had it not been for the learned hand of Nash Buckingham in its initial planning stage.

So, I have a personal reason for being here tonight. The name of Nash Buckingham will be enshrined in the hearts of Missouri sportsmen and conservationists as long as the memory of that great pioneering movement may endure.

I speak not only for the Fish & Wildlife Service here tonight, but I speak for the sportsmen of my native state when I say that I welcome the opportunity to accord to Nash Buckingham this honor which is being accorded.

PRESENTATION OF 1962
OUTDOORSMAN OF THE YEAR AWARD
TO NASH BUCKINGHAM
BY LOWELL E. KRIEG
Vice-President and General Manager, Winchester-Western,
Olin Mathieson Chemical Corporation, January 18, 1963,
Lockhaven Country Club, Alton, Illinois

Secretary Briggs; Directors Durand, Lodge, and Towell; distinguished guests... May I extend both Winchester's official and my personal appreciation for your attendance at this final banquet of the Fourth Annual Winchester-Western Seminar on Firearms and Ammunition Development.

As I look about me, I wonder if there were ever before so many leaders in the shooting sports gathered together for one occasion? While the number of persons is relatively small, the quality is first rate – And this is as it should be for this particular banquet because we have a singular honor tonight.

As I am sure most of you know by now, we are going to make the presentation of the 1962 Outdoorsman of the Year Award to a certain distinguished young gentleman who – according to custom – will remain nameless for a few more paragraphs!

Gentlemen, as you know, I am a relative newcomer in the sporting firearms world. When I was told the results of this year's balloting by the outdoor press, I requested a full biography of the winner. I took it home with me one night and after the house had quieted down – I have six children – I took out what the staff had prepared on this gentleman the nation's outdoor writers considered so important.

Frankly, I was stunned. It seemed as if I was reading the accomplishments of a combination Frank Merriwell, Tom Swift, Dan'l Boone, Jim Bridger, Johnny Appleseed, Zane Gray, Robert Service, Gentleman Jim Jeffries, Jim Thorpe, and maybe even a little of Robert E. Lee! How could one man cover so much territory, do so much and still find time to turn out a series of books which now are considered classics in their field? I still don't know the answer. If I find out, you can rest assured the formula will be liberally applied in New Haven.

Nash Buckingham.

The name even sounds like the man. Distinguished, literate, courtly – a gentleman-sportsman representative of the very best in the world of sports, conservation, and the outdoors in general.

Let me recount some of his accomplishments. Born on May 31, 1880 in Memphis – and, incidentally, still resident there with Mrs. Buckingham – and graduated from Harvard, Class of 1902, and the University of Tennessee Law School, Nash Buckingham was a four-letter man in football, baseball, track, and boxing. He is the oldest living captain of a University of Tennessee football team.

After graduation, he became a sports reporter for the *Memphis Commercial Appeal*, but somehow found time to become the Southern Amateur Heavyweight Boxing Champion in 1910 at New Orleans. He held the title for five years and had a berth for the Olympics until boxing was cancelled from that year's program. He also played semi-pro football and pro baseball with the old South Atlantic league. By the way, he also found time to get married to Miss Irma Jones In 1910.

Nash never gave up his first love in sports, though; from his earliest days on the old Beaver Dam Lake near Tunica, Mississippi and the

Wapanoca Club in Arkansas, Nash Buckingham was a hunter first, last, and always. Perhaps I should say a conservationist-hunter, because his love of duck hunting soon turned to a dedicated, lifelong concern for migratory waterfowl. As he watched the hunting excesses and depletion of our ducks and other waterfowl, his interest forged him into a militant conservationist.

He had moved West and bought a ranch soon after his marriage. It was on this ranch – ninety miles by horseback to the nearest doctor – that he began his career as an outdoor writer, and many of these early stories were pointed toward the saving of game as well as shooting. His wanderlust took him to the big game trails of Alaska and he became a horse wrangler and guide for dude outfits until World War I brought him back home to become a sergeant in Company I, First Tennessee Infantry. After the war, Nash returned to become a companion of the shanty boatmen of the Mississippi and to begin his career as one of the country's foremost field trial judges.

I am particularly proud to list the next step in Nash Buckingham's career. In 1925, the old Western Cartridge Company – now part of Olin's Winchester-Western Division – created the first conservation game management job in industry. Nash Buckingham was named Director of Game Restoration and was based right here in Alton, Illinois. It was to our everlasting benefit that he stayed three years before he left to become the Executive Secretary of the American Wildfowlers in Washington, D.C. I might add that – in spite of being employed by a company whose business was the sale of shotgun shells – he led the fight for Federal regulations to limit the capacity of semi-automatic and repeating shotguns to three shells when used in the hunting of migratory waterfowl. As some conservationists have pointed out, this single act might be one of the greatest boons in the preservation of our migratory ducks and geese.

As a researcher for the U. S. Department of Interior; as Executive Secretary of the American Wildfowlers Association – subsequently absorbed by More Game Birds for America and later to become Ducks Unlimited; as Waterfowl Examiner for the U. S. Biological Survey; as Director of the American Wildlife Institute; as Field Director of Ducks Unlimited; as a founder of the Outdoor Writers Association of America, Nash Buckingham has preached the gospel of game restoration and conservation from one end of the country to the other.

He has never backed off from a fight in the protection of our wildlife heritage, and he has been a conscience to our selfish interests –

be they industrial abuses or simple game hogs. Much of the credit for the preservation and restoration of wildfowl nesting grounds in the United States and Canada surely belongs to him. He certainly has been responsible for a good part of the reorganization of various state game departments and the passage of Federal laws limiting bag limits and seasons for migratory waterfowl. He was at the forefront of the fight for the Federal Duck Stamp to provide additional funds for the acquisition of wetlands.

There is no end to his accomplishments, and I for one hope that there will be no end for many years to come. I do not believe that America can afford to lose its Nash Buckinghams. We need their pens, their spirit of principle and no compromise and, mostly, we need their example. They are our consciences. They keep us all in line – and, I think that is as it should be.

Nash Buckingham – scholar, sportsman, horse-wrangler, conservationist, hunter, boxer, great athlete, teller-of-tales of the outdoors…and gentleman …will you please step forward to receive the 1962 Winchester Outdoorsman of the Year Award.

Please let me read this inscription: "Winchester…in behalf of the Nation's Outdoor Writers herewith names Nash Buckingham Outdoorsman of the Year 1962 as the man who through his prominence and personal example has done most to increase interest in our American heritage of good marksmanship and sportsmanship in the field."

Congratulations. And as a token of our respect and so that your honor will ever be present to all witnesses in the field, we are greatly pleased to present you with this custom-made presentation Winchester Model 21 shotgun with suitable inscription designating the recipient and the occasion of this award.

My address to the assemblage gathered for the banquet honoring me as the 1962 Winchester-Western Outdoorsman of the Year

Mr. Olin, Mr. Krieg, Mr. Kelty, Mr. Casteel, Colonel Durand, Dr. Kozicky – honored guests of Olin Mathieson Winchester-Western Seminar.

Having recovered somewhat from a state of shock since notification of my award as Winchester's Outdoorsman of the Year, my major obligation is, with a very low bow, to give thanks to each and every one of those writing men and women who have made this such an unforgettable evening for an octogenarian gun addict on the far slope.

I am proud to meet on equal footage, yardage, and eyesight the second generation of our nation's firearms and ballistic writers whose work is still a delight to me. Many of you have blazed trails into the strange lands that I shall never see – save on the map. And I sorrow that I cannot see at this board those splendid gentlemen with whose typewriters and by whose campfires I shared the salt – Townie Whelen, E. C. Crossman, Paul Curtis, and the incomparable Hal Sheldon. I give you true thanks and a firm handclasp, too, for myself, and proudly on behalf of my honorable ancestors.

Somehow, I seem to have grown up with Winchester. I recall, as a tot, with my older brother and younger sister, having our footprints drawn on paper and sent to a gentleman who had charge of a Sioux Indian reservation and we were sent beaded moccasins made by the womenfolk of chiefs Gaul and Rain-In-The-Face of Custer's Last Stand fame. His name was Irby Bennett and when, grown up a bit, I met him, he was district manager, in Memphis, Tennessee, our home, for the great Winchester Repeating Arms Company and a shooting companion of my Dad.

Mr. Bennett gave me an 1890 Model, lever action twelve-bore that same year and my first solo duck hunts at the famous old Beaver Dam and Wapanoca clubs in Mississippi and Arkansas were with that stalwart old piece. My first ducks, geese, and swans fell to its hand-loaded charges.

As a school exam prize, Mr. Bennett offered the first Model 1893 pump Winchester to reach the State of Tennessee. My older brother, Miles, a better wildfowl and upland game shot than most of his elders, won it. But with that loving generosity that was to mark his life, he gave it to me. I whittled off its half pistol-grip with my jackknife and had an old German gunsmith lay a solid steel rib down its solid-frame tube. Undoubtedly, it was the first ribbed Winchester shotgun in existence – and I have it yet. My nephew was raised on it.

Then came the old .44-40 rifle, numerous "twenty-twos," and a Model

Nash addressing the dinner company after the presentation. John Olin is on Nash's left, and Dru Pippen from Missouri is on his right.

254

1895 box magazine .30-06 shooting the two-twenty grain rimmed Krag cartridge. That Winchester traveled with me for years, from Eastern moose-bogs to Western sheep country under the peaks. In the early '20's I gave the old Winchester to the late Blair Lowrance for use on his plantation along Horseshoe Lake, Arkansas. In recent years Blair's retired Army kinsman, Major Carlos U. Lowrance, visiting the plantation, still gets his buck with the old Winchester.

From about 1907 came years on the trap shooting circuit. I had, as a youth, watched open-mouthed and wide-eyed, the shooting greats – Buffalo Bill, Annie Oakley, Brewer, Dr. Carver, J. A. R. Elliot, and flyer and target greats. In my earliest trap shooting period, I achieved a wonderful friendship with the late Captain Harold Money, the young Englishman who came over with his father and won fame as winner of the Cartaret Live Bird Handicap. He became one of Western's first salesmen, when as the late Mr. F. W. Olin used to express it, "We had a couple of loading machines in a cornfield at East Alton."

Young Money had a flair for taming all sorts of moles, mice, and reptiles. One day he turned loose a tiny snake in the sales office and so frightened the girls that Mr. "F. W." sacked him. He transferred to Winchester and stardom. It was Harold Money who became the titlist of my book, *De Shootinest Gent'man*.

After World War I, I entered the jobbing, wholesale, and retail sporting goods field and again Mr. Irby Bennett, now highly placed with Winchester, re-enters the picture. Our firm merchandised carloads of the major lines. Eventually, Western predominated because of Super-X. But Mr. Bennett could not go along with Winchester's expansion program, and, after mature deliberation, he resigned and became a vice-president of the Western Cartridge Company. All too soon thereafter he passed on, beloved and respected by all who knew him.

During my sporting goods days of the early '20's, in addition to the advent of Super-X and Xpert, I also witnessed and tested magnum three-inch loads of copper-coated shot shot in over-bored shotguns. Along there, too, I became obsessed with the conclusion that the arms and ammunition industry had better begin giving some attention to the management, propagation, and preservation of waterfowl and upland game bird populations, or else. Even then, they were under too heavy an attack. I began writing "pieces" along such lines in the *Sporting Goods Dealer* magazine of whose national sporting goods board I was a member.

A young executive of the Western Cartridge Company, of East Alton, Illinois – John Olin – this gentleman siting beside me – began reading them.

In June of 1925 I became Director of Western's Department of Game Restoration – the first of its kind in the industry. That word "restoration" has covered a lot of mileage – and still has a long track ahead of it.

But, thanks again to John Olin, it fell into association with the word "biology." John Olin once said to me: "We'll never get anywhere with this problem until we strap it down by science and operate on it like a guinea pig." How right he has been – and how hard he has pushed. On December 21, 1931, the Olins acquired the Winchester Repeating Arms Company. Industry makes strange bedfellows but chickens still come home to roost.

Now, gentlemen, as to this chaste firearms award which John Olin has handed me, my position is reminiscent of a story told me one morning in an Arkansas duckblind by ex-Governor Lloyd Stark of Missouri. He said: "During my first campaign, a bearded old squirrel-turner in a backwoods, sequestered Ozark county took a liking to me, campaigned hard, and carried the county for me, too. He said, 'Lloyd, I went to the bridge with ye, we made it, and I oughta git sumpn' pretty nice.' 'Right you are,' said I, 'What's on your mind?' He said, 'How about my becomin' your Commissioner of Taxation and Banking?' Startled, I stammered, 'Well, Ed, I wasn't thinking exactly along such lines – you are still a good hunter and a fine shot – now it may surprise hell out of you, Ed, but I had you in mind for Head Guard at the Missouri State Penitentiary.' And Ed said, 'Well, Lloyd, it may surprise hell out of *you*, but I'll take it.'"

Yes, gentlemen, you see some oddities in men and guns as you mush the trails of the Red Gods. There was the day the late Windsor White, of Cleveland, Ohio and I were quail shooting on the late Hundley May's plantation, next door to the Ames Plantation where we helped judge the National Field Trial Champion Stake for so many years. We took rain-refuge in a Negro tenant's home and hanging over his cavernous brick fireplace was an old double-barreled hammer gun. Something odd about it attracted my attention, so I took it down. The right tube was 32 inches, with its inner lining intact; the left only 26 inches.

I said to the tenant, "Do you still shoot it this way?" "Oh, yes suh," he replied. "I calls it 'Ol Nub. I shoots d' long shots with th' right barl' an' d' short ones with th' lef'." When the rain stopped, I fired a quail load across the smooth mud-surface around the well – and you couldn't have flown a gnat through the pattern. Maybe the gun industry has missed a bet.

In the Houston Bottoms now covered by the waters of Sardis Lake, Mississippi, I met a grizzled squirrel hunter and his dog. He carried a 32-inch solid-frame Model 1897 Winchester pump gun. Its slightly discolored muzzle attracted my attention, and I discovered that he had rechoked it, as he put it, to kill squirrels from the highest trees in the bottoms. He had done it by heating the muzzle red-hot for about three inches and then tapping it to somewhere between a 16 and 20-bore. That one stopped me, but as he had six squirrels and two big swamp rabbits, I was in no position to become either critic or analyst.

So gentlemen, tramps the marching song of powder, lead, and steel – and let us be proud of the company we have kept as it passes in review. In memory I seem to hear the magnificent basso of Eugene Cowles singing his "Armorers Song" – wasn't it from "Robin Hood?"

> The sword is a weapon to conquer worlds
> I honor the man who shakes it
> But what is he, or can he be
> Compared to the man who makes it –
> Let the Hammer on the anvil go Clang – Clang – Clang

And because – for when may this company meet again? – we are of, by, and for the gunmakers, let us stick with them from the first to bore Kaintuck, Decherd, or Hawken – to the last rifle built in defense of this dear land. Beat back the bills that leave homes defenseless. Vote away the importations of junk surplus. For when the chips go down it is to the gunmakers that our people turn and they and only they can let the hammer on the anvil go clang, clang, clang.

And so, in very truth, gentlemen, as I accept this beautiful weapon, I see it through the eyes of a lad of ten and his 1890 lever-action Winchester and in deepest gratitude I give you back the years. Years now brinked with crisis but companioned by adage. First – "what is, is." Next – "today to me, tomorrow to thee." And, when we begin taking ourselves a bit too seriously, harken to the ancient Sage of Cathay who wrote upon his rice paper: "No man hath all the knowledge – even a monkey falls out of a tree."

But I am reminded here of lines from my old fraternity's initiation ritual when we neophytes left the presences of our peers – "And now, kind sirs, the hour waxeth late and I would fain hasten onward toward Mount Minerva." But for the sake of my little great-grandson, let me leave you with this thought:

Let us all look forward, prayerfully, to that day when the hands of comprehension and reason will knock at the doors of our brains and a Voice will cry out: "Get up – the dawn of a better understanding is breaking." Soon the sunrise will pinken vast rolling sea wastes across which Irish and Celts and Vikings drove their bull-hided, idol-headed, striped-sailed rowboats to plant civilizations still unknown from Mexico to Labrador. It will, that sunrise, bless the spirits that are Jamestown's, lave the barnacles of fabled Plymouth Rock, creep through the still narrow streets of Olde Boston Towne, whiten the massive shaft of Bunker Hill, and cross that bridge at Concord.

It will suffuse the Eastern ranges and come to stand with averted eyes beside the frozen horrors of Valley Forge – only to lunge forward to Cowpens, Monmouth, King's Mountain, and the glorious victory at Yorktown. It will kneel with bowed head beside the dust-to-dust and ashes-to-ashes of Gettysburg and Appomattox, on and on to the Wilderness, Cold Harbor, Sharpsburg, Harper's Ferry, Fredericksburg, Stone's River, Missionary Ridge, Chickamauga, Franklin, Atlanta, Donelson, and Shiloh – that gory vortex of human emotions that by the will of God helped regain a nation's poise.

It will mantle the Blue Ridge, the Cumberland, and Smoky Mountains, peering down into sequestered gulches where little feet and lunch baskets still climb to country schools with cracked bells calling to these havens the "heel and blood that will never perish." With resplendent reflection it will enhance the pallid cotton fields of Dixie's domain, cross "Ole Miss," and bring the 'morrow to the lowing herds of the nation's beeflands. It will embrown the tasseled silk of the tall corn and enrich the tawny, tossing seas of wheat in whose golden hearts (so sing the poets) lie health and wealth and strength for all the nation.

It will sweep and cross the Great Plains, penetrating phantom dust clouds from the thundering herds of bison and wild horses – roaming prairie and Badlands under the Indians who owned the land in God's fee-simple. They fought us to a standstill and lost, but as good Americans they came to the flag and to die as our brothers from the Argonne to Mount Suribachi.

It will climb the ever-heightening mesas and hogbacks, rising, rising barrier-like in the distance – foot by foot along the bloodstained moccasin tracks of Lewis and Clark's intrepids as they scaled the ramparts and battlements of the Rockies to consummate the most tremendous transaction in empires in the history of the world. It will glint upon hoary mountain peaks and shimmer along the craggy, rim-rocked backbone of the Continental Divide.

And then, with the scent of salt and spruce in its nostrils and the din and turbulence of great rivers in its ears, it will swoop down across the stupendous green wilderness of the Pacific slope, to brush and gild the portals of the Golden Gate. Again the hands of comprehension and reason will knock. Again, that Voice. Easily recognizable now and carrying the challenge of sharp finality. The Voice that scourged money lenders from the temple – but yet – the Voice that uttered the tenderest, the most heartening, the most proudly unequivocal statement ever to fall upon the ears of mankind. "I am – I am the Way and the Truth and the Life. Get up – and come out into the grandeurs and the glories of a more moral, a more tolerant, a more determined, freedom-loving, God-fearing United States of America – reborn – for this is God's Great Day in the Morning."

Goodnight, gentlemen – and goodbye.

PART V

EPILOGUE
BY
DR. DYRK HALSTEAD

Writing the epilogue to Nash Buckingham's autobiography is, I think, a rather ambivalent honor – like delivering a eulogy. You're flattered to have been asked, but you really wish the occasion had never arisen in the first place. That's especially true in this case. I wish Nash were still here and his pen still alive. This story was intended to be finished about 1963. Or as Nash put it, "The Olin award was about the getting off place."

This epilogue is intended to detail the last eight years of his life. It is quite tempting for me to include some facts that he didn't write about in the autobiography. There are nearly 2200 letters, many articles, and photos crowding my files. It's anybody's guess why he didn't include them. But this is *his* book, and we have endeavored to publish it as Nash would have. It would have been a lot more fun for me to write about the triumphs of his life. I'll leave that to the biographers. Unfortunately, the final years were anything but triumphant. That's why this final section is bittersweet for me – grateful for the privilege but sorry for the content. It's about a giant of a man ingloriously succumbing to advancing years.

Nash's first evidence of aging were problems with his hearing and his sight. Since the mid-1940's Nash has become increasingly deaf, no doubt due to the pounding of countless rounds through the Becker 12 gauge magnum he so loved. This limited his ability to use the telephone effectively; hence, through his misfortune, we are left with a plethora of letters. It is no coincidence that he saved virtually every correspondence from about 1948, undoubtedly to refresh his memory when the time came. By 1955, there were many requests from his reading audience to do an autobiography. However, he was just finishing *National Field Trial Champions* with co-author Bill Brown and was contemplating a biography of Herb Parsons, the Winchester "trick shooter." Nash never told Herb's story for want of an interested publisher. He then assembled the last of his books, *De Shootinest Gent'man and Other Hunting Tales*, published in 1961. The autobiography was to follow.

Unfortunately, a cataract in his right eye was seriously beginning to affect his vision. I'm sure the ensuing operation was more intended to improve his shooting than his proficiency at the typewriter, although it accomplished both. Cataracts are clouding of the eye's lens, a normally clear ovoid structure located just behind the pupil. Advancing age, among other causes, can allow the lens to become cloudy. In 1963, the treatment was to remove the lens, then fit the patient with strong glasses which took over the function of the lens. While vision didn't return to normal, it did permit folks much improved near vision; distant vision was another story, however. Many of the post-cataract operation photos of Nash taken when he was shooting show him wearing a very dark lens over his non-dominant eye. This was his attempt to disallow the left eye from automatically focusing on a target since it was the stronger of the two. His only other option was to shoot from the left shoulder. Try it both ways sometime; I'm sure you'll understand Nash's choice. Incidentally, cataract surgery has come a long way the past thirty years. They remove the defective lens then surgically implant a new one. In most cases, vision is better than before the cataract even started.

Sadly, Nash apparently had no health insurance at that time, and Medicare wasn't a reality until 1968. The royalties from *National Field Trial Champions* and the Nelson edition of *De Shootinest Gent'man* were short-lived. Fortunately Nash had some wealthy friends, one of whom lived in Washington – Jim Brinkley. Jim saw to it that the eye operation was paid for. Nash's letter to Jim of May 9, 1963, states, "I want to assign the full returns of any sort (from the autobiography) to you, until it is paid out…The minute my eye's able, I'll be back on the job, my general health is sound. But I want to get my mind at rest and protect you. I'm sure you get what I mean. If we can get a contract, the advance would be enough to help me pay you back."

Nash never forgot the favor; look at the dedication of this book.

The operation was a success by 1963 standards. That September found Nash back in the dove field. The dark glasses did have one other hitch – he lost his depth perception. Unfortunately for all of us, we require both eyes to judge distances. As difficult as it must have been for him to relearn his shooting technique, he didn't get discouraged. He told his friends that he "got to fire a whole lot more shells." Nash wasn't one to let petty problems ruin his shooting – truly a man after my own heart.

In 1960, Nash was eighty years old. Although his mind was as sharp as ever and his literary genius still intact, the demand for his material had waned. Editors were looking for "how-to" and "how many were killed" articles. Eugene V. Connett, possibly the greatest outdoor publisher ever (he published the *Derrydales*), prophetically told Nash in 1955, "The outdoor press is an enigma to me and has been for many years. I like to recall the old days of *Forest and Stream* and *Outing*. How different those great papers were…Today's young 'sportsmen' don't seem very interested in the past; all they want is more game to kill, and more deadly ammunition to kill it with." While some of Nash's writing was didactic, most was prosaic or "classic." To his eternal credit, he never gave in to the fashion of the day. Unfortunately, it contributed to his economic demise – and the worst was yet to come.

About that time, he noticed an ad in *The American Field* for *Field Trial Champions*. He wrote to Bill Brown, co-author of the book and publisher of the *Field*, inquiring as to why the book was being offered and why he wasn't receiving royalties. Nash felt the reply was evasive. Nash then wrote to Lurton Blassingame, his agent, who also wrote to Brown. Apparently, Brown had purchased the "remainders" from Stackpole at cost and was offering them for sale. Nothing illegal, but it didn't do anything for Nash's and Bill's friendship.

To make matters worse, Nash had brokered the sale of Wapanoca Lake, his early shooting grounds, to the Federal government on behalf of the then-current owners. Nash's understanding was that he was to receive a commission of $25,000 based on a verbal agreement with the owners. After the sale, he got a check for $1000 which he promptly returned. Friendly negotiations failed to resolve the matter. Nash consulted his friend, Walter Chandler, the senior partner in the law firm of Chandler, Manire and Chandler. Mr. Chandler's letter of June 13, 1963 makes it apparent that Nash intended to use the Wapanoca proceeds for the cataract operation. It states:

"Your letter of June 11 received, and I am delighted that you have had the cataract operation, because it would have been necessary regardless of our efforts to settle the claim against the Crittenden Farms people. I hope that your sight comes back twenty-twenty.

"I have had several conferences with (the Wapanoca attorney) but I have been unwilling to reduce my suggested settlement figure from $10,000, and he has been explaining that his people are not in accord on any substantial settlement of your claim, although he feels that some substantial progress has been made in that direction. However, he will not give me a definite offer, and I have notified him that I will bring suit immediately. He has replied that we possibly can settle after the suit is brought. There is no use to wait on these people any longer, and I am preparing the papers

in the suit and will ask for $25,000. I believe we can win
this case before a jury, and, when court meets in the Fall,
we should be ready for trial."

On June 18, 1963 the complaint was filed in the Circuit Court of
Shelby County, Tennessee stating that the "Plaintiff, Nash Buckingham,
sues the above named defendants (Individually and as Shareholders
of Property Formerly Known as Wapanoca Hunting Club in Crittendon
County, Arkansas) jointly and severally for the sum of Twenty-Five
Thousand Dollars..."

Wapanoca was to bestow one last gift on Nash. On August 15, 1963,
Mr. Chandler wrote to tell him that he had received a check for $8500
paid in settlement of his claim against Wapanoca Hunting Club, et. al.
This story would not be complete without my relating one last fact. In 1968,
Nash was contacted by the Federal government to comment on the status
of the Wapanoca Wildlife Refuge. Without malice, he complied with
their request.

The settlement of the Wapanoca matter did provide a brief financial respite
to Nash. A few weeks later, he was elected to the Field Trial Hall of Fame.
Nash had been "in the running" the previous year but was not elected. There
are many letters expressing indignation at Nash's early defeat; some even
accused the vote tallying to have been less than honest. The fact that Nash
didn't mention his election in his letters to his friends makes me feel as
though he had become "soured" on the idea of the Hall of Fame. He certainly
had misgivings about the running of the National Field Trial Championship,
feeling as though it was not the "class" event it once was. Nonetheless, Nash
accepted the honor graciously and irrespective of his suspicions, was certainly
deserving. He included his acceptance speech in his autobiography.

Shortly after the filing of the Wapanoca matter in Circuit Court, Nash sent
the initial draft of this autobiography to Lurton Blassingame who received it
on June 21, 1963. They had discussed the possibility of having a collaborator
work with Nash to organize the text. Bob Crowell, the owner of T.Y. Crowell
Company, was selected as the publisher some months prior. Crowell suggested,
and both Blassingame and Nash concurred, that the emphasis be
on "conservation, what's happened to hunting over the years, and why?"
There are many letters and writing of Buckingham's that I enjoy emmensely.
You can feel his passion. No letter better summarizes what Nash Buckingham
meant than the cover letter he sent with the autobiography. It is reprinted
here in its entirety.

I98 S McLean Memphis Tenn
May 6th 63

Mr. Lurton Blassingame
IO East 43rd New York I7 New York.

Dear Lurton-;
            The enclosed is not the finished product;its an attempt
to illustrate some of the facets of my perhaps too-many sided career of
forty years in the Conservation field alone. The OLIN award was about
the getting-off place.
            I think Mr. Crowell is correct as to the autobiography
's slant--''what's the cause of wildlife's decline'' rather than mere
recitation of prodigous shooting episodes, etc.Sure,I know what's the
matter;it's all around us--automobile strangulation, roads into the
last fence-row, enormous population increases with rat-breedings from
scum,steady infiltration of lowered standards in everything, and, as to
waterfowl and upland game, more than fifty years of burning the candle
at both ends.Slyly blaming waterfowl declines wholly on droughts in
Canada,while,down the flyways, subjecting the resource to a complascent
and downright incompetent bureaucracy, lap-dogged by higher-up political figures, and beset,from the public aspect by rings of.criminal duck
bootleggers,an inadequate Federal enforcement, and a 40% body of whats
known as licensed duck stamp buyers that is actually stealing more duc
-ks than the professionals. 60% of the duck stamp buyers are pretty go
od, cooperative guys,but even the law has turned against them. Attached
is a fair sample,and, it is a well known fact that the Federal Judicia
-ry ''dislikes'' trying ''waterfowl cases''. As a result,criminal rings
broken up, reform almost instantly.It took us twenty years to get duck
bootlegging made a felony;and we can't get excess bag limits made so,
when,in the aggregate,theyre worse than the professional thieves. As nn
enforcement agent I have seen things to sicken one.But,it is all coming
to a head,that is, if have the guts to remain a nation long enough.
Sooner than you dream, practically all farm land will be posted against
''public'' or ''free shooting''.. There will be per diem charges. More
and more commercial shooting preserves will arise.And the states will
acquire what's left and let what's left of the public--shoot on them-
for a reasonable fee,or stay off.And that's the European system come
home. As of today,industrial,state and Federal forests are over-run by
vandals, arsonists and game hogs,largely politically protected,and,it
is this class which, when routed out,turn at once to their Congressmen
to protect them by having the game agents fired or transferred.
            The Wildlife Service has ONE--not over two--Undercover agents.
State Game Commission have built themselves into far better standing.
Conservation-so called-is between two fires.Other than as ''reporters'
of current conservation dope,the outdoor magazines,as to leadership,
simply aren't worth a damn.Now all this sound embittered, hard,but we
old-time,hard-bitten wildlife cops know it.Administration follows admi
-nistration-it's all the same.I've never seena piece of worthwhile wild
life legislation,evolve from Washington;theyve come from individual or
group brains and push.
                    (Over)

267

I have,literally, bales of letters, reports, and verifications for
everything I say.
I have set down here just a few incidents,with letters to cover.
About 8 years ago the Magnum shot-shell situation got so bad in Califor
- nia that I had to come out of retirement,so to speak,and get that
settled.
The Governments refusal to shoot half-days,with the resource in declin-
-is criminal,but kept so by political pressures,mostly from California
. They won't block .4IO's on migrants. Countless thousands are crippled
. Right now, there is a stop order on information as to the situation
;more ''managed news''. In the past two seasons the sale of duck stamps
(and they are to be collateral for the ''crash loan'') must have declined over half a million.
     And the hell of it is that all they would have to do is either
close the flyways for a season or two; or, shoot half days,with a
30 or 40 days season,seasons the same in all four flyways, and excess
bag limits of 4 a day,made felonies.You would see a quick and tremendo
-us change for the better.
     I wish you'd go over all these enclosures,slanted a bit along the
lines of your contact with Mr. Crowell, I have hundreds of pictures.I
have my football teams at Univ of Tenn nineteen hundred one-and two.I
have the AAUS heavweight pix,with the Secretary's notation that I could
have made the team to the Olympics.Other rare old prints,and the plate
awards.
     When I get this eye-job(the right eye) over wit the twenty
first,I'll be in shape around September to get with a collaborator and
settle down to the job.What bothers me is the continuity of such a job
-because there are so many fields. That's where I need advice and direction. So mull thoru these notes and pictures and let me hear from
you. I think you've done a wonderful job in interesting Mr. Crowell and
I believe that we can work out something that could have a powerful eff
-ect on Conservation and gunning's future.

               With all good wishes.
                                   Nash Buckingham.

PS   It has taken five years of incessant labor by a few of the Outdoor
     Writers Association to pull that once effective and potentially
     powerful outfit back into the gold standard of Conservation.We
     need and we intending getting,a mobilized public press to tell the
     story I've outlined here.And they could be such a book's biggest
     booster.

By mid-July, Nash had requested that the manuscript be returned to him. Lurton mentioned it very briefly on two other occasions that November. Why had Nash not pursued this? The whole idea seemed to have evaporated. The answer was not to be found in our files. In January of 1990, Steve Smith, the Editorial Director of Countrysport Press, called to tell me that one of Nash's friends had heard about the autobiography and wanted us to have access to his letters. Lea Lawrence had known Nash since the late 1940's and had worked with Nash on a couple of projects in the early 60's. Lea began his career as a freelance writer after leaving the Tennessee Game and Fish Commission in 1966 and also used Lurton Blassingame as his agent. Lurton suggested that Lea help Nash "modernize" several articles that Nash had written and was trying to get published. (Lea compiled with the request and Nash sold the articles to quality publications, one to *Outdoor Life* and two to *The American Sportsman.* They were among the last that Nash ever published.)

In January 1967, Lea was visiting Nash in Memphis and was asked to collaborate on the autobiography. In Lea's correspondence to me, he states, "I was flattered by this offer, of course, since I considered Nash to be the greatest outdoor writer ever, and I accepted without hesitation. I was going to 'ghost' my part, but Nash would have none of that. He insisted that it be a 'by Nash Buckingham with H. Lea Lawrence,' or a 'Nash Buckingham and H. Lea Lawrence' work. The plans for this got underway, and Nash began putting things together...He showed me a lot of material and photographs that were to be included...The project stopped cold when Irma suffered a major stroke...and Nash was so distressed that he preferred not to concern himself with other things. As a result, no further progress was made."

Nash's letter to Lea on January 11, 1967, tells what happened with Crowell:

> "Crowell was going to put a 'Ghost' with me two years
> ago, but the terms didn't suit, so we backed off. It's a big
> story and a lot of dirty linen to be washed, a task I don't
> particularly fancy."

Lea had also worked with Nash on a movie produced by the Tennessee Game & Fish Commission on the running of the 1964 National Championship. The film was shown at the drawing of the 1965 Nationals, which ended in disaster due to a lack of birds. Rube Scott, the plantation manager, was taken to task for the decade ("scapegoated" was the word that

Nash used), but Nash quickly recognized the truth, that being that the trustees from the Bank of Boston and the "politicians" from the University were shooting the grounds. Nash knew this was not something that the Ames would have approved had they been alive. After a few well-placed letters threatening to expose the situation, Nash wrote to his close friend, John Bailey, on January 6, 1966, stating: "No one but you and me and a few others know what really caused the quail to disappear from the Championship courses. I surer'n hell stopped THAT to honor Mr. and Mrs. Ames, and it better stay stopped."

Irma had been intermittently ill for a number of years. Nash made and cancelled many outings, his undying loyalty to his "Unquenchable Star" taking precedence. He never complained about his meager circumstances, which were continually worsening. Letters and manuscripts were written on the backs of insurance notices and other "used" paper that found its way to Nash's desk. He expressed sincere gratitude for the gifts of wild game that his friends bestowed. It was, at times, the only meat that he and Irma had in the house. I pause to try to understand this man and the contradictory nature of the later years. He was friends with some of the most influential and wealthy men in the country and continued to correspond with them. How painful it must have been to decline their invitations to shoot and remain part of that world he so cherished. But advancing age, with its attendant infirmities and living on near-poverty income, could not rob this man of his dignity. That's what made Nash Buckingham great.

Nash's writing had slowed dramatically since the publication of the Nelson edition of *De Shootinest Gent'man*. The *Delta Review* published an article called "It Takes More Than a Pretty Face to Make a Field Trial Champion," in 1967. Nash submitted a longer text with photos to the editors, but was "ashamed" of the final form of the article, according to his private correspondence. In June of 1968, *Outdoor Life* ran "Big Shots," one of the pieces that Lea Lawrence had assisted with. Judging by the number of letters he received, there were a lot of folks glad to see him back at the typewriter.

He still continued to hunt Beaver Dam, almost exclusively with his close friend, Dr. William Andrews, a Memphis surgeon. Nash was in his mid-eighties, but never hesitated to do his part breaking ice, carrying decoys, or preparing the blind. He and Dr. Andrews even took their close friend Bob Anderson shooting when Bob was confined to a wheelchair due to crippling arthritis. They lifted him in and out of the boat and blind. Despite his own pathetic situation, Nash said, "I could just cry for Bob Anderson," and he meant it.

Dr. Andrews was a great help to Nash and Irma during the last few years in Memphis, more so than most of us will ever realize. Dr. Andrews is himself a modest, gentile, man of the old school. It's no wonder that he and Nash got along so famously. It's also my understanding that Dr. Andrews has compiled his recollections of Nash and that they will soon be in print. I'm looking forward to it.

On February 20, 1968, Irma fell at home and fractured her hip. She was taken to Baptist Hospital were Dr. Andrews supervised what became a rather prolonged recovery. It was mid-May before she was allowed to return home. Nash was able to avert financial disaster for two reasons. First, Medicare had become an entity and paid most of the hospitalization expenses. More importantly, Nash sold two articles to *The American Sportsman* magazine, receiving $1100 upon acceptance of the manuscripts. *The American Sportsman* was a relatively short-lived quarterly, being published from 1968 to 1970. Unfortunately, its demise was engendered by the subscription price of $25 per year and because it appealed to a limited audience, the true "sportsmen." It was, however, fitting that a writer of Nash Buckingham's stature have two of his last published pieces in that fine magazine. There is a striking irony here. In a letter of March 12, 1968, the editor of *The American Sportsman* wrote Lurton Blassingame stating, "Mr. Buckingham's piece is a pleasure to read and just what we had hoped for. It's so good, in fact, that I'd like to request just a bit more. On page 14 he refers to hunting 'signs' he learned from Negro guides; I wonder if he could give a few more paragraphs of description of how such a day was spent: when they started, how they got there, procedure in the field, what was served for breakfast, what the clubhouse was like – just a few elements to typify the whole feeling of a gentleman's hunting club of the time." That's the type of material that the magazine was looking for – pure Buckingham. The irony is that both Nash and the magazine died the same year, broke, due to a shrinking audience.

Outdoor Life ran "Gone are the Honkers" in the May 1969 issue. That story mentioned another incident that Nash had at O.K. Sandbar, one of his old goose-hunting grounds. Robert Elman, the editor for *The American Sportsman* read the story and wrote Nash asking to see a manuscript of the other incident with the understanding that he may or may not be able to use it. Elman declined after reading the story, probably because his publication was nearing its demise.

Nash then sent the piece to *The American Rifleman* in October 1969. An associate editor wrote, "Thanks very much for letting us see, 'My Best Remembered Goose Hunt.' We like it and would like to buy it for $150 if that figure is agreeable to you. We would have to trim it down a bit in length, but I think we can do it without losing the flavor. And you would see a xerox of the

Strolling Nash's Most Dramatic Race Isn't in the Record Books

ON FEB. 20, in Nashville, Nash Buckingham, Memphis author and sportsman, will be inducted into the Tennessee Sports Hall of Fame.

It is an honor he well deserves on his accomplishments both as an athlete and as a sports writer.

As a young athlete, he was a four-letter man at the University of Tennessee — football, baseball, track and boxing. He is the oldest living captain of a Tennessee football team. He led it in 1902.

Buckingham

Prior to that he was a member of the original Memphis Chickasaws, baseball team, in 1899.

In later years Nash became famous as a bird-dog expert and field-trial judge, and as an author of hunting and fishing stories.

These and many other accomplishments will be remembered and told when Nash goes into the Hall of Fame. But his most dramatic athletic feat won't be mentioned. It didn't go into the record books, and only a few people saw him in action. But he still chuckles when he thinks about it, and still regards it as one of the most satisfying victories of his long career. He scored it in an impromptu footrace in an isolated little meadow in the Colorado Rockies 64 years ago!

★ ★ ★

The Challenge

NASH AND A FELLOW MEMPHIAN, Bayard Snowden, had gone out there for a season of fishing, and were boarding with a rancher who had accommodations for a few sportsmen. Among the vacationists were a tall, sinewy, loudmouthed and wealthy man of about 30, his wife and two friends, all from the East.

One Sunday afternoon Nash and Bayard saw quite a commotion down in the little valley — the other guests and a group of ranchers and cowboys were down there — so they went to see what it was all about.

They learned the tall, loudmouthed guest had just won a footrace from a much older man — Mr. Mack, a rancher of about 50. He and Mr. Mack had got into an argument over their footracing ability, and a contest and a bet had developed. The vacationist bet $250 against Mr. Mack's team of horses that he could outrun him to a big rock up on the mountain. A challenge like that from a bragging tenderfoot couldn't be ignored. The rancher accepted it — and lost.

So, when Nash and Bayard arrived on the scene, old Loudmouth was strutting around. The Memphians listened to him a few moments in silence, and then Bayard Snowden spoke up.

"I know a man who can beat you running," he said quietly.

"Who is he?" demanded Loudmouth. "Bring him on. Want to bet $10,000?"

"No, I don't want to bet $10,000," Mr. Snowden said. "But you've won Mr. Mack's team, so I'll put up $250 against that. And, in addition, I'll bet you room and board for two for the whole summer."

★ ★ ★

On the Spot

SUDDENLY it dawned on Nash that he was the man Mr. Snowden had in mind! And he looked at the lean, leggy vacationist and got trembly. He gave Mr. Snowden a hey-wait-a-minute look, and motioned him aside.

"Watch yourself," he cautioned. "You don't know anything about that fellow. He looks as if he can run."

"Aw, he talks too much," Mr. Snowden said. "Let's teach him a lesson." And he turned and walked back to the group.

"All right, it's a bet," Loudmouth said. "Get your man."

Mr. Snowden nodded towards Nash. "There he is."

Loudmouth looked at the broad-shouldered, heavy young man — and smiled. "What distance you want to run?"

"Oh, anything up to a quarter mile," Nash replied. He was on the spot.

They agreed on a 100-yard dash, and the distance was stepped off parallel with a cowpath, and the runners prepared for the race. Loudmouth went to the ranch house and got a pair of sneakers he had in his baggage, and Nash got a pair of boxing shoes he had brought along. They stripped to their drawers.

A cowboy with a big shootin' iron was selected as the starter. As they went to the post before a handful of spectators, Nash was scareder than he had ever been before thousands of fans watching him in an important football game. He knew he was a pretty good sprinter, especially for a hefty fellow—could do 100 in 10.4 seconds in football togs — but old Loudmouth was really built for speed. And imagine the humiliation of getting beat by such a braggart after the way Bayard Snowden had talked.

"All right, get ready," drawled the cowboy starter as he raised his gun. And immediately Nash's fears left him — swept away in a flash as he eyed his opponent. Instead of getting down on his hands, as all experienced runners did, old Loudmouth stoop up on the mark and merely leaned forward. And that, of course, indicated he was a novice. No matter how natural a runner he was, he would be duck soup.

Nash dug in, got down and all set.

BANG!

He shot away from his mark and tore down the cowpath like a wild man with bees in his drawers. He had a lead of several yards before the greenhorn Loudmouth got into high, and Nash was stilll going away when his opponent quit at the 80-yard mark. A cheer went up from the cowboys.

He and Mr. Snowden gave back to Mr. Mack the team they won from Loudmouth, and spent the rest of the summer there free. Loudmouth's wife gave him an awful rawhiding for being such a sap, and from that day on he fished more and talked less.

Yes, when Nash Buckingham thinks back over his many athletic triumphs, that race down the cowpath ranks high among those that gave him great satisfaction.

edited version, so you could raise hell if you didn't like it!"

The edited xerox was returned to Nash in March 1970, accompanied by a form letter asking Nash to review it and "make any additions or deletions you feel are absolutely essential for correctness." It was signed by Ashley Halsey, Jr., Editor. On the back of the same letter, in handwriting now barely legible from a recent stroke, Nash writes:

> Dear Mr. Ashley Halsey-:,
>
> There's little can be done with this as parts are missing from text – in two places the text ends. I tried to do the best here and there but I'd like to see a good clear relating. Sorry.
>
> Nash Buckingham

The letter and manuscript were returned to Nash. On June 18, 1970 he made a note, in much improved handwriting, that said, "The xerox was such a mess that I notified them of my dissatisfaction – and have never heard from them since other than a threat to cancel…(They should) have rejected the mss [manuscript] instead of ruining it. They should be ashamed." Well, perhaps they need not to have been ashamed, but it does reflect what the outdoor press wanted at the time – less nostalgia and ethic and more "blood-sport." Even at ninety and poor, Nash remained the principled man he always was.

For whatever reasons, there seems to have been a slow evolution back to aesthetic, creative writing as evidenced by the growing popularity of publications such as *Sporting Classics, Gray's*, etc. There would be no more fitting tribute to Nash Buckingham than to see widespread support of this type of writing and a return to the outdoor ethics that he espoused.

Irma did reasonably well during the last half of 1968 and until October 1969, when she fell and injured her pelvis. She had been wanting to move to Knoxville to live with her daughter, son-in-law, and grandchildren for some months. After Dr. Andrews released Irma from the hospital, they made final preparations for the move that I am sure was one of the greatest hardships Nash endured. Nothing, however, was more important than Irma's happiness. In a letter to his friend John Bailey, he writes, "We hope to get away by the 20th (Nov. 1969), and it's a job, but my dear love wants to get to and see her babies, so that's the way it's going to be if I die trying." These were, no doubt, painful words written by a man who was leaving the city he had loved for more than eighty-nine years.

On February 20, 1970, Nash was inducted into the Tennessee Sports Hall of Fame. This was a fitting honor, given his early, overall athletic prowess. He was also the oldest living captain of a University of Tennessee football team. There are many letters of congratulations, some written in response to Nash having told their author about the award, contained in the files. Andy Holt, President of the University of Tennessee, and Cecil Loeb, Mayor of Memphis, were among the first to have written.

By early spring Irma was to be confined to a nursing home for the last time. Nash continued to visit as regularly as he could find a ride; he never learned to drive a car. It must have been a terribly painful, at times lonely, existence watching his wife of sixty years slowly succumb to advancing age. He told several of his friends that he wanted to outlive her "by about one day, just to make sure that everything went all right." Fate would have it that he was to be denied that wish.

In October of 1970, scarcely more than a month after he enjoyed his last hunt, he was hospitalized with a stroke. It initially halted all his writing. But Nash refused to accept what was almost certain fate and by December he was back at the typewriter. His handwriting was deplorable still, but even that recovered remarkably just before his death. He was elated at his own recuperation and I am certain that this prompted him to renew his efforts to write another book he had been contemplating while in Knoxville. On January 22, 1970, he wrote to John Bailey about these matters:

"Recuperation from a series of congestive chills prevented me from telling you how much we appreciated your lovely Christmas card. My first illness in 91 years. But at least I have managed to beat the rap. My beloved mate of 61 years is holding her own at the nursing home, and I am trying to put together a last book of rather unusual mixed contents."

When I initially read this letter, I assumed that Nash was trying to resurrect the autobiography. In our files, however, were letters with pieces attached that Nash had requested from various publications. Most notable were stories from *Field & Stream* and *Outdoor Life* with cover letters that had been written in 1970 in the same file with several unpublished works. It was hard for me to envision how he intended for this to be used in the autobiography, if at all. Then, as luck would have it, I found a clipping from the *Knoxville News-Sentinel* dated Sunday, March 21, 1971, ten days after Nash died. Sam Venable, a young outdoor writer who befriended Nash in Knoxville, published an interview with Nash's daughter. The headline stated that "Buckingham Had New Book 'Ready'." It went on to quote his daughter as follows, "He had planned to make it a series of short stories and reminiscences...It's title was to be

'Once Upon A Time.' He contacted *Field & Stream* several weeks ago for a copy of a story he wrote for them in 1946...When the material arrived, he told me, 'this will finish it'...Nash had worked on the latest piece for quite some time last year before suffering a stroke on October 26. After that I put away his typewriter, thinking he would never use it again. But then, about three weeks before his death, he started working on the book once more. He almost had it finished."

His daughter went on to say that they weren't certain as to what they would do with the manuscript, because there was a lot of "housecleaning" to do.

I can tell you two things unequivocally: The "housecleaning" was done and that nothing happened to the manuscript – until Robert Urich and I bought it. I'll let you guess what's going to happen to it now.

I have intentionally refrained from addressing Nash's continued involvement on the conservation front. That's what he wanted the autobiography to accomplish. I hope it has done so admirably.

Suffice it to say, however, that he remained deeply committed, with his pen and in his lifestyle, to those efforts about which you have read. He never stopped writing to Congressman, conservation groups, editors, and the like about the status and direction that wildlife resources needed. That message is more relevant today than it ever was. For me to have written about that, I feel, would have undermined the intent of this autobiography. And besides, I'm sure it's apparent by now that I couldn't have done it near as well as the Master himself.

Nash Buckingham died in his sleep on March 10, 1971. George Bird Evans once said, "How kind it is that most of us never know when we have fired our last shell." Truer words could not have been spoken about Nash Buckingham. How sad it is for me to close this story with his death. The passing of this man, almost a prophet, signaled the passing of an era, a way of life. My hope is that we can resurrect a little bit of this man with this book and its message.

The obituaries were eloquent. Nash's friend, Paul Flowers, author of the "Greenhouse" column in the *Memphis Press-Scimitar*, wrote:

"For three quarters of a century before the words 'ecology' and 'total environment' existed outside the dictionary, Nash Buckingham was sounding an eloquent reminder that scientists, engineers, politicians, cannot outguess God. His message always was 'give nature a chance; she will have the last word.'

"Nash's voice is still, but his message will echo down the corridors of time, and generations to come will breathe prayers of thanks that some of our heritage was preserved, because of his counsel.

"His life spanned a century, less nine years, and it was a life lived to the utmost; he was a man of many facets. On a challenge he played a calliope in a circus parade. He engineered creation of a wildlife sanctuary in the center of the Mississippi flyway. His books occupied places of honor on the shelves of an alcove at Abercrombie & Fitch in New York. He was acclaimed as one of the finest wingshots of his time."

But I suppose that Warner Nagel, in the preface to *Hallowed Years*, distilled the essence of Nash Buckingham by saying:

> To know the outdoors and to love it, to use it and enjoy it in the light of that understanding and love, to fight keenly and fairly whatever threatens to spoil it, to share with others every golden experience gained – surely these add up to stature in any true sportsman's code. To follow these concepts is to take the poor old tarnished, battered, prostituted word "sportsman" has become and make it the clean and honest trademark it was meant to be. Hunting with Nash, in the flesh and on paper, makes a man think about things like that.

BIBLIOGRAPHY

Books By Nash Buckingham

De Shootinest Gent'man and Other Tales

    The Derrydale Press, 1934, 240 pgs. Limited edition of 950 copies, numbered. Blue simulated morocco binding with Dr. Edgar Burke canvasback ducks medallion on cover. Original selling price: $7.50. Col. H.P. Sheldon introduction.

    G.P. Putnam's Sons, New York, 1943. 240 pgs. Blue cloth covers and dust jacket. Original selling price: $2.50. This edition went into various printings.

    Premier Press, 1984. 240 pgs. Limited edition of 3,000 copies, numbered. Blue bonded leather binding. Original selling price: $49.00. James A. Casada introduction. Sheldon introduction omitted.

De Shootinest Gent'man

    Charles Scribner's Sons, New York, 1941. 24 pgs. Linen board covers with green dust jacket. Original selling price: $2.00. Robert Ball illustrations. A rather difficult-to-locate book consisting of one (titled) story.

De Shootin'est Gent'man and Other Hunting Tales

    Thomas Nelson and Sons, New York, 1961. 246 pgs. Deluxe edition of 260 copies. Hamilton Green illustrations. Werner O. Nagel introduction. Col. Sheldon introduction omitted. Nagel was technical editor for the Missouri Conservation Commission and hunted with Nash Buckingham. This edition contains "De Shootinest Gent'man" and "The XIVth of John." The balance of the stories are different from the original Derrydale edition.

    Thomas Nelson and Sons, Nelson Sporting Edition, 1961. 246 pgs. Blue cloth with illustrated dust jacket. Original selling price: $7.50. Trade edition.

Mark Right! Tales of Shooting and Fishing

    The Derrydale Press, 1936. 250 pgs. Limited edition of 1,250 copies, numbered. Dark red cloth binding with Dr. Edgar Burke bobwhite quail medallion on cover and glassine wrapper. Original selling price: $7.50. Nash Buckingham preface plus extracts from John Bailey, his diary.

    G.P. Putnam's Sons, New York, 1944. 196 pgs. Mahogany cloth covers with green dust jacket. Original selling price: $2.50. Col. William H. Hobson foreword (appears in this edition only). Hobson was Col., Infantry, U.S. Army, Fort Benning, GA and Buckingham's friend.

Ole Miss'

    The Derrydale Press, 1937, 242 pgs. Limited edition of 1,250 copies, numbered, Maroon cloth with Dr. Edgar Burke Canada geese medallion on cover. Original selling price: $7.50. Paul A. Curtis foreword. Richard Bishop frontis.

    G.P. Putnam's Sons, New York, 1946. 178 pgs. Dark green cloth covers with light green dust jacket. Original selling price: $2.75.

    Premier Press, 1986. 242 pgs. Limited edition of 3,000 copies, numbered. Turquoise bonded leather binding. Original selling price: $49.00. Jim Casada introduction.

Blood Lines, Tales of Shooting and Fishing

    The Derrydale Press, 1938. 227 pgs. Limited edition of 1,250 copies, numbered. Maroon cloth with Dr. Edgar Burke mallard duck medallion on cover. Original selling price: $7.50. Henry P. Davis foreword. Davis was the Dog Editor for *Sports Afield*.

    G.P. Putnam's Sons, New York, 1947. 192 pgs. Tan linen with black dust jacket. Original selling price: $2.75. Henry P. Davis foreword.

    Premier Press, 1988. 227 pgs. Limited edition of 3,000 copies, numbered. Dark blue bonded leather binding. Original selling price: $49.00. Jim Casada introduction.

Tattered Coat

    G.P. Putnam's Sons, New York, 1944. 210 pgs. Deluxe edition of 995 copies, signed and numbered. Linen covers with Arthur Fuller medallion. Edward Cave foreword. Cave was editor of *Recreation* (which later merged with *Outdoor Life*) and printed "De Shootinest Gent'man" in 1916.

    G.P. Putnam's Sons (regular edition), 1944. 210 pgs. Dark red binding with light sienna dust jacket. Original selling price: $2.75. Edward Cave foreword.

Game Bag, Tales of Shooting and Fishing

    G.P. Putnam's Sons, New York, 1945. 185 pgs. Deluxe edition of 1,250 copies, signed and numbered. Green cloth covers with quarter linen. H.P.A.M. Hoecker illustrations. Paul Flowers "fo'ward." Flowers was a newspaperman who wrote the "Greenhouse Column" for the *Commercial Appeal* in Memphis, to which Buckingham submitted occasional letters.

    G.P. Putnam's Sons (regular edition), 1945. 185 pgs. Bright red cloth binding with dark green dust jacket. Original selling price: $2.75. Paul Flowers "fo'ward."

Hallowed Years

    The Stackpole Company, Harrisburg, Pennsylvania, 1953. 209 pgs. Brown board covers with wine and light green dust jacket. Werner O. Nagel preface. Nagel was Director of Public Relations and Editor of the Missouri Conservationist. He hunted with Nash Buckingham. Introduction by the late Col. H.P. Sheldon, "The Saga of Bo-Whoop."

BOOKS CO-AUTHORED BY NASH BUCKINGHAM

William F. Brown and Nash Buckingham.

National Field Trial Champions, An Authentic and Detailed History of The National Field Trial Championship Association Since Its Inception in 1896.

    The Stackpole Company, Harrisburg, Pennsylvania. 1955. 520 pgs. Deluxe edition of 50 copies, signed and numbered. Leather covers. Henry L. Betten, Henry P. Davis and Dr. T. Benton King forewords.

    The Stackpole Company, Harrisburg, Pennsylvanis, 1955. 520 pgs. Imitation leather covers with dark green dust jacket. Henry L. Betten, Henry P. Davis and Dr. T. Benton King forewords. Trade edition.

BOOKS ABOUT NASH BUCKINGHAM
BOOKS WITH INFORMATION ABOUT NASH BUCKINGHAM

Evans, George Bird

The Upland Shooting Life

    Alfred A. Knopf, New York, 1971. 301 pgs. plus index. Original selling price: $10.00.
        Buckingham, Nash: 139, 182-84, 276
        Buckingham, Irma: 182-84
        American Wildfowlers: 182

Evans, George Bird

The Best of Nash Buckingham

    Winchester Press, New York, 1973. 320 pgs. plus bibliography. Selected, edited and annotated by George Bird Evans. Brown cloth with photographic dust jacket. Milton C. Weiler endpapers. Original selling price: $10.00. Note: Weiler endpapers are not present on later printings of this book.

    A sensitive, insightful look at a man and his writings by one of the foremost bird hunter/writers who also bred bird dogs. The annotations for each reprinted Buckingham story would make a book by themselves.

Evans, George Bird

Troubles With Bird Dogs and What To Do About Them

    Winchester, New York, 1975. 307 pgs.
        Buckingham, Nash: 144, 194, 204, 236, 264-68, 294

    Old Hemlock, Bruceton Mills, West Virginia, 1985. Limited edition of 1,500 copies, signed and numbered.

    Old Hemlock, 1985. Regular edition.

Bashline, L. James and Saults, Dan, (editors)

America's Great Outdoors

    J. G. Ferguson Publishing Company, Chicago, Illinois, 1976. An anthology of 200 years of writing with collected illustrations. Buckingham, Nash: 141, 227, 229-231, 264

Evans, George Bird

Opus 10: Men Who Shot and Wrote About It

    Old Hemlock, Bruceton Mills, West Virginia, 1983. 203 pgs. Limited edition of 990 copies, signed and numbered. Navy blue coarse linen covers in light grey slipcase.

Buckingham, Nash: 1880-1971: 146-155
Buckingham, Nash: 196, 199-201

Evans, George Bird (editor)
Dear John:, Nash Buckingham's Letters to John Bailey
  Old Hemlock, Bruceton Mills, West Virginia, 1984. 205 pgs. Limited edition of 575 numbered and signed copies.
  Old Hemlock, 1984. 205 pgs. Regular edition.
    An evocative look at friendship, companionship and hunting experiences shared by two gentlemen and friends.

BOOKS THAT CONTAIN NASH BUCKINGHAM STORIES

Phillips, John C. and Hill, Lewis W.
Classics of the American Shooting Field: A Mixed Bag for the Kindly Sportsman,1783-1926
  Houghton Mifflin, Boston and New York, 1930. Deluxe edition of 150, signed and numbered.
    Buckingham, Nash: De Shootinest Gent'man, 1916

Bigelow, Horation
Gunnerman's Gold
  Standard Publications, West Virginia, 1943. Memories of fifty years afield with a scatter gun. Limited edition of 1,000 copies. Nash Buckingham introduction.

Kelley, Robert E., (editor)
The Sportsman's Anthology
  New York, 1944
  Buckingham, Nash: Salute to Youth

Sheldon, Col. H.P.
Tranquility
  A.S. Barnes, 1945. Nash Buckingham introduction.

The Field & Stream Reader
  Doubleday and Company, Inc., New York, 1946.
    Buckingham, Nash: The Brownie Company, Ltd. (Tattered Coat)

Brown, J. Hammond (editor)
Outdoors Unlimited
  A.S. Barnes and Company, New York, 1947. A collection of great hunting and fishing tales selected by the editors of the country's leading outdoor magazines.
    Buckingham, Nash: Great Day In The Morning
                      Red Letter Days with Quail
                      Surrender to Youth (Ole Miss')

Godfrey, Joe Jr. and Dufresne, Frank, (editors)
The Great Outdoors
  Brown & Bigelow, St. Paul, Minnesota, 1947. The where, when and how of hunting and fishing, including a new dictionary of sportsmen's terms.
    Buckingham, Nash: Quail Shooting

Jacobs, Charles R., (editor)
Official Hunting Book: How, When and Where to Hunt in North America.
  Crown Publishers, New York, 1950.
  Buckingham, Nash: Waterfowl Flyways of North America: Middle and Lower Mississippi Flyway.
                    Dove Tactics
                    Common Sense Hunting
                    Start 'Em Off Right

Grey, Hugh and McCluskey, Ross, (editors)
The Waterfowl Gunners Book
  Henry Holt and Company, New York, 1955. Memorable articles and stories selected from the pages of

America's Number One sportsman's magazine.
Buckingham, Nash: Bob White, Down 'T Aberbeen (*Field & Stream*, September, 1913)

Camp, Raymond R., (editor)
Hunting Trails
Appleton-Century-Crofts, New York, 1961.
Buckingham, Nash: Broccoli

Bashline, L. James and Saults, Dan, (editors)
America's Great Outdoors
J.G. Ferguson Publishing Co., Chicago, Illinois, 1976. An anthology of 200 years of writing with collected illustrations.
Buckingham, Nash:

Evans, George Bird, (editor)
The Bird Dog Book
The Amwell Press, Clinton, New Jersey, 1979. Limited edition of 1,000 copies, signed and numbered.
Original selling price: $37.50
Buckingham, Nash and Brown, William: Mary Montrose
Buckingham, Nash: The Family Honor (De Shootinest Gent'man)
Not Unsung (Tattered Coat)
The Amwell Press, Clinton, New Jersey, 1989. Trade edition, slipcased. Original selling price: $30.00

Evans, George Bird, (editor)
The Upland Gunners Book
The Amwell Press, Clinton, New Jersey, 1979. Limited edition of 1,000 copies, signed and numbered.
Buckingham, Nash: Bobwhite Blue, Bobwhite Gray! (De Shootinest Gent'man)
The Dove (*Field & Stream*, January 1947)
The Amwell Press, Clinton, New Jersey. Original selling price: $30.00 Trade edition.

Williamson, F.P.
The Waterfowl Gunners Book
The Amwell Press, Clinton, New Jersey, 1979. Limited edition of 1,000 copies, signed and numbered.
Buckingham, Nash: De Shootinest Gent'man (*Recreation*, 1916)
The Amwell Press, Clinton, New Jersey. Origional selling price: $30.00 Trade edition.

Underwood, Lamar, (editor)
The Bobwhite Quail Book
The Amwell Press, Clinton, New Jersey, 1982. Limited edition of 1,000 copies, signed and numbered.
Original selling price: $25.00.
Buckingham, Nash: Bobs of the Bayou Bank (Mark Right!)
Pipeline "Pottiges" (The American Field, 1959, De Shootinest Gent'man, 1961)
Carry Me Back (Hallowed Years)
Play House (Field & Stream, January, 1929, De Shootinest Gent'man)
Bobwhite Blue, Bobwhite Gray! (De Shootinest Gent'man)

Underwood, Lamar, (editor)
The Duck Hunter's Book
The Amwell Press, Clinton, New Jersey, 1982. Limited edition of 1,000 copies, signed and numbered.
Original selling price: $25.00
Buckingham, Nash: Are We Shooting 8 Gauge Guns? (Gun Digest, 1960, De Shootinest Gent'man, 1961
Great Day In The Morning (Field & Stream, 1941, Tattered Coat)
What Rarer Day (De Shootinest Gent'man, 1934)
Hail and Farewell (Mark Right!)

MAGAZINE ARTICLES BY NASH BUCKINGHAM

The American Field
December 7, 1940:   Figment of Destiny
December 6, 1941   Permanent Truce

December 4, 1943   Brimstone
December 2, 1944   Beatae Memoriae
December 2, 1950   The Hallowed Years
December 1, 1951   Death Stalked the Springstand
December 6, 1952   "When Time Who Steals Our Years Away"
December 3, 1955   Voices of Orphans and Old Folks
December 1, 1956   Memories of the National Championship
December 7, 1957   Old Minstrels Harp Their Lays!
December 5, 1959   Pipeline "Pottiges"
December 3, 1960   Blow, Blow – and Blow the Ducks Down
December 1, 1962   Recall to Eden
December 5, 1964   Goodbye and Good Luck!
December 3, 1966   Yankee – Don't Go Home!!

American Game
October/November, 1929 Letter regarding toxic poisoning of ducks

The American Rifleman
January, 1948   Jump Shooting's Joys
June, 1948   Let Your Subconscious Alone
October, 1949   "All Purpose" Shotgun Myth
November, 1952   Get Thee Behind Me, Satan!

The American Sportsman
Fall, 1968   Birdy Dogs
Winter, 1969   The Prodigal Years

Country Life
October, 1939   Sportsman's Paradise

Field & Stream
August, 1920   My Daddy's Gun
October, 1920   My Dog Jim
September, 1921   Quail Story
October, 1921   Rich Man – Poor Man
November, 1921   Moose Story
January, 1922   Bark Horn
March, 1922   Thou and Thy Gun Bearer
November, 1922   All Over Gawd's Heaven
January, 1923   Bob-White
February, 1923   I Wish
May, 1923   Anti-Automatic
June, 1923   The Closed Creel
March, 1924   Lost Voices
November, 1924   The Ropes of Goose Shooting
March, 1926   Sell Ole Dan?
January, 1927   Decoys on Fresh Water
September, 1927   Me and Capri
December, 1927   All in the Day's Work
January, 1928   The Neglected Duck Call
July, 1928   Thar She Putts!
January, 1929   Play House
April, 1930   The Family Honor
October, 1930   Golden Sedge and Whirring Wings
September, 1931   Eye-See, Not Hear-Say
November, 1931   What Rarer Day?
December, 1931   The XIVth of John
May, 1934   Norias Annie Wins
May, 1935   Homewood Flirtatious Wins

May, 1936	Beauty in the Sedge
May, 1937	Calling All Champions
May, 1939	Setter in the Sun
October, 1939	Write Your Own Ticket
November, 1939	P-u-l-l!
May, 1940	Lester's Enjoy Wahoo Enjoys
March, 1941	Leaf Among Leaves
April, 1941	Great Day in the Morning!
May, 1941	Ariel – Prince of Prairie and Sedgelands
October, 1941	The Brownie Company, Ltd.
December, 1941	The Sally Hole
May, 1942	Dog of Destiny
May, 1943	They Do Come Back – Ariel Wins Again
September, 1943	The Great Reprisal
December, 1943	Valley of Contentment
April, 1944	And Still Champion Ariel!
May, 1945	Bird Dog for the Ages
August, 1945	What Really Happens Out Quail Shooting?
October, 1945	Bird Dog Blinkers
February, 1946	The Gallows Bear
Feburary, 1946	In Memoriam
May, 1946	Zev Wins National
December, 1946	Lady
January, 1947	The Dove
March, 1947	Tri-State Duck Survey
April, 1947	Remember?
May, 1947	Bird Dog of Destiny
October, 1947	Duck Shooting's Two Ultra "Musts"
February, 1948	They Do Come Back
May, 1948	Golden Jubilee Dog
September, 1948	So You Want to Be a Wing Shot
March, 1949	The Champagne Pointer
May, 1949	Sierra Joan Wins National Field Trial
June, 1949	The Cricket Field
September, 1949	Heads of Tails It's Doves!
May, 1950	Brownie Doone Sees It Through
July, 1950	Drake's Debut
September, 1950	Tight Place
October, 1950	Calling All Ducks
March, 1951	The High Sign
May, 1951	National Field Trial
November, 1955	Great Day in the Morning (reprint from April, 1941)

Gun Digest

1959	The Dove
1950	Are We Shooting 8-Gauge Guns?

Harvard Monthly (first published piece)

February, 1900	Uncle Willis, Skimpy, and the Cotton Bale

Hunting Dog

February, 1969	Hunting Dogs Think

Life

January 24, 1944	Quail Shooting In Tennessee; famous sportsman-author hunts birds in the uplands of the Grand Junction country.

National Sportsman Magazine

October, 1924	The Palm of Victory

August, 1934   Hail and Farewell

Outdoor America (monthly magazine of the Izaak Walton League)
May, 1927
August, 1937   While There's Life

Outdoor Life
June, 1918   It Reminded Him
October, 1920   In the Southlands Open Season
January, 1921   How!
January, 1924   To the Spirit of the Covered Wagon
July, 1925   Consolation
September, 1927   Duck Scarcity – and Its Remedy
October, 1927   Some Bird Dog Deals
November, 1927   De Shootinest Gent'man
February, 1928   A Shootin' Po' Soul
March, 1929   To an Ol' Cullud Fren'
March, 1929   The Coaster (Part I)
April, 1929   (Part II)
August, 1952   Duke
December, 1953   A Remembering Fellow
September, 1955   Magnum Opus
June, 1968   Big Shots
June, 1969   Gone Are the Honkers
September, 1971   Feeling Like a Goose

Recreation
September, 1916   De Shootinest Gent'man

Scribners Magazine
August, 1936   With Mrs. Allen Tate Gordon: B From Bull's Foot

Southern Outdoors
July/August, 1955   The Best All-Round Gun Dog I Ever Saw (Part I)
September/October, 1955   (Part II)

Sports Afield
January, 1943   First and Last Days
January, 1944   Januaries Afield
April, 1945   Ghost Trout

REFERENCES USED TO PREPARE THIS BIBLIOGRAPHY:

Evans, George Bird (editor)
The Best of Nash Buckingham
Winchester Press, 1973. 320 pgs. plus bibliography

Evans, Kay – who so graciously answered my questions and curiosities

Frazier, Don
Recognizing Derrydale Press Books
Privately printed, 1983.

Bibliography prepared by
Carol McNally
Fair Chase, Inc.
Box 880
Twin Lakes, WI 53181
414-279-5478

Other Titles
by
Countrysport Press

BEST GUNS by *Michael McIntosh*

THE BIG BORE RIFLE: The Book of Fine Magazine & Double Rifles .375-.700 Calibers by *Michael McIntosh*

CALL OF THE QUAIL: A Tribute to the Gentleman Game Bird

EASTERN UPLAND SHOOTING by *Dr. Charles C. Norris*

GAME SHOOTING: The Definitive Book on the Churchill Method of Instinctive Wingshooting and Sporting Clays by *Robert Churchill and Macdonald Hastings*

THE GRAND PASSAGE: A Chronicle of North American Waterfowling

RETRIEVER TRAINING: The Cotton Pershall Method by *Bobby N. George, Jr.*

SHOTGUNNER'S NOTEBOOK: The Advice and Reflections of a Wingshooter by *Gene Hill*

The following Countrysport Press titles are also available in DELUXE LIMITED EDITIONS:

BEST GUNS

THE BIG-BORE RIFLE: The Book of Fine Magazine & Double Rifles .375-.700 Calibers

CALL OF THE QUAIL: A Tribute to the Gentleman Game Bird

EASTERN UPLAND SHOOTING

THE GRAND PASSAGE: A Chronicle of North American Waterfowling

"MR. BUCK": The Autobiography of Nash Buckingham

SHOTGUNNER'S NOTEBOOK: The Advice and Reflections of a Wingshooter

The Countrysport limited editions feature:
*deluxe leather binding
*gilt-edged top papers
*ribbon bookmark
*specially commissioned gold foil cover art
*commemorative title page bearing the edition size

288